POLITICAL GUMBO

POLITICAL GUMBO
A Collection of Editorial Cartoons

Walt Handelsman

Foreword by Jim Amoss

PELICAN PUBLISHING COMPANY
Gretna 1994

To Jodie and J. D.:
Thanks for giving me the freedom to be nuts

Special thanks to Jim Amoss, Kenny Harrison, and John Pope for helping me pull this book together

The word "Pelican" and the depiction of a pelican are trademarks of
Pelican Publishing Company, Inc., and are registered in the U.S. Patent and Trademark Office.

Library of Congress Cataloging-in-Publication Data

Handelsman, Walt.
  Political gumbo : a collection of editorial cartoons / Walt
Handelsman ; foreword by Jim Amoss.
    p. cm.
  ISBN 1-56554-054-9
  1. United States—Politics and government—1989-1993—Caricatures
and cartoons. 2. Louisiana—Politics and government—1951- -
-Caricatures and cartoons. 3. American wit and humor, Pictorial-
-Louisiana—New Orleans. 4. Editorial cartoons—Louisiana—New
Orleans. I. Title.
E881.H35 1994
973.929'0207—dc20   94-6025
                                    CIP

Manufactured in the United States of America
Published by Pelican Publishing Company, Inc.
1101 Monroe Street, Gretna, Louisiana 70053

Contents

Foreword

The first thing an editor notices about Walt Handelsman is that he's funny—outrageously so. To make an editor giggle during a typical news-room day requires serious tickling. Walt does it with an arsenal of playful-ness, absurdity, and sheer nerve.

The second thing an editor notices is that the man can't spell. We're talk-ing a Quayle-caliber deficiency. In fact, there is great hidden irony in Walt's cartoon spoofing the former vice-president's "potatoe" gaffe. There but for his editor's perpetual vigilance goes Walt.

Of course, both qualities—outrageous humor and bad spelling—are essential to the successful newspaper cartoonist. The bad spelling distracts the editor, numbing his squeamish instincts and allowing the cartoonist to get away with another cartooning outrage.

And in Louisiana, fortunately for Walt, there is no dearth of outrage. Walt has had such tragicomic subject matter as a gambling governor, a rud-derless legislature, and a bevy of city politicians who would be the envy of cartoonists everywhere.

But his most serious local target to date was the racially divisive 1991 Louisiana governor's race of neo-Nazi David Duke. When Duke made the runoff that fall, the newspaper realized it had to speak to its readers at full volume. We spared no opportunity to tell what stuff Duke was made of. But Walt wielded humor in the best tradition of Chaplin vs. Hitler. He recognized that the most effective way to deflate Duke was to puncture his self-importance, to cloak him relentlessly in the Klan sheets he had conveniently shed. Walt's image of the hooded Duke as the Energizer bunny who never stops running or Duke irrepressibly giving a Heil Hitler salute were more devastating than editorial prose.

Walt also possesses this essential trait of the best newspaper cartoonists: He has made himself a part of his town. By embracing New Orleans, Walt has earned his right, in the eyes of *Times-Picayune* readers, to cheer and deride our best and worst—gifted musicians and corrupt politicians, balmy winters and beastly summers, Saints victorious and Saints disgraced.

The city's charm and quirkiness become him, for they match his own. At the same time, Walt's wide scope makes him an astute national commentator. The result is a good chemistry and sharp-witted cartoons that have won him two National Headliner awards, Sigma Delta Chi's award for editorial cartooning, as well as a place in the hearts of *Times-Picayune* readers. This collection of Walt's best will delight his old audience and win over a new one.

JIM AMOSS
Editor, *The Times-Picayune*

Inside the Beltway

Rambling from the Dan Quayle "potatoe" patch to the complex corridors of healthcare reform, a cartoonist needs an endless supply of ink to keep up with this crowd.

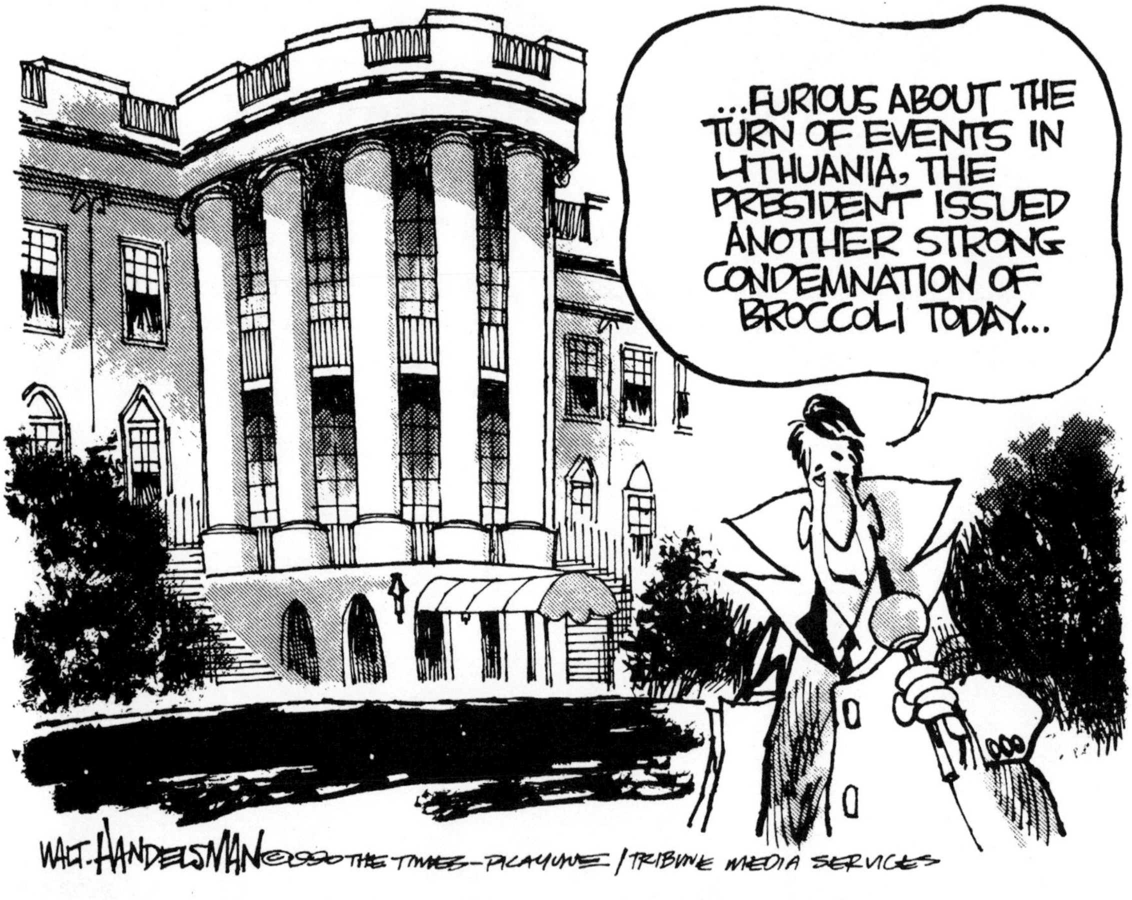
...FURIOUS ABOUT THE TURN OF EVENTS IN LITHUANIA, THE PRESIDENT ISSUED ANOTHER STRONG CONDEMNATION OF BROCCOLI TODAY...
WALT. HANDELSMAN ©1990 THE TIMES-PICAYUNE / TRIBUNE MEDIA SERVICES

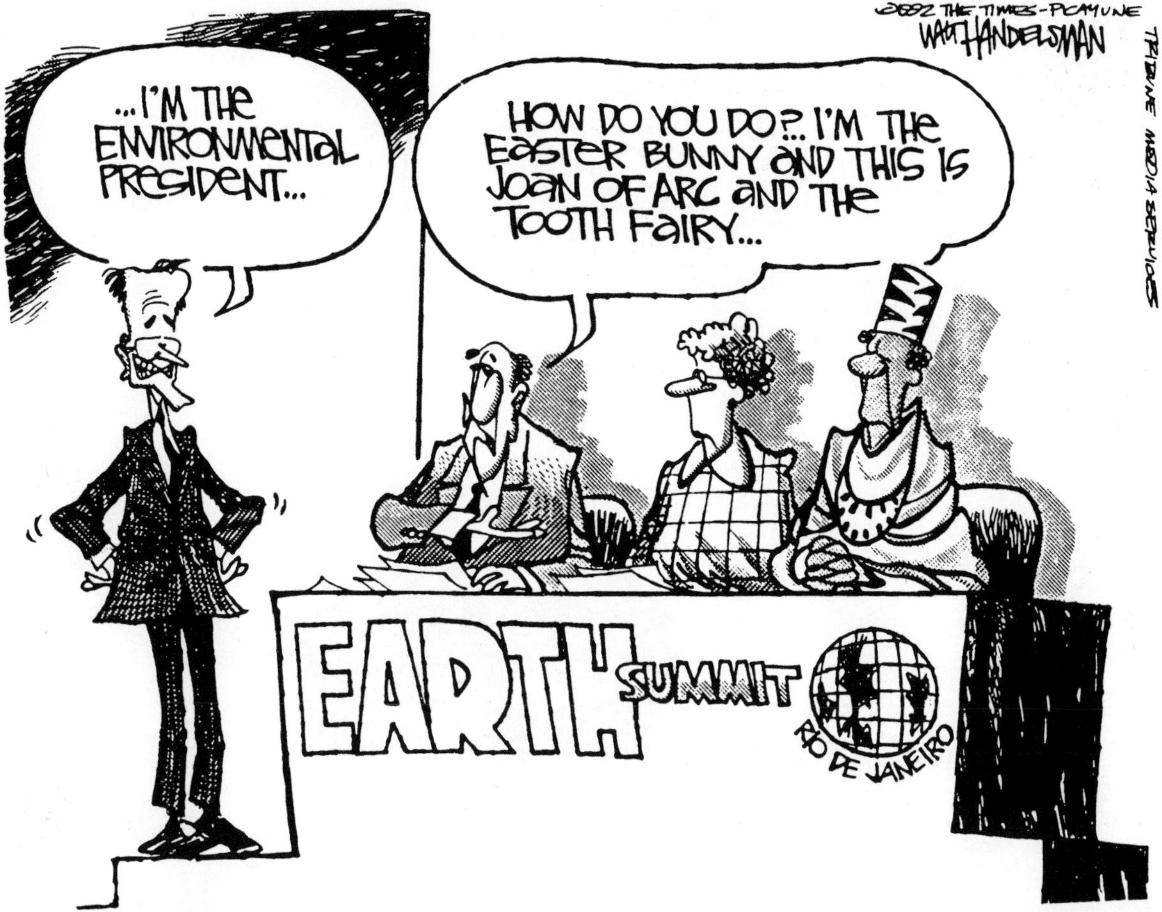
©1992 THE TIMES-PICAYUNE
WALT HANDELSMAN
TRIBUNE MEDIA SERVICES
...I'M THE ENVIRONMENTAL PRESIDENT...
HOW DO YOU DO?... I'M THE EASTER BUNNY AND THIS IS JOAN OF ARC AND THE TOOTH FAIRY...
EARTH SUMMIT
RIO DE JANEIRO

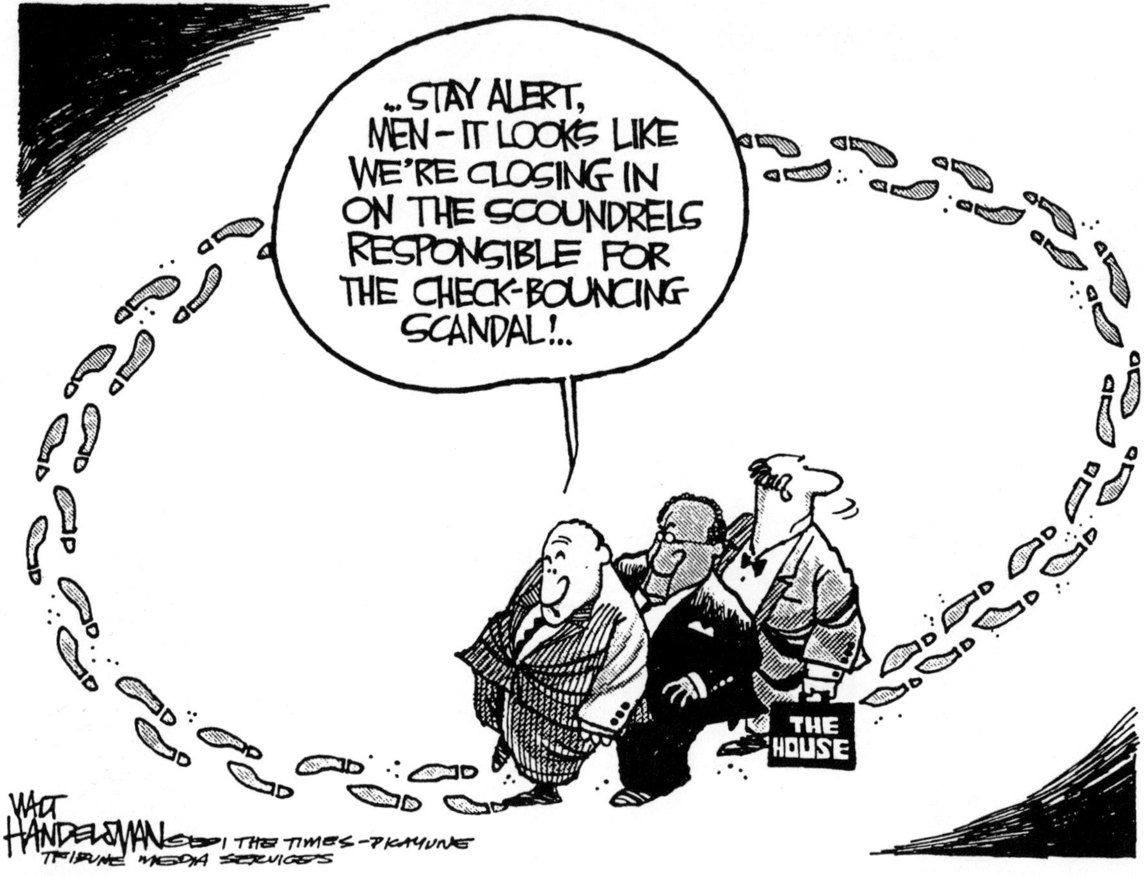
...STAY ALERT, MEN - IT LOOKS LIKE WE'RE CLOSING IN ON THE SCOUNDRELS RESPONSIBLE FOR THE CHECK-BOUNCING SCANDAL!..
THE HOUSE
WALT HANDELSMAN

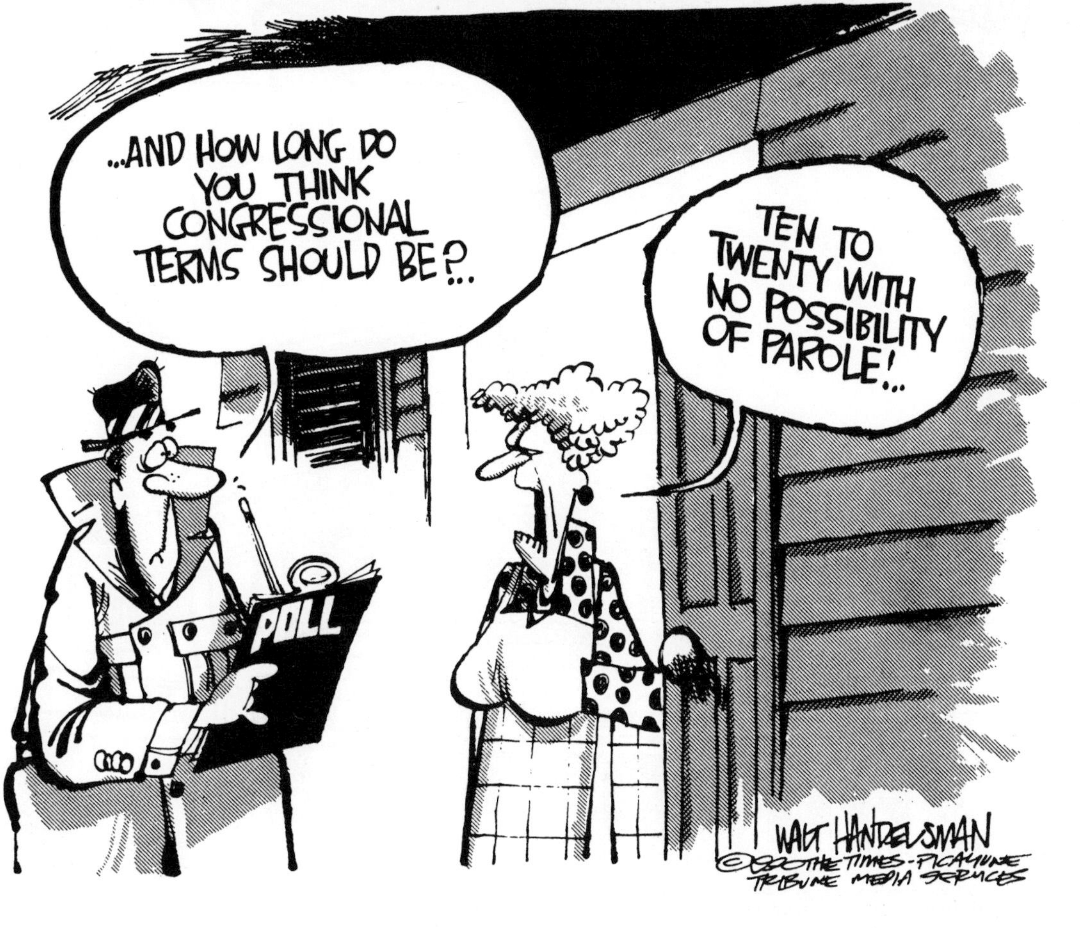
...AND HOW LONG DO YOU THINK CONGRESSIONAL TERMS SHOULD BE?...
TEN TO TWENTY WITH NO POSSIBILITY OF PAROLE!...
POLL
WALT HANDELSMAN
©1990 THE TIMES-PICAYUNE TRIBUNE MEDIA SERVICES

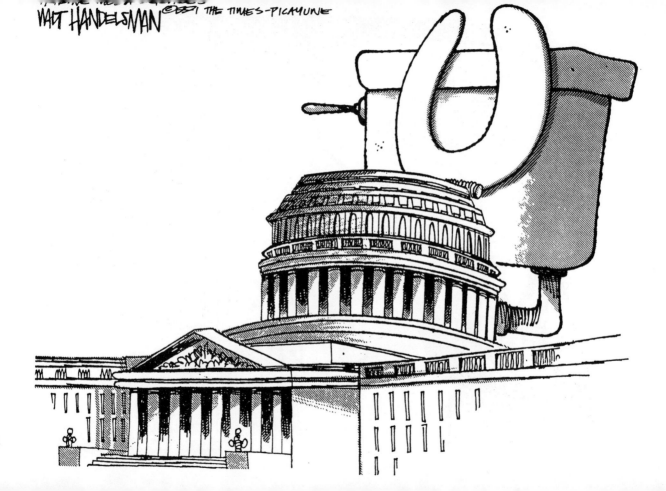

WALT HANDELSMAN ©1991 THE TIMES-PICAYUNE

14

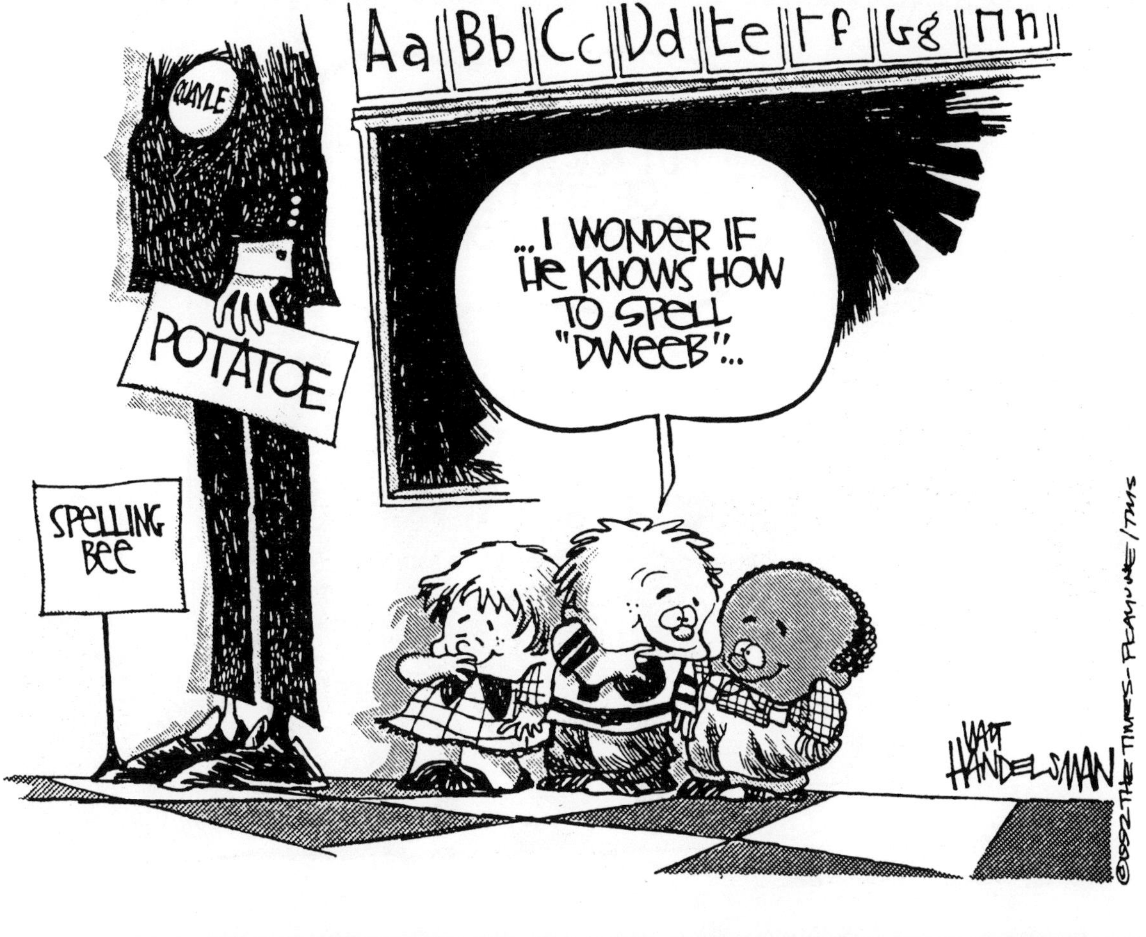

Aa Bb Cc Dd Ee Ff Gg Hh
QUAYLE
POTATOE
SPELLING BEE
...I WONDER IF HE KNOWS HOW TO SPELL "DWEEB"!...
WALT HANDELSMAN
©1992 THE TIMES-PICAYUNE/TMS

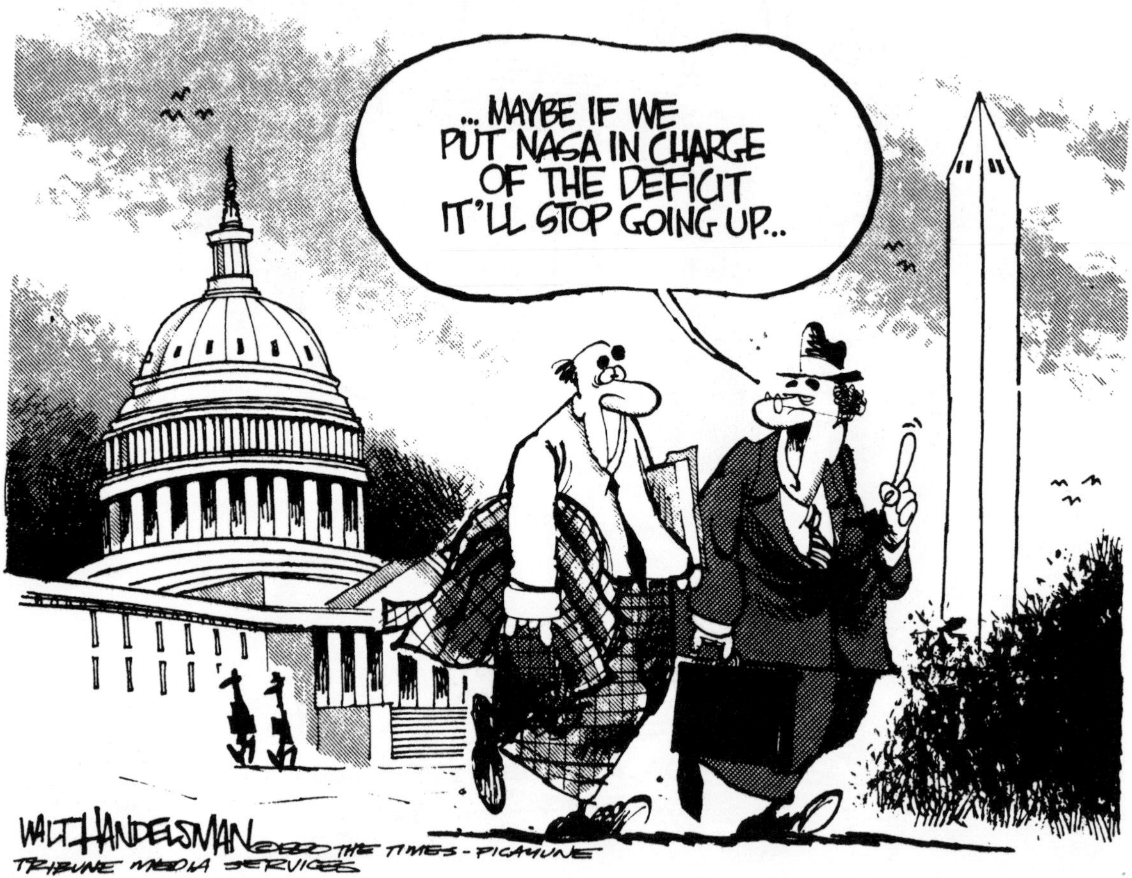
... MAYBE IF WE PUT NASA IN CHARGE OF THE DEFICIT IT'LL STOP GOING UP...
WALT HANDELSMAN ©1990 THE TIMES-PICAYUNE
TRIBUNE MEDIA SERVICES

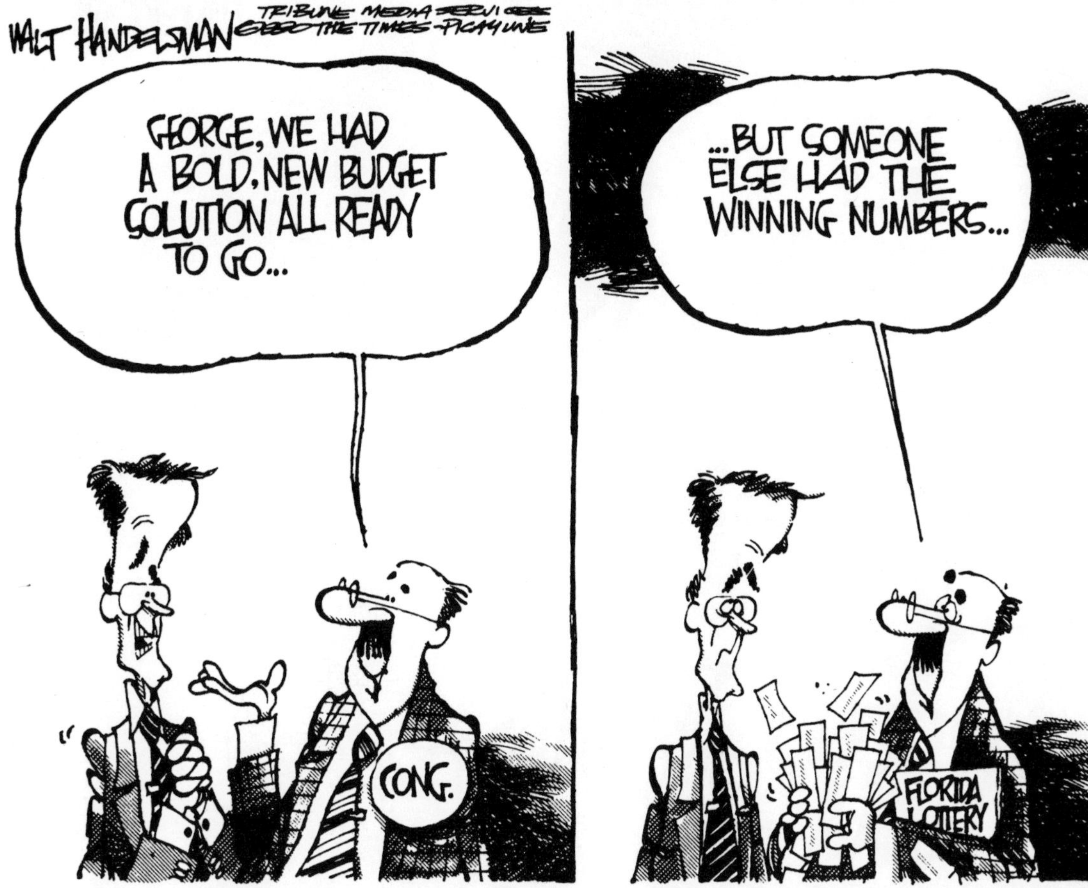
WALT HANDELSMAN
TRIBUNE MEDIA SERVICES
©1990 THE TIMES-PICAYUNE
GEORGE, WE HAD A BOLD, NEW BUDGET SOLUTION ALL READY TO GO...
CONG.
...BUT SOMEONE ELSE HAD THE WINNING NUMBERS...
FLORIDA LOTTERY

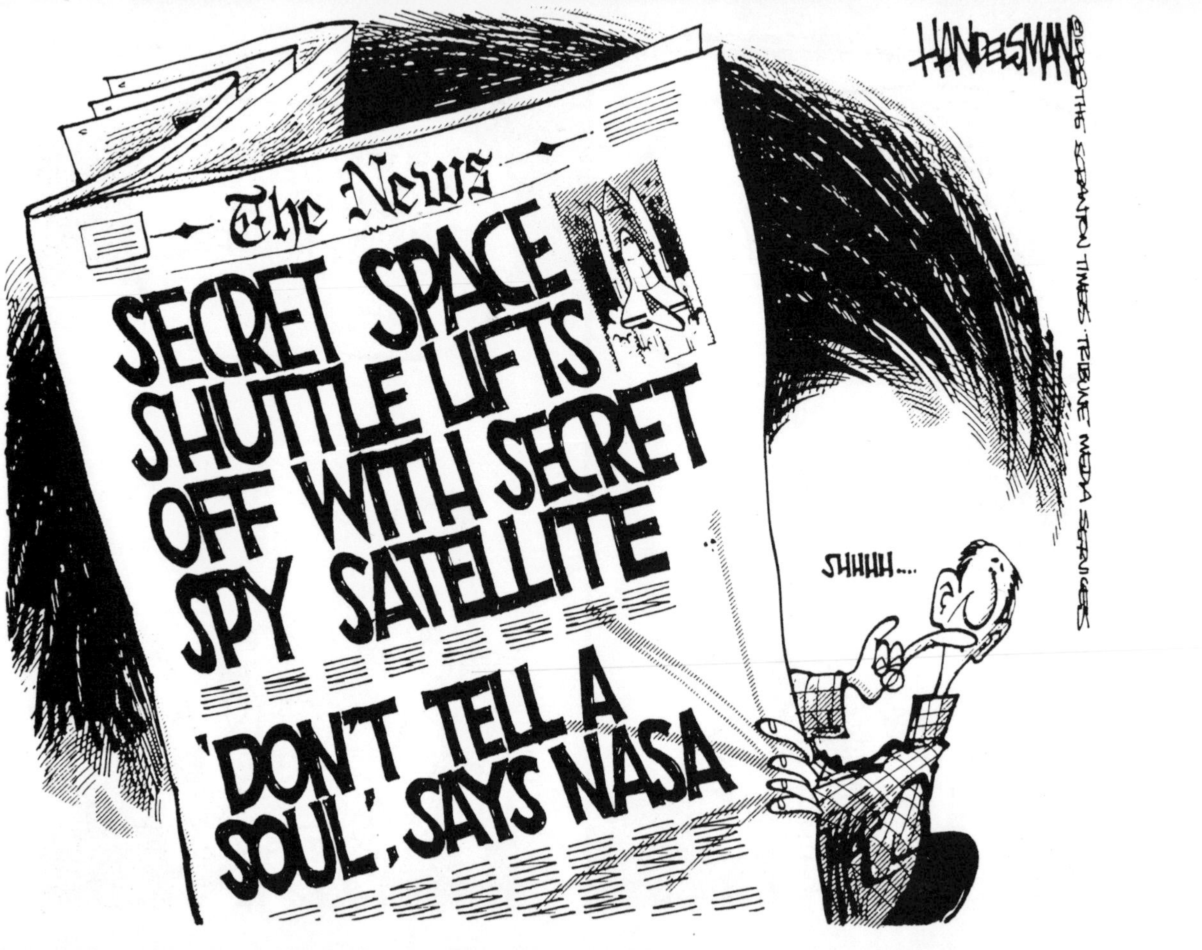
HANDELSMAN
©1990 THE SCRANTON TIMES · TRIBUNE MEDIA SERVICES
The News
SECRET SPACE SHUTTLE LIFTS OFF WITH SECRET SPY SATELLITE
'DON'T TELL A SOUL', SAYS NASA
SHHHH....

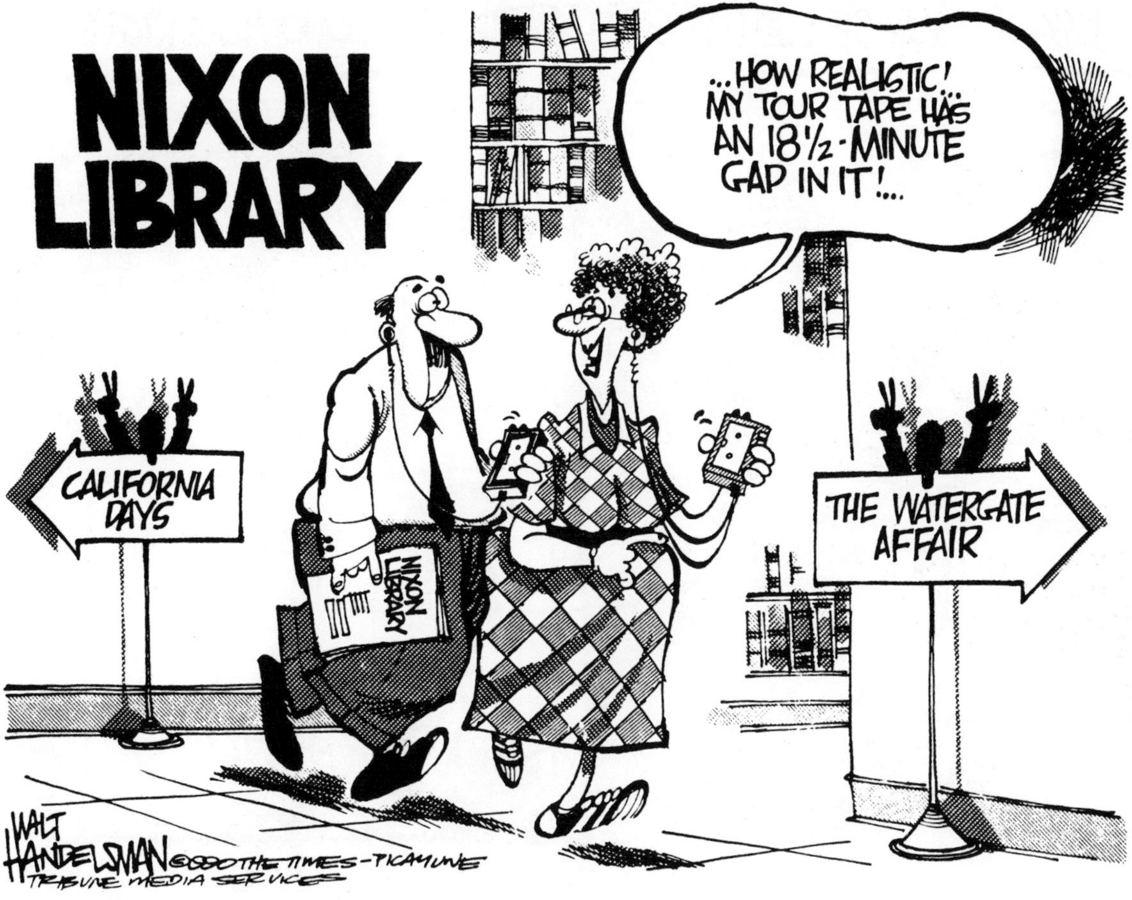
NIXON LIBRARY
...HOW REALISTIC! MY TOUR TAPE HAS AN 18½-MINUTE GAP IN IT!...
CALIFORNIA DAYS
NIXON LIBRARY
THE WATERGATE AFFAIR
WALT HANDELSMAN ©1990 THE TIMES-PICAYUNE
TRIBUNE MEDIA SERVICES

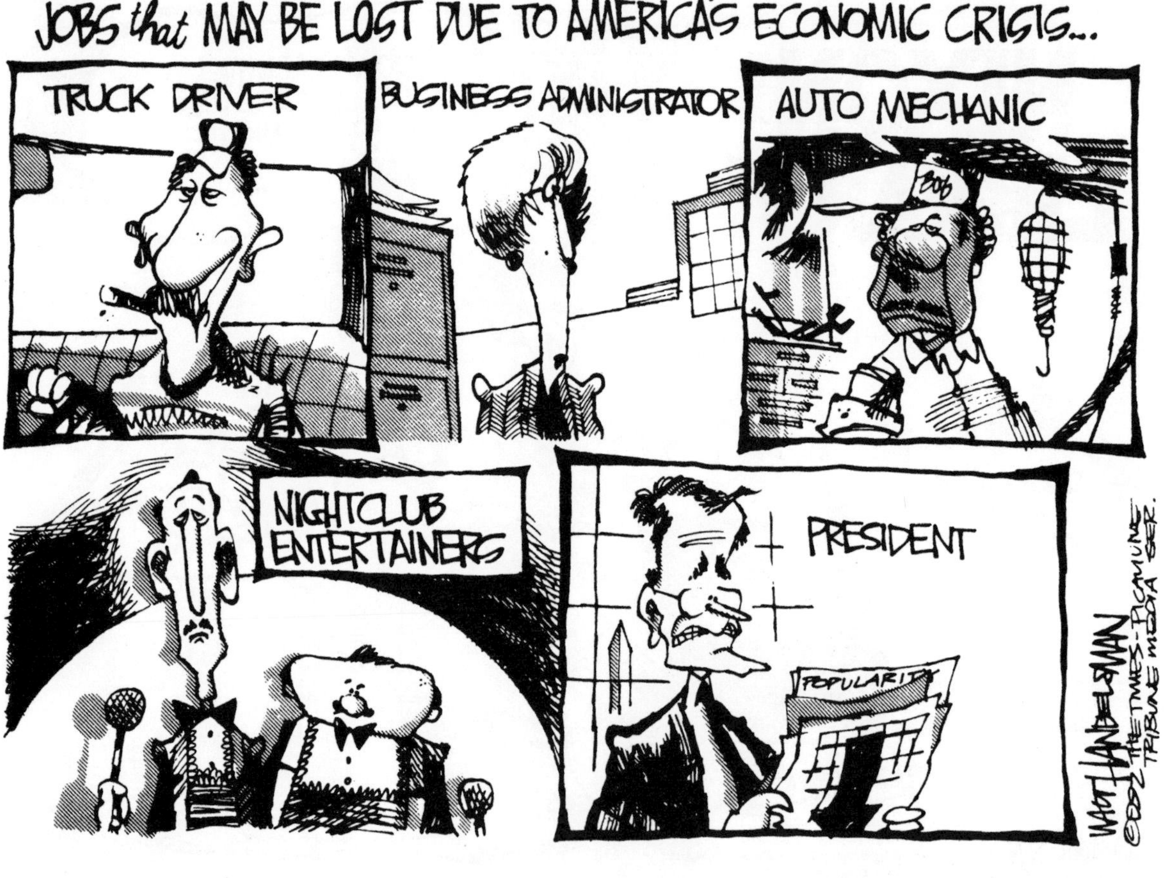

JOBS that MAY BE LOST DUE TO AMERICA'S ECONOMIC CRISIS...
TRUCK DRIVER
BUSINESS ADMINISTRATOR
AUTO MECHANIC
BOB
NIGHTCLUB ENTERTAINERS
PRESIDENT
POPULARITY
WALT HANDELSMAN
THE TIMES-PICAYUNE
TRIBUNE MEDIA SER.

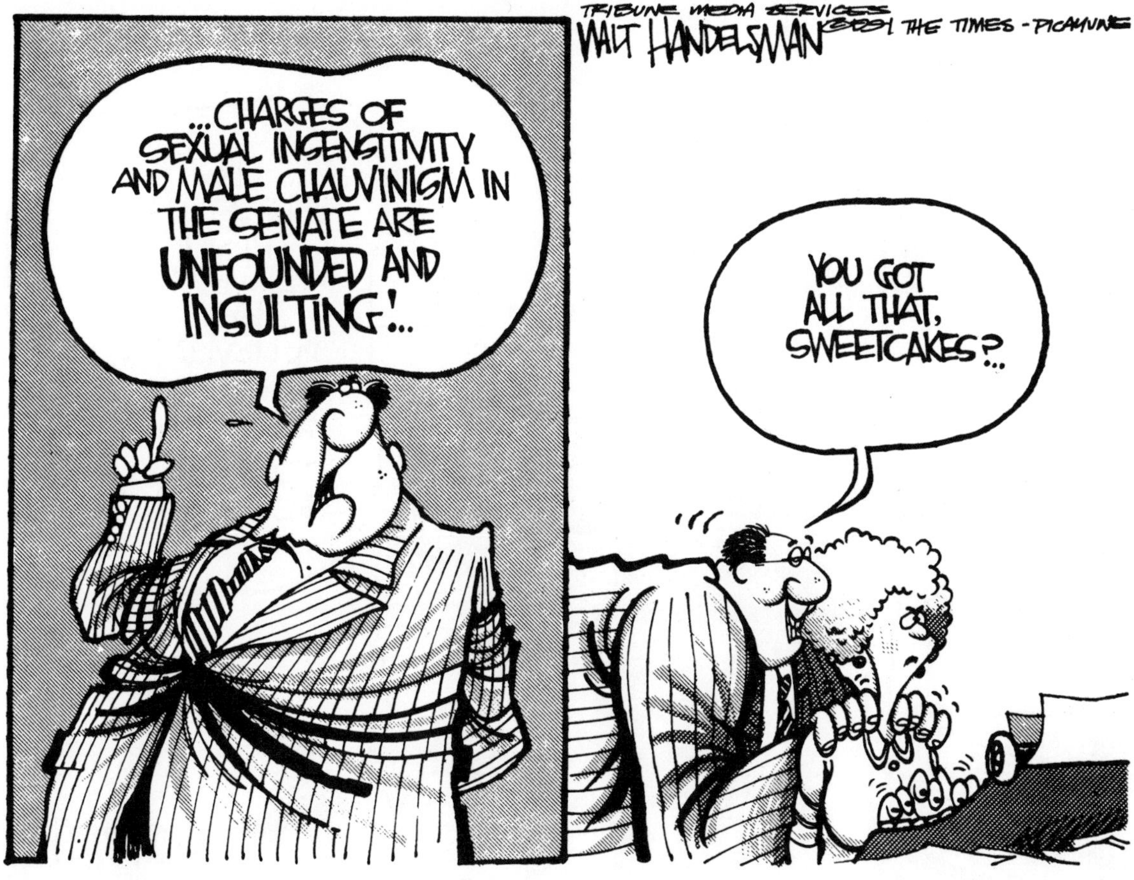
TRIBUNE MEDIA SERVICES
WALT HANDELSMAN ©1991 THE TIMES - PICAYUNE
...CHARGES OF SEXUAL INSENSITIVITY AND MALE CHAUVINISM IN THE SENATE ARE UNFOUNDED AND INSULTING!...
YOU GOT ALL THAT, SWEETCAKES?...

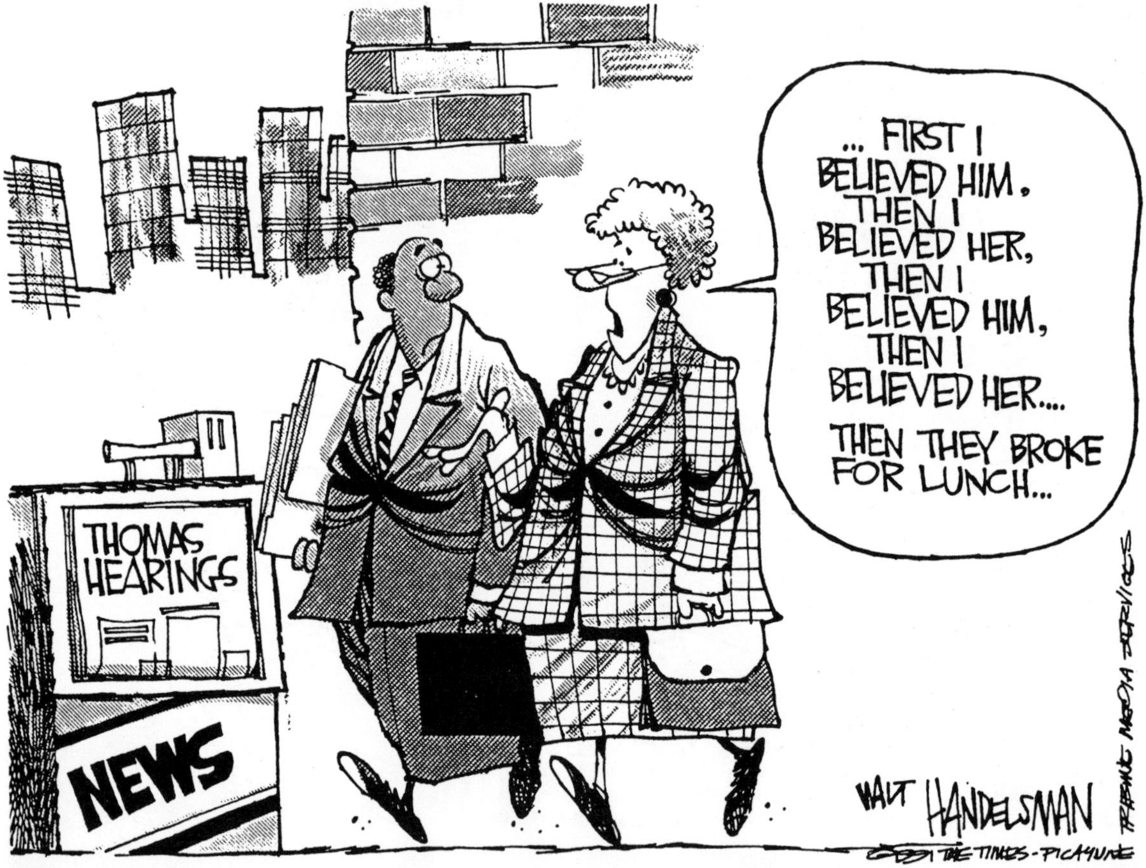

... FIRST I BELIEVED HIM. THEN I BELIEVED HER, THEN I BELIEVED HIM, THEN I BELIEVED HER....
THEN THEY BROKE FOR LUNCH...
THOMAS HEARINGS
NEWS
WALT HANDELSMAN
©1991 THE TIMES-PICAYUNE
TRIBUNE MEDIA SERVICES

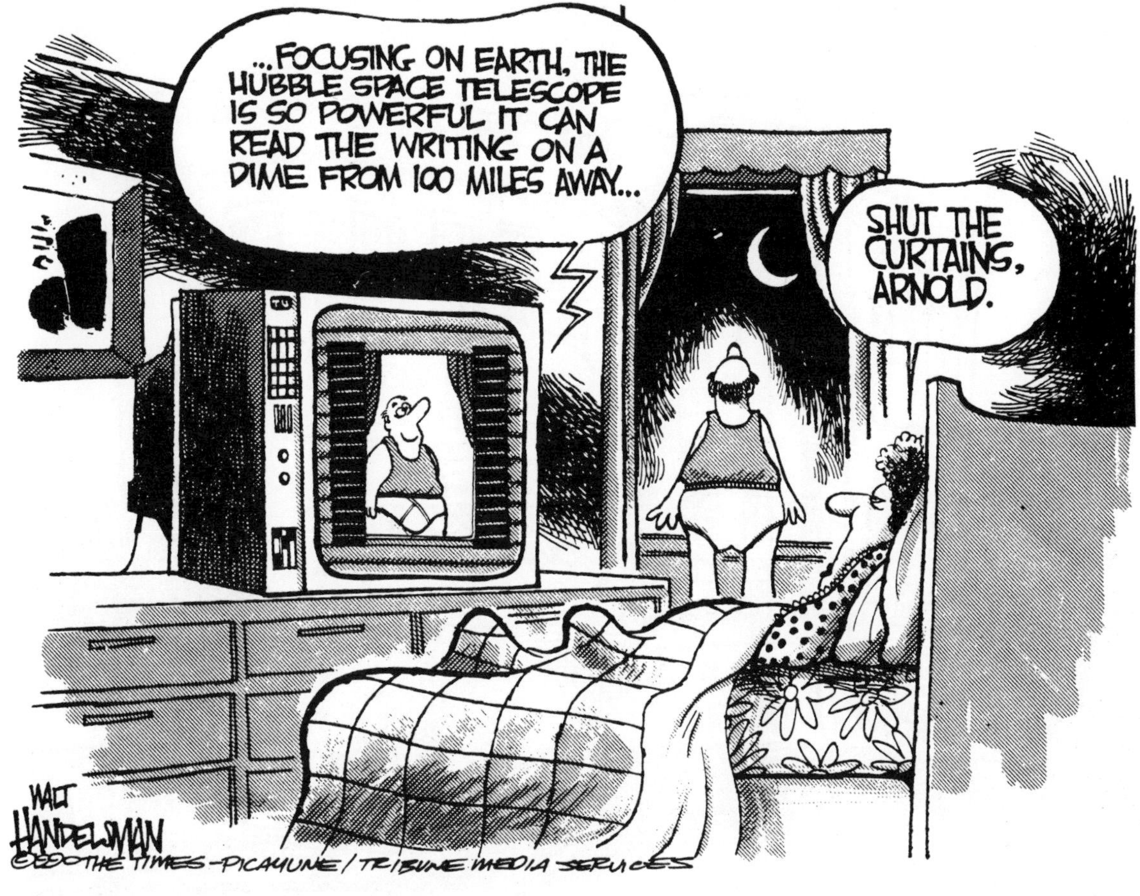
...FOCUSING ON EARTH, THE HUBBLE SPACE TELESCOPE IS SO POWERFUL IT CAN READ THE WRITING ON A DIME FROM 100 MILES AWAY...
SHUT THE CURTAINS, ARNOLD.
WALT HANDELSMAN
©1990 THE TIMES-PICAYUNE/TRIBUNE MEDIA SERVICES

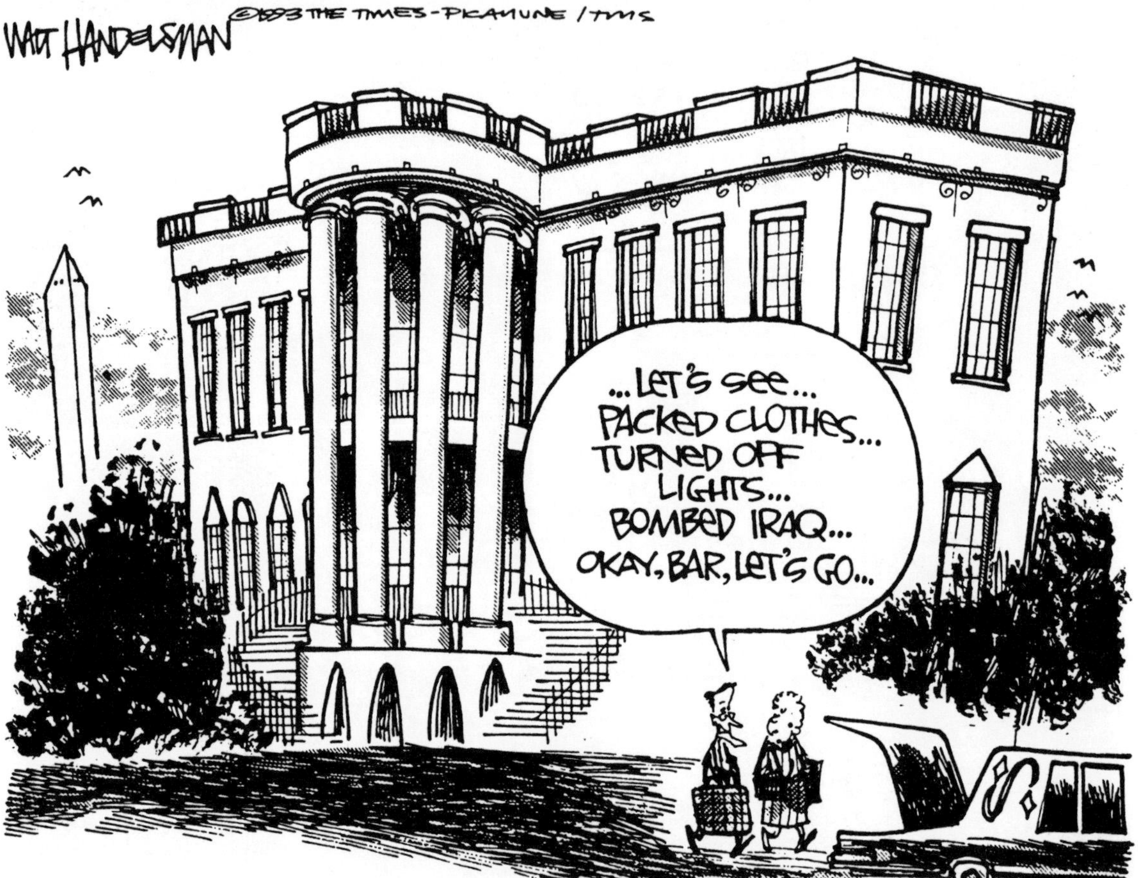
WALT HANDELSMAN
©1993 THE TIMES-PICAYUNE / TMS
...LET'S SEE...
PACKED CLOTHES...
TURNED OFF
LIGHTS...
BOMBED IRAQ...
OKAY, BAR, LET'S GO...

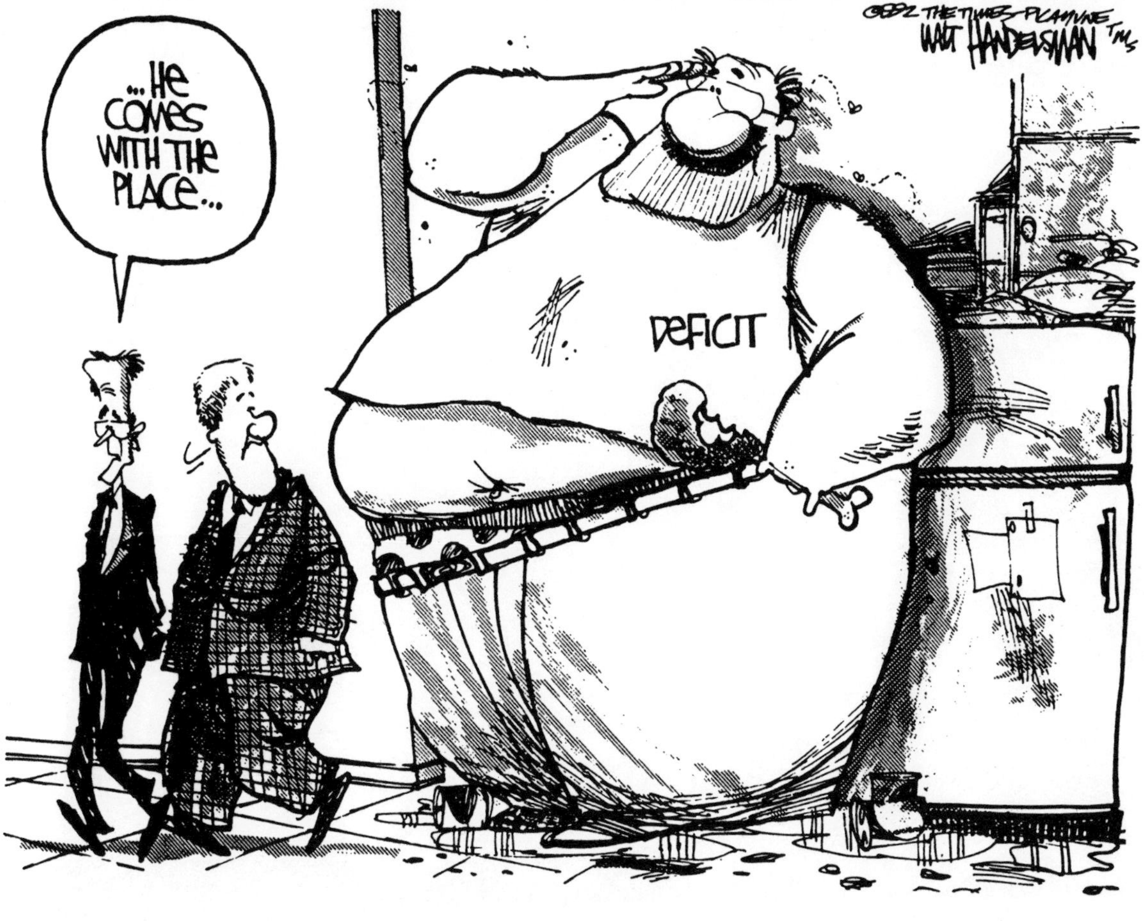
...HE COMES WITH THE PLACE...
DEFICIT
©1992 THE TIMES-PICAYUNE
WALT HANDELSMAN
TMS

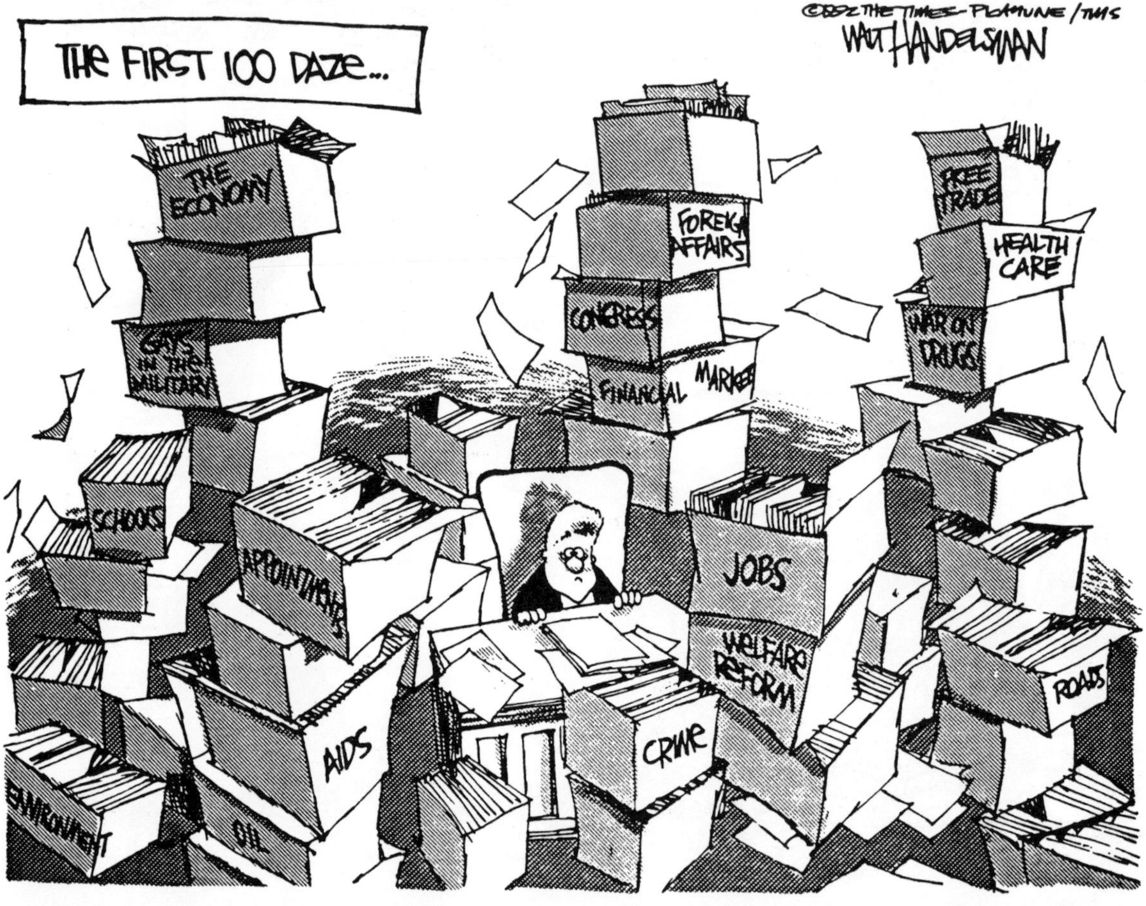
THE FIRST 100 DAZE...
©1992 THE TIMES-PICAYUNE / TMS
WALT HANDELSMAN
THE ECONOMY
GAYS IN THE MILITARY
SCHOOLS
APPOINTMENTS
ENVIRONMENT
OIL
AIDS
FOREIGN AFFAIRS
CONGRESS
FINANCIAL MARKETS
JOBS
WELFARE REFORM
CRIME
FREE TRADE
HEALTH CARE
WAR ON DRUGS
ROADS

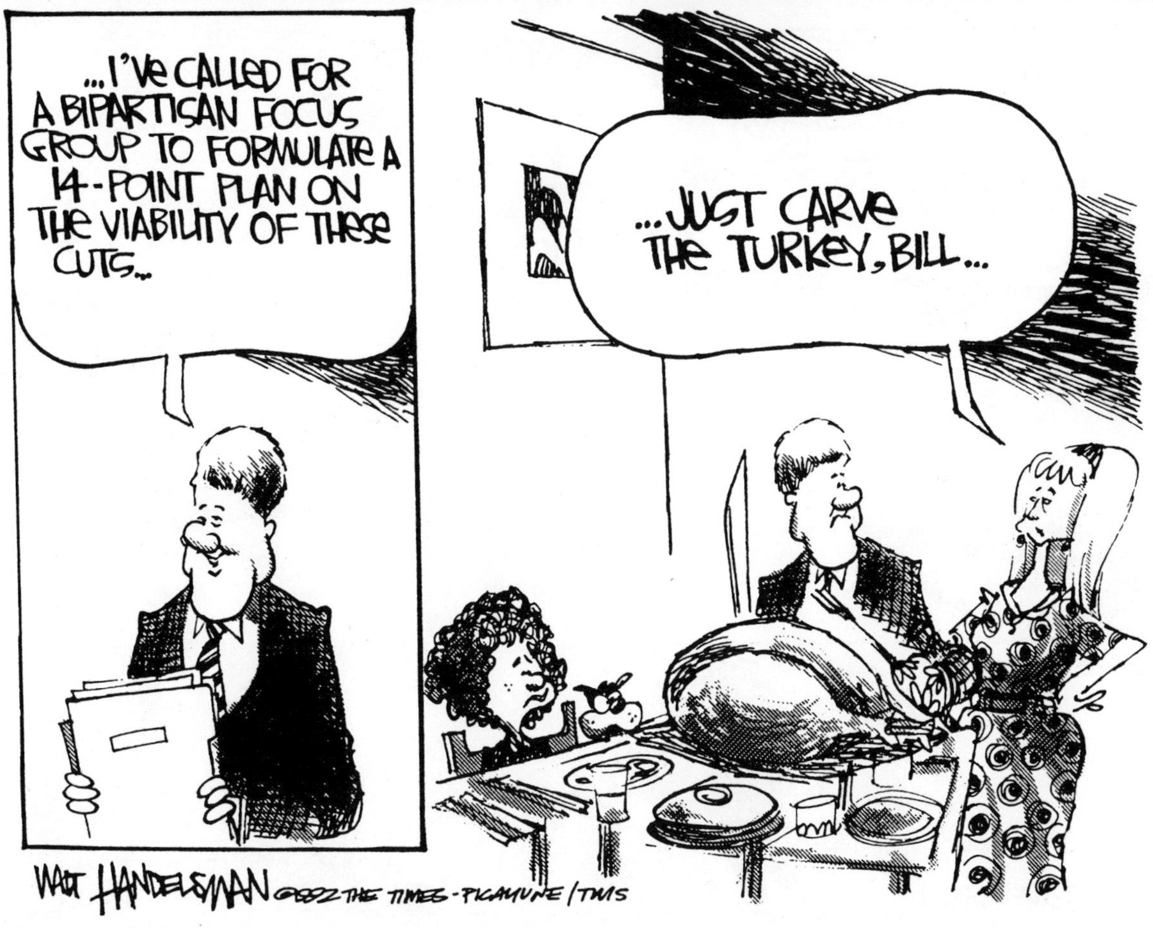
...I'VE CALLED FOR A BIPARTISAN FOCUS GROUP TO FORMULATE A 14-POINT PLAN ON THE VIABILITY OF THESE CUTS...
...JUST CARVE THE TURKEY, BILL...
WALT HANDELSMAN ©1992 THE TIMES-PICAYUNE / TMS

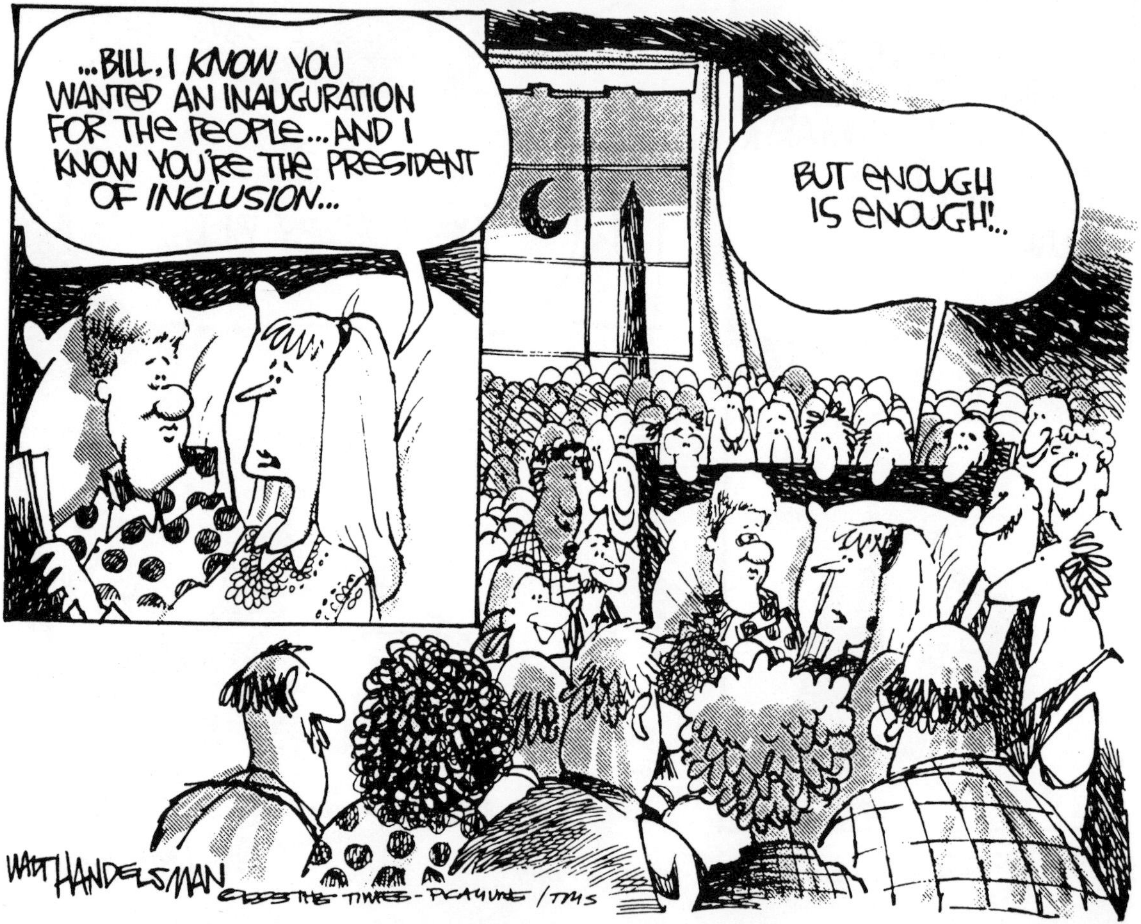
...BILL, I *KNOW* YOU WANTED AN INAUGURATION FOR THE PEOPLE... AND I KNOW YOU'RE THE PRESIDENT OF *INCLUSION*...
BUT ENOUGH IS ENOUGH!...
WALT HANDELSMAN
THE TIMES-PICAYUNE / TMS

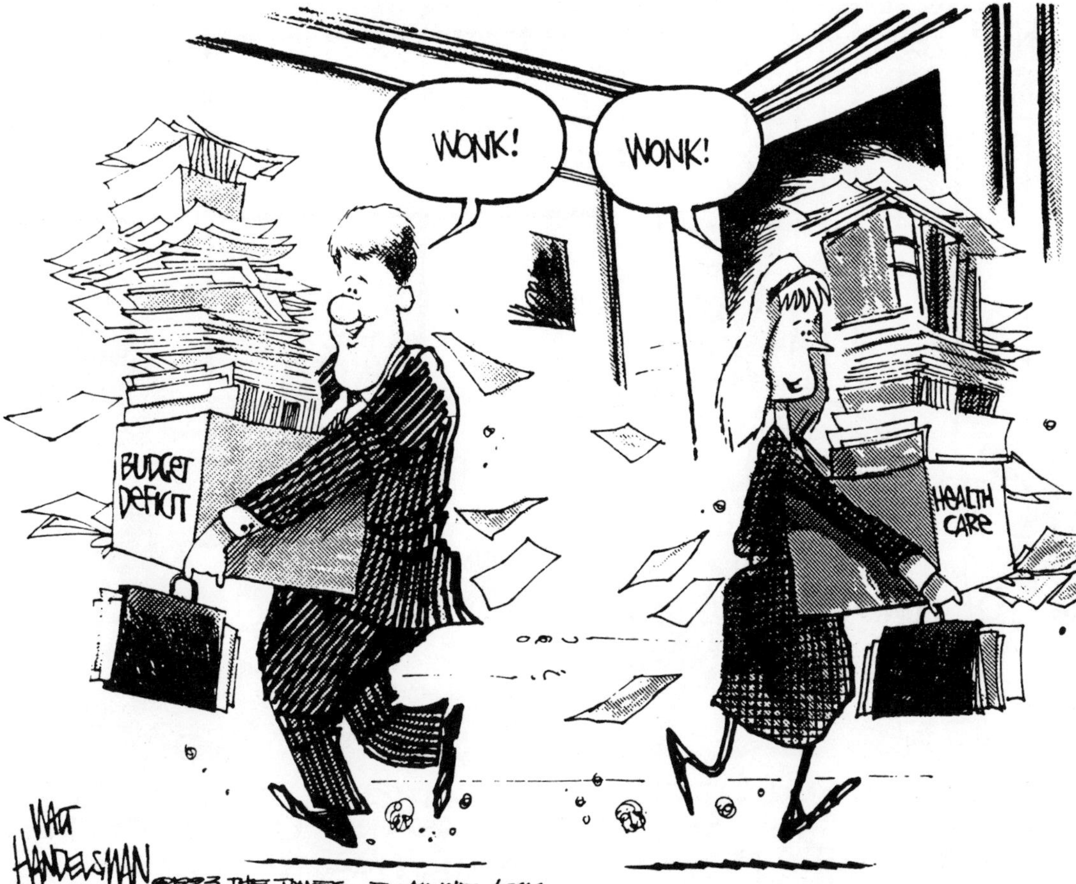
WONK!
WONK!
BUDGET DEFICIT
HEALTH CARE
WALT HANDELSMAN ©1993 THE TIMES - PICAYUNE /TMS

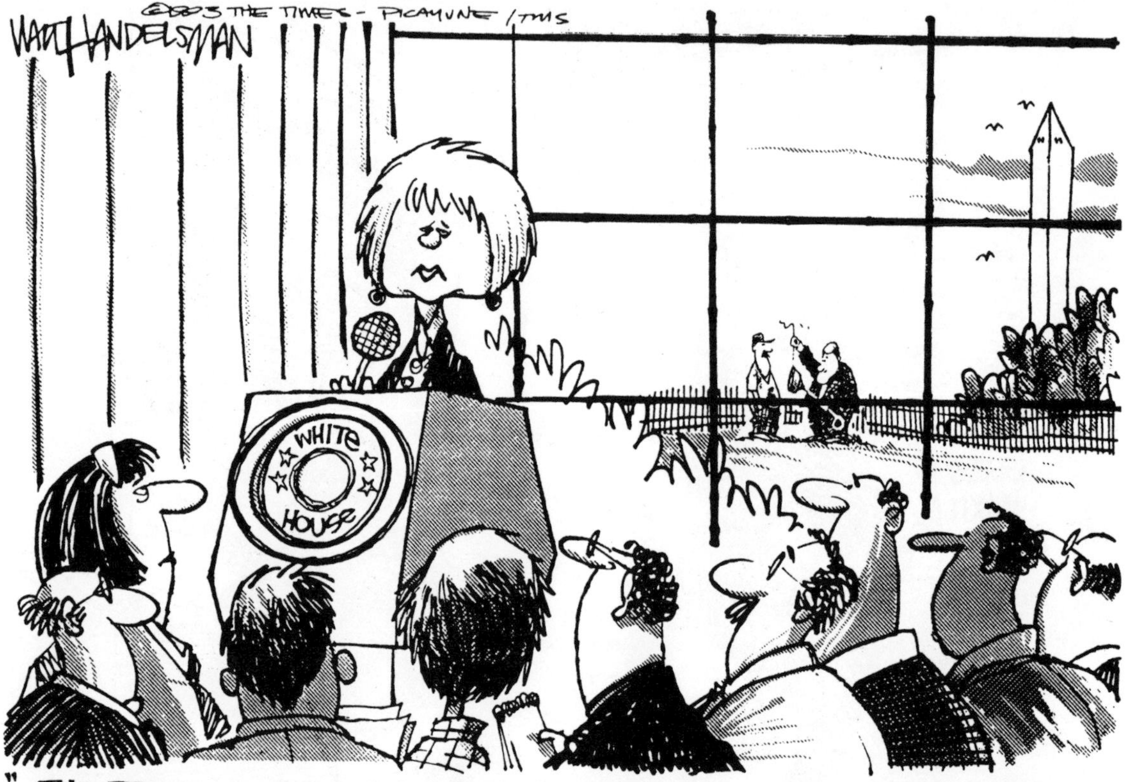
©2003 THE TIMES-PICAYUNE / TMS
WALT HANDELSMAN
WHITE HOUSE

"...THE PRESIDENT WILL ADDRESS YOUR CRITICISM OF HIS MICRO-MANAGEMENT STYLE, JUST AS SOON AS HE'S FINISHED HELPING THE GARDENER PUT A NEW STRING IN THE WEED WACKER..."

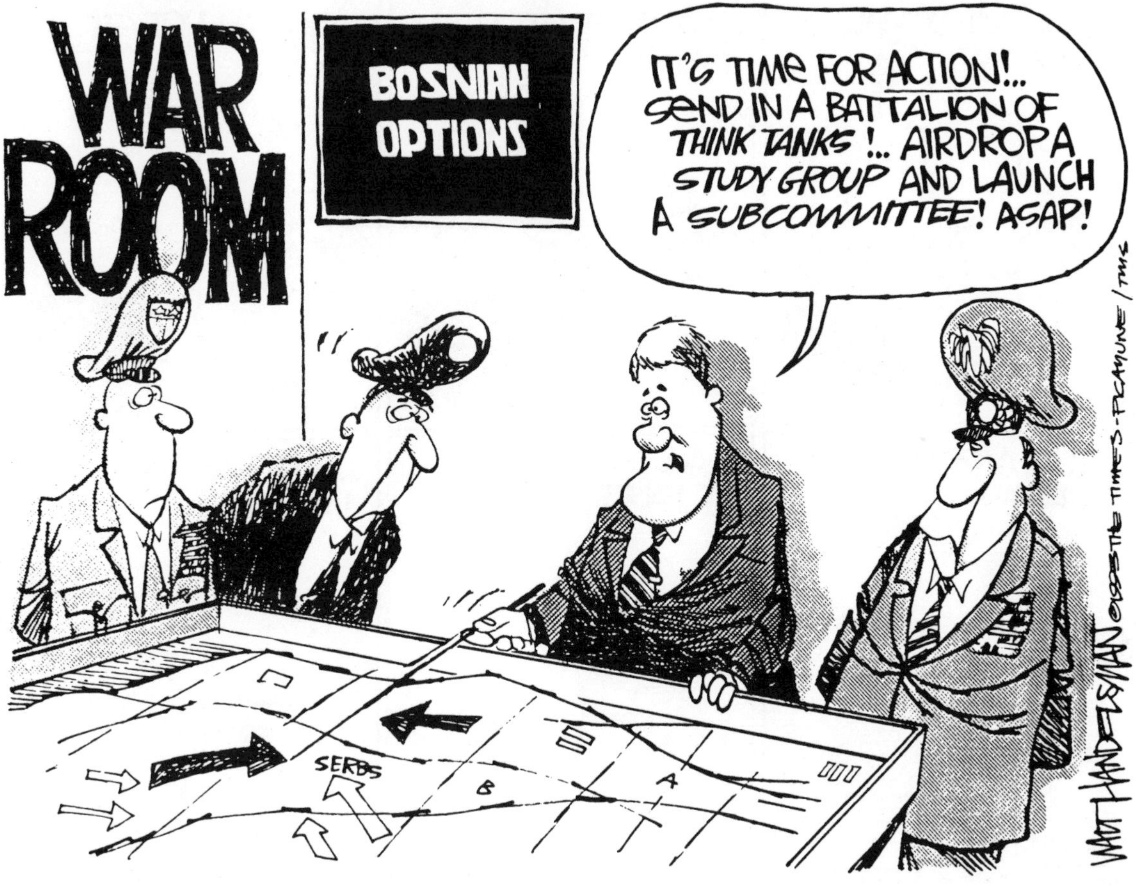
WAR ROOM
BOSNIAN OPTIONS
IT'S TIME FOR ACTION!... SEND IN A BATTALION OF THINK TANKS!... AIRDROP A STUDY GROUP AND LAUNCH A SUBCOMMITTEE! ASAP!
SERBS
B
A
WALT HANDELSMAN
THE TIMES-PICAYUNE / TMS

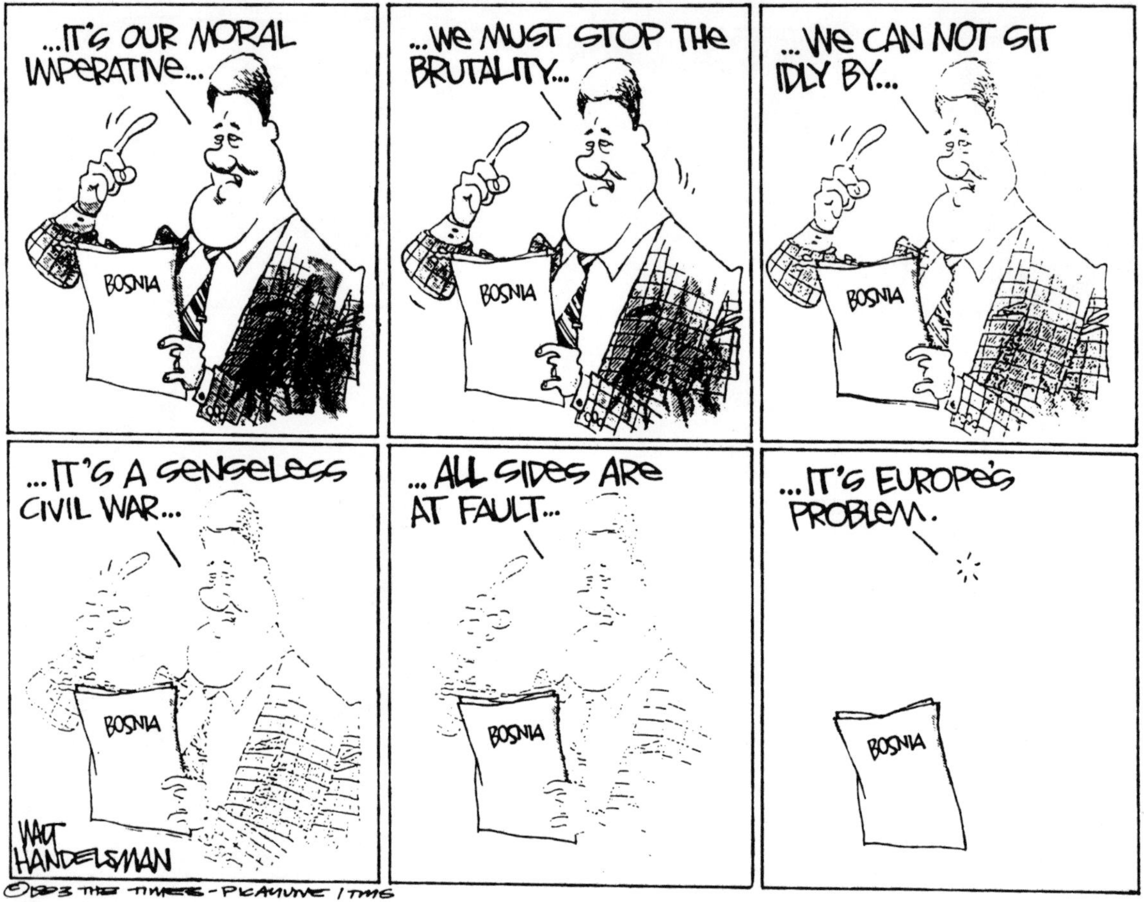
...IT'S OUR MORAL IMPERATIVE...
BOSNIA
...WE MUST STOP THE BRUTALITY...
BOSNIA
...WE CAN NOT SIT IDLY BY...
BOSNIA
...IT'S A SENSELESS CIVIL WAR...
BOSNIA
WALT HANDELSMAN
...ALL SIDES ARE AT FAULT...
BOSNIA
...IT'S EUROPE'S PROBLEM.
BOSNIA

©1993 THE TIMES-PICAYUNE / TMS

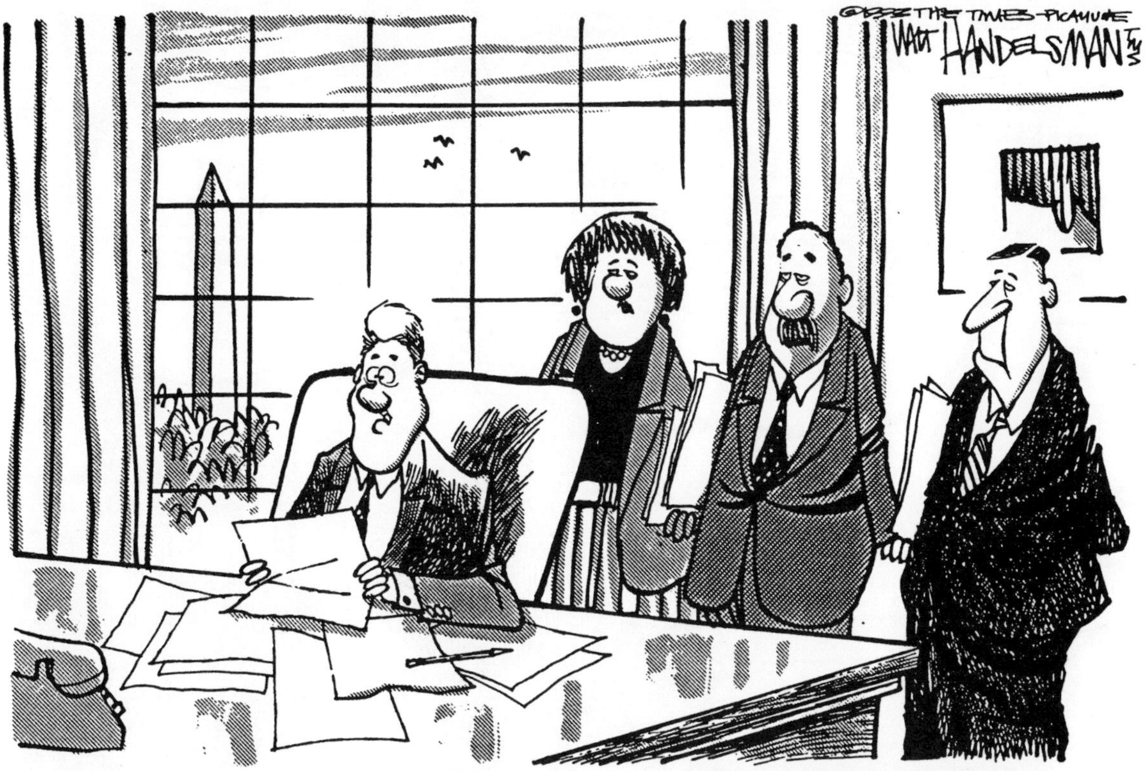
THE TIMES-PICAYUNE
WALT HANDELSMAN

"...IS THIS MY BOSNIA COMPROMISE... MY HAITIAN REFUGEE COMPROMISE... MY GAYS IN THE MILITARY COMPROMISE... OR MY BUDGET COMPROMISE..?"

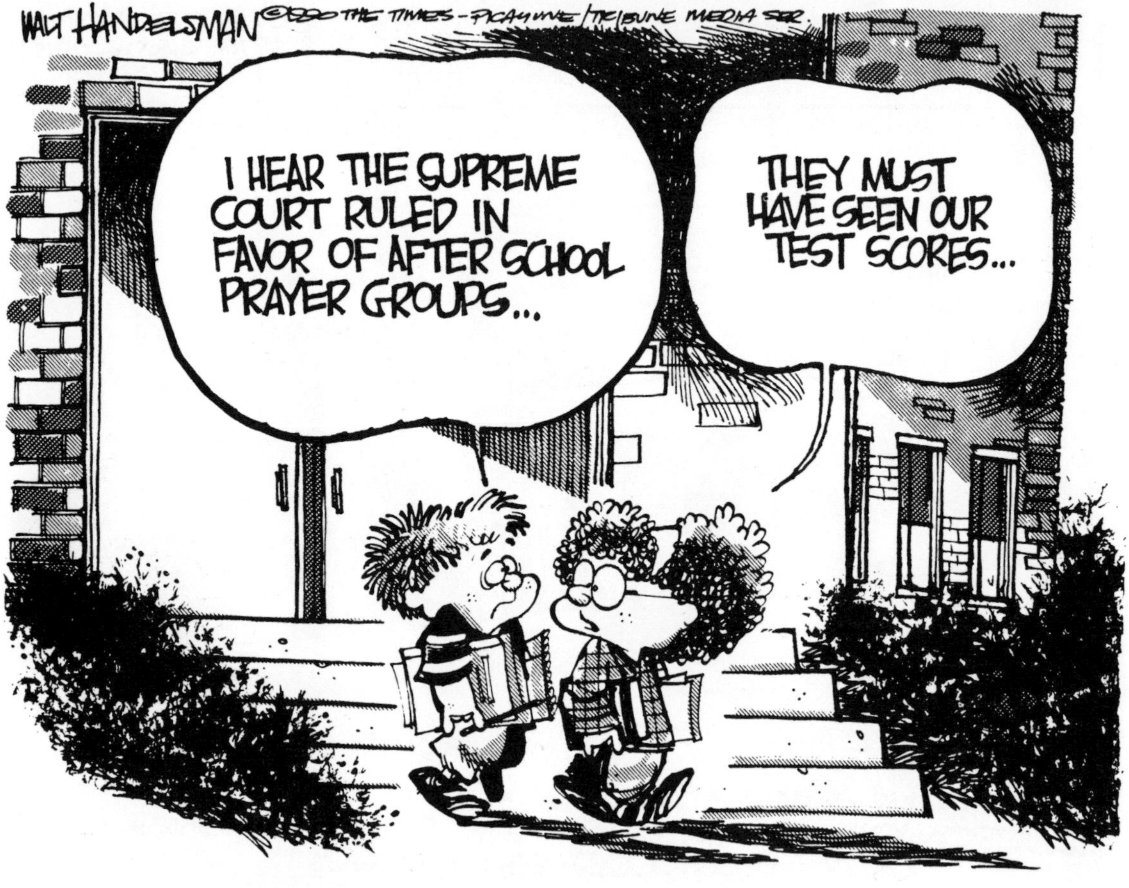
WALT HANDELSMAN ©1990 THE TIMES-PICAYUNE / TRIBUNE MEDIA SER.
I HEAR THE SUPREME COURT RULED IN FAVOR OF AFTER SCHOOL PRAYER GROUPS...
THEY MUST HAVE SEEN OUR TEST SCORES...

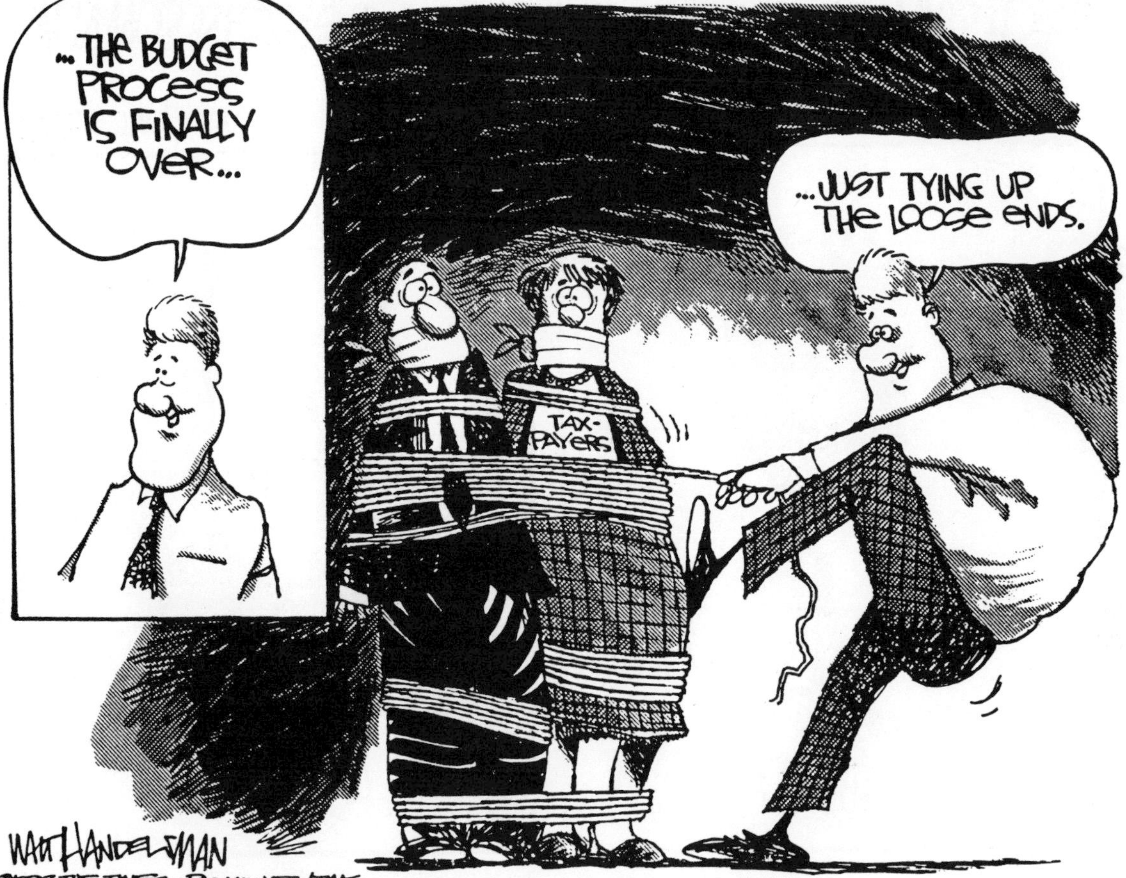
...THE BUDGET PROCESS IS FINALLY OVER...
...JUST TYING UP THE LOOSE ENDS.
TAX-PAYERS
WALT HANDELSMAN
©1993 THE TIMES-PICAYUNE /TMS

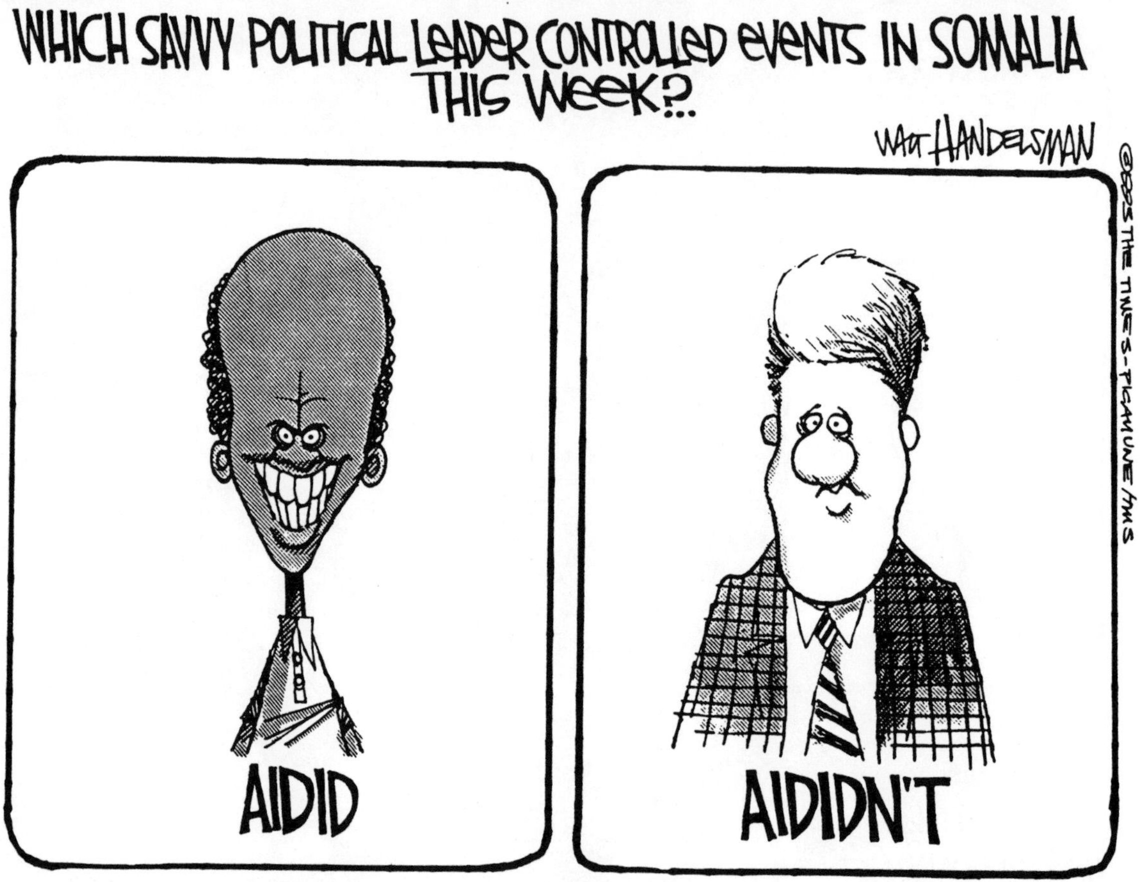
WHICH SAVVY POLITICAL LEADER CONTROLLED EVENTS IN SOMALIA THIS WEEK?...
WALT HANDELSMAN
THE TIMES-PICAYUNE/TMS
AIDID
AIDIDN'T

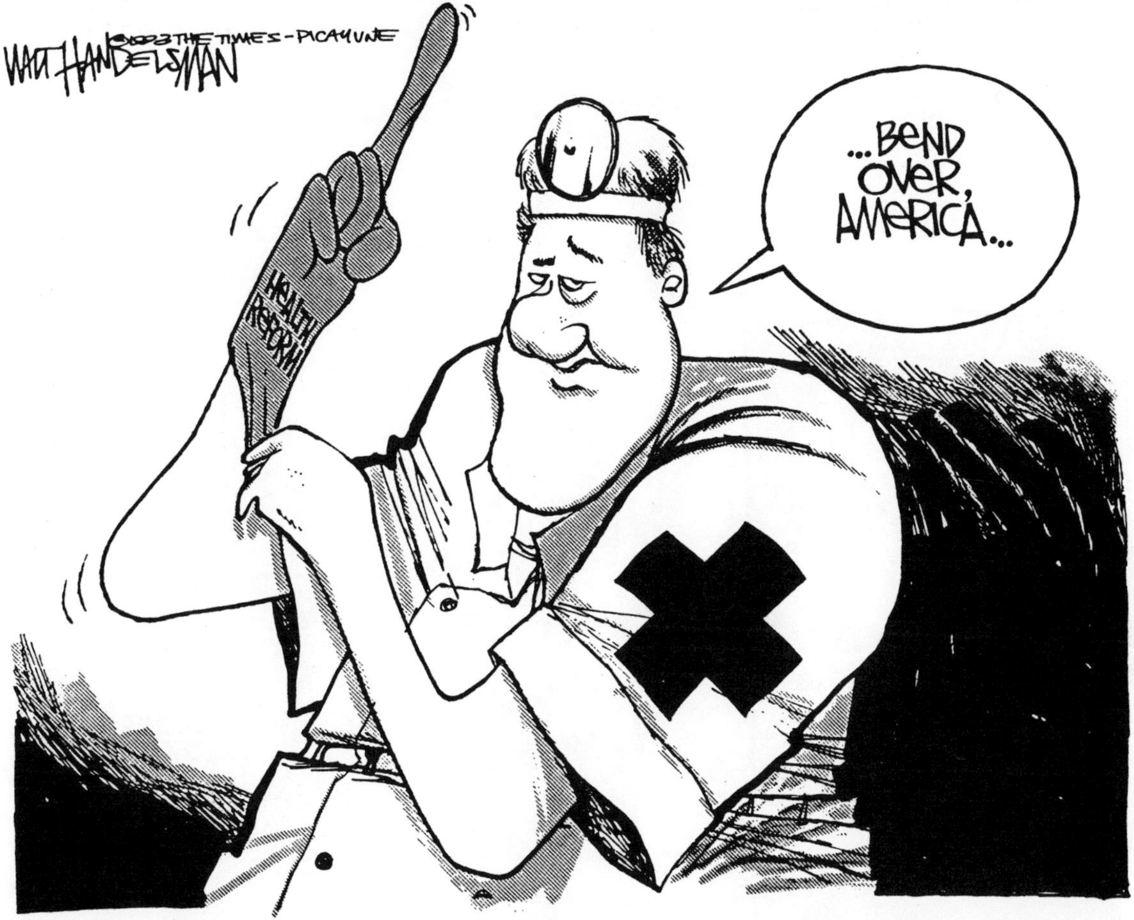
WALT HANDELSMAN ©2003 THE TIMES-PICAYUNE
HEALTH REFORM
...BEND OVER, AMERICA...

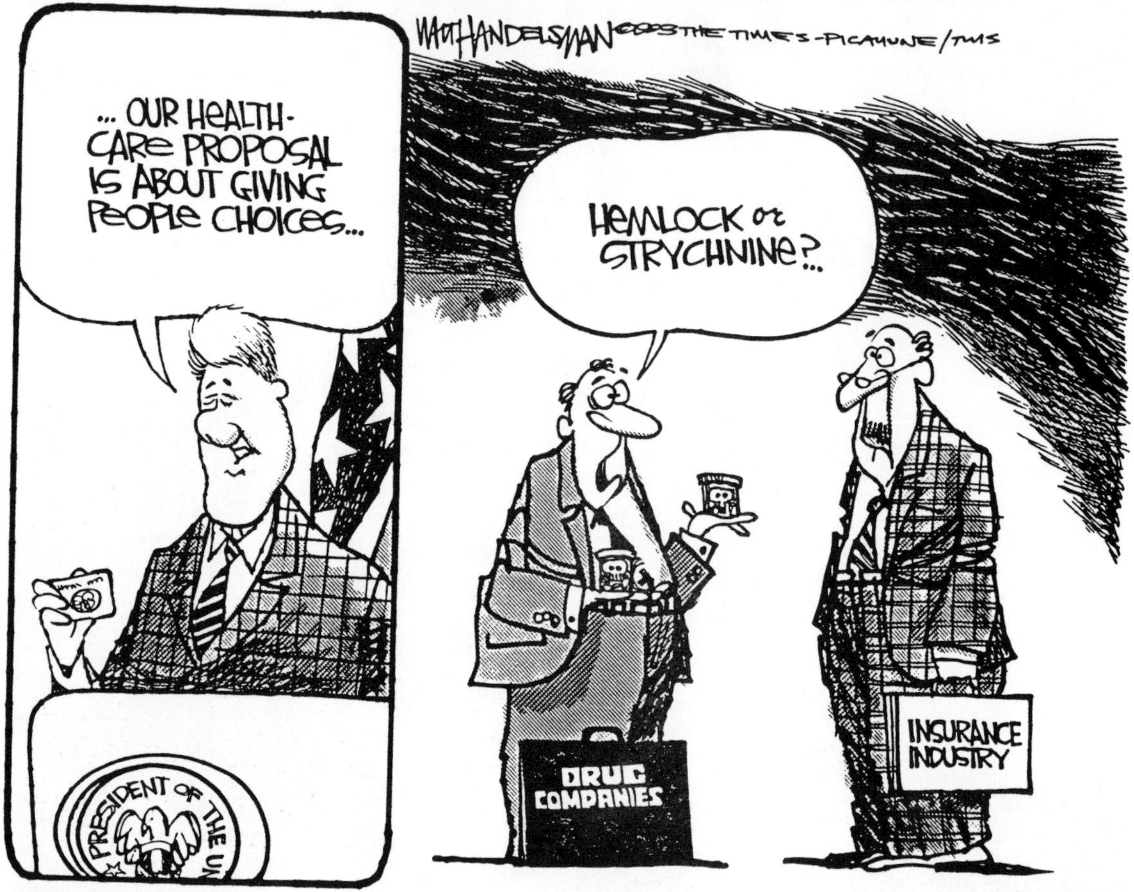

WALT HANDELSMAN ©1993 THE TIMES-PICAYUNE/TMS
... OUR HEALTH-CARE PROPOSAL IS ABOUT GIVING PEOPLE CHOICES...
HEMLOCK or STRYCHNINE?...
PRESIDENT OF THE U
DRUG COMPANIES
INSURANCE INDUSTRY

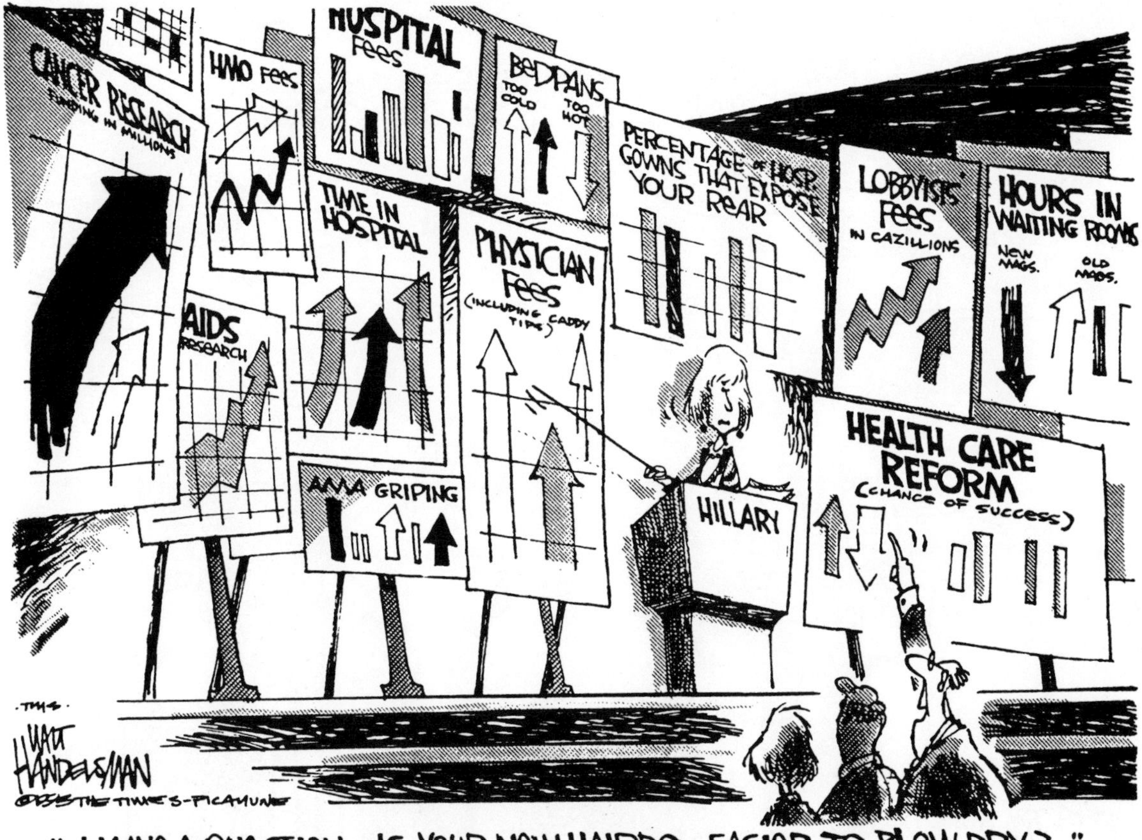
CANCER RESEARCH
FUNDING IN MILLIONS
HMO FEES
HOSPITAL
FEES
BEDPANS
TOO COLD
TOO HOT
PERCENTAGE OF HOSP. GOWNS THAT EXPOSE YOUR REAR
LOBBYISTS' FEES
IN CAZILLIONS
HOURS IN WAITING ROOMS
NEW MAGS.
OLD MAGS.
TIME IN HOSPITAL
PHYSICIAN FEES
(INCLUDING CADDY TIPS)
AIDS RESEARCH
AMA GRIPING
HILLARY
HEALTH CARE REFORM
(CHANCE OF SUCCESS)
WALT HANDELSMAN
©93 THE TIMES-PICAYUNE

"...I HAVE A QUESTION... IS YOUR NEW HAIRDO EASIER TO BLOW DRY?..."

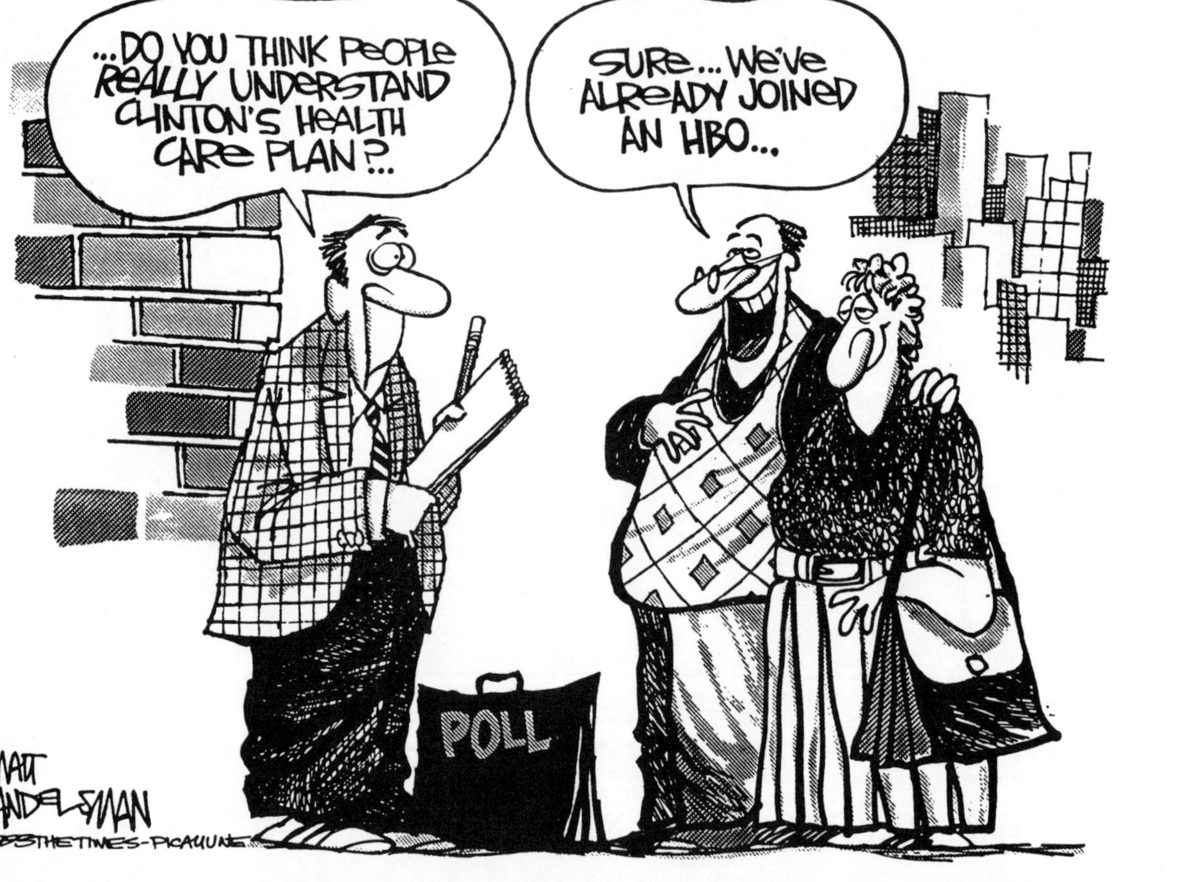
...DO YOU THINK PEOPLE REALLY UNDERSTAND CLINTON'S HEALTH CARE PLAN?...
SURE... WE'VE ALREADY JOINED AN HBO...
POLL
WALT HANDELSMAN
©1993 THE TIMES-PICAYUNE

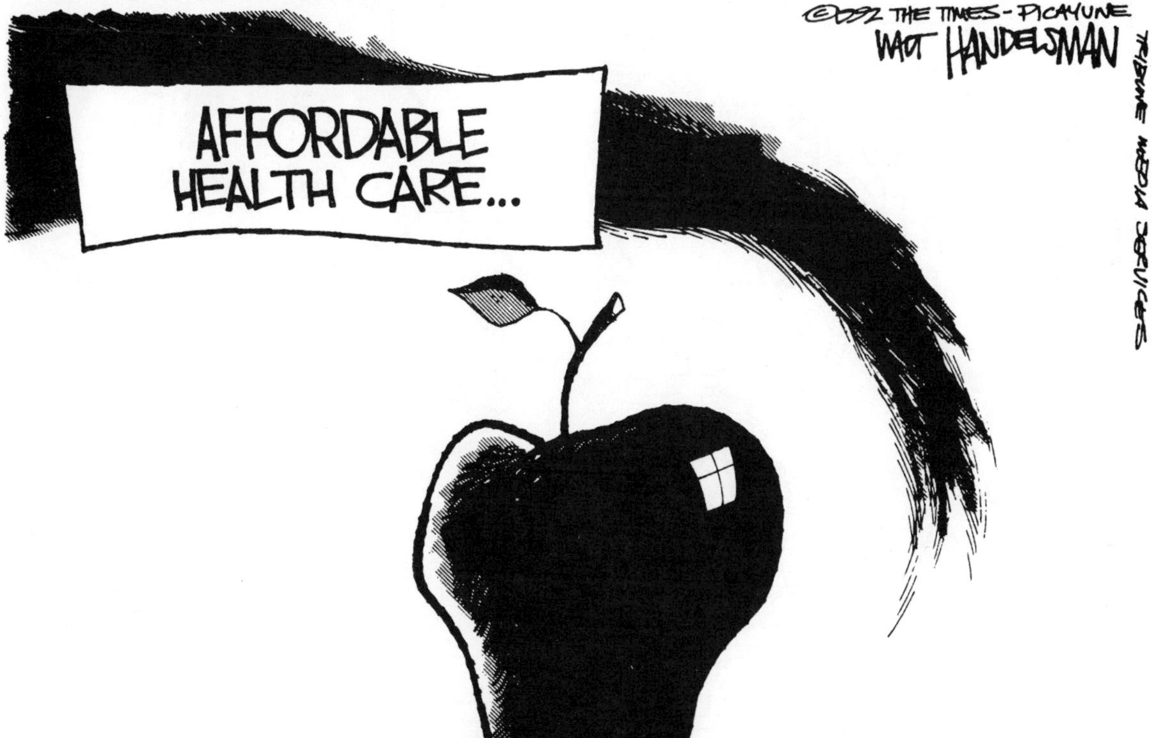

AFFORDABLE HEALTH CARE...
©1992 THE TIMES-PICAYUNE
WALT HANDELSMAN
TRIBUNE MEDIA SERVICES

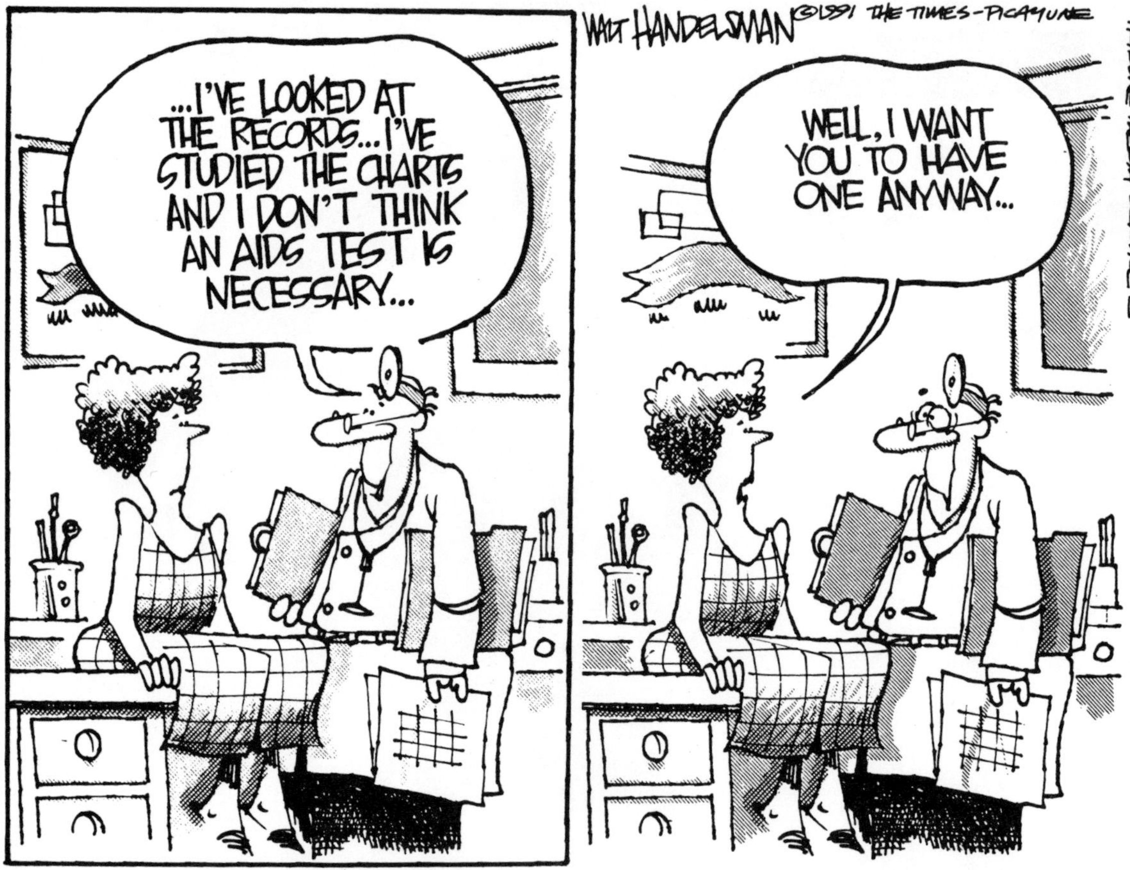
WALT HANDELSMAN ©1991 THE TIMES-PICAYUNE
TRIBUNE MEDIA SERVICES
...I'VE LOOKED AT THE RECORDS... I'VE STUDIED THE CHARTS AND I DON'T THINK AN AIDS TEST IS NECESSARY...
WELL, I WANT YOU TO HAVE ONE ANYWAY...

The 1992
Presidential Campaign

A saxphone-playing Elvis wannabe, the environment/education/family values President, and the little billionaire with the big ears . . . don't forget to vote.

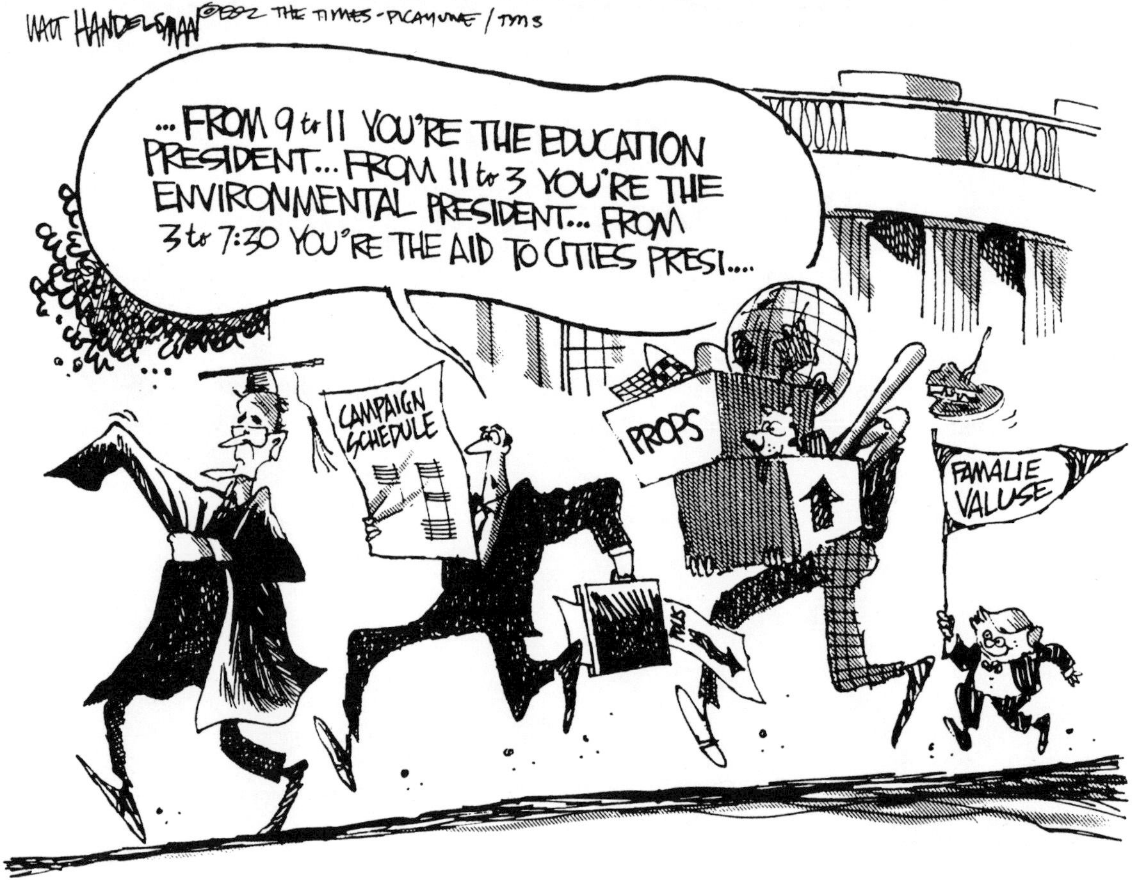
WALT HANDELSMAN ©1992 THE TIMES-PICAYUNE / TMS
...FROM 9 to 11 YOU'RE THE EDUCATION PRESIDENT... FROM 11 to 3 YOU'RE THE ENVIRONMENTAL PRESIDENT... FROM 3 to 7:30 YOU'RE THE AID TO CITIES PRESI....
CAMPAIGN SCHEDULE
PROPS
FAMALIE VALUSE

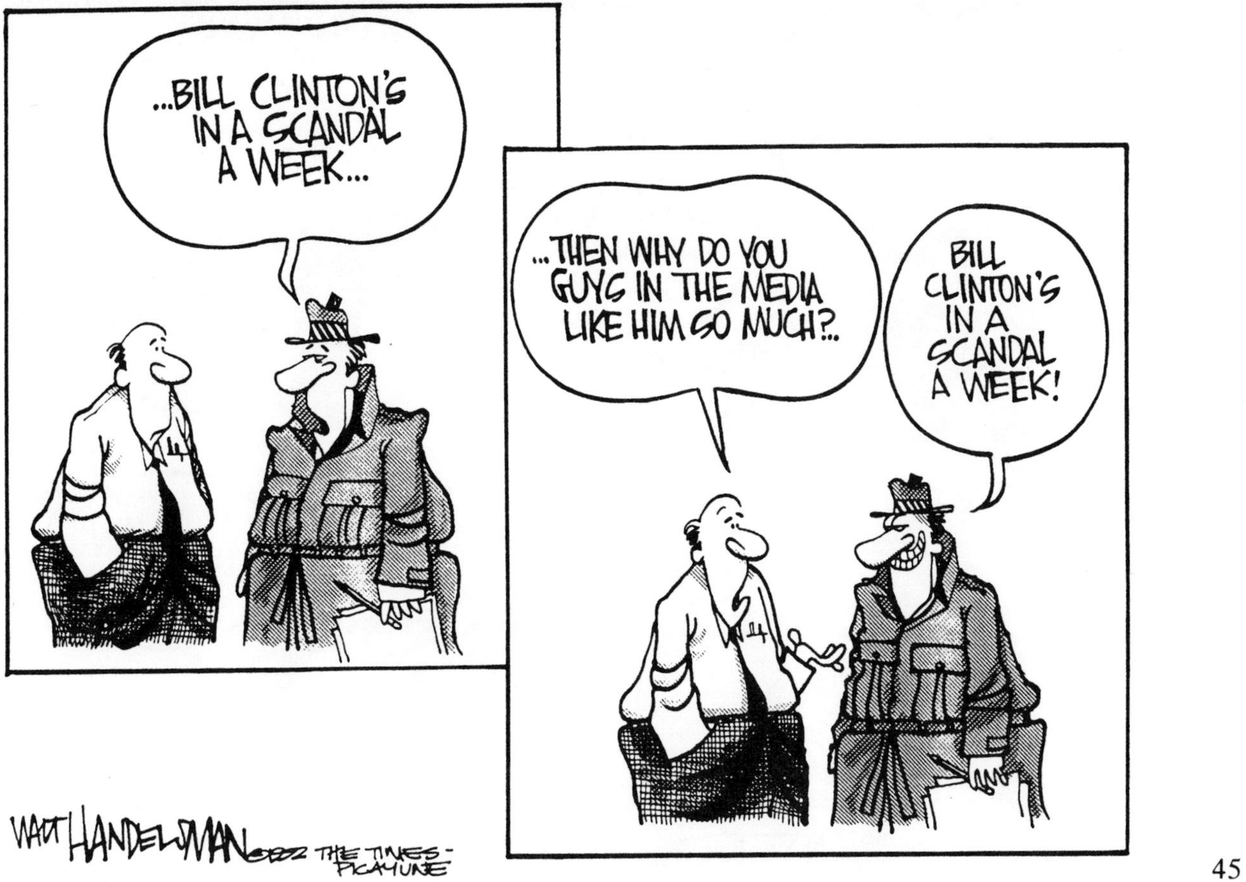
...BILL CLINTON'S IN A SCANDAL A WEEK...
...THEN WHY DO YOU GUYS IN THE MEDIA LIKE HIM SO MUCH?..
BILL CLINTON'S IN A SCANDAL A WEEK!
WALT HANDELSMAN
THE TIMES-PICAYUNE

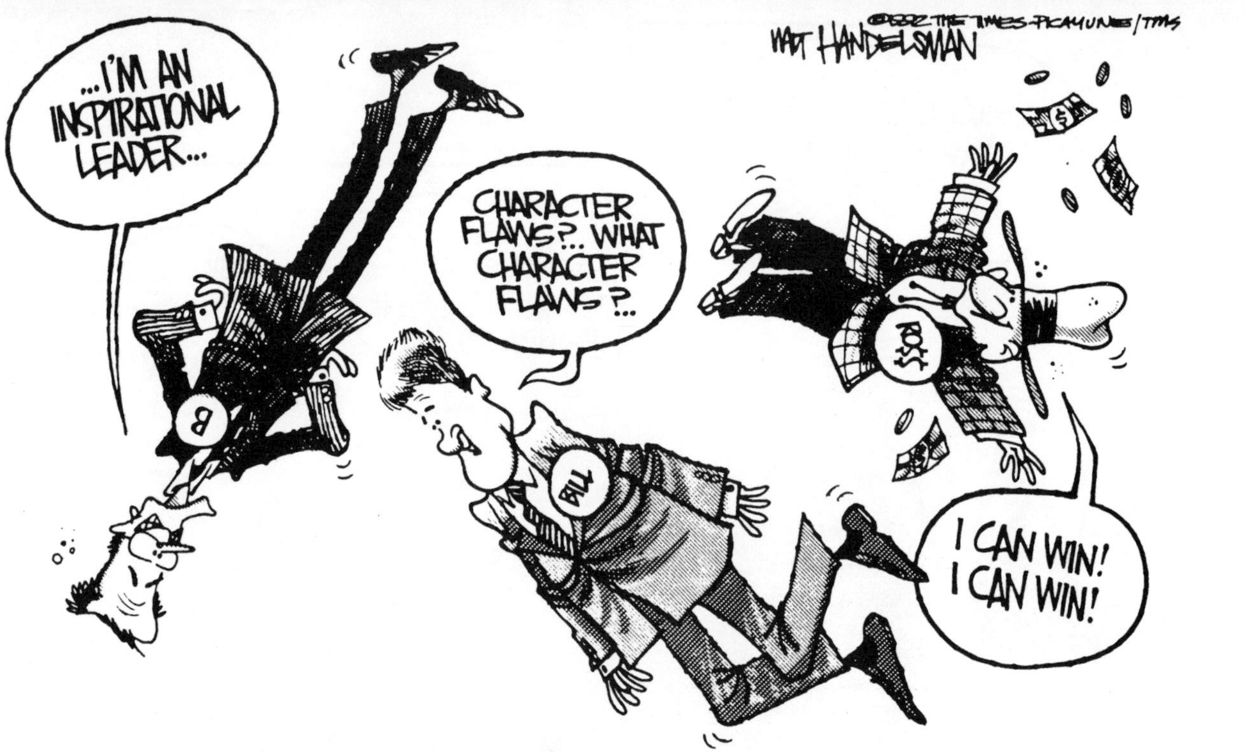
©1992 THE TIMES-PICAYUNE/TMS
WALT HANDELSMAN
...I'M AN INSPIRATIONAL LEADER...
CHARACTER FLAWS?... WHAT CHARACTER FLAWS?...
I CAN WIN! I CAN WIN!
B
BILL
ROSS

...ANOTHER 3-MAN SPACEWALK...

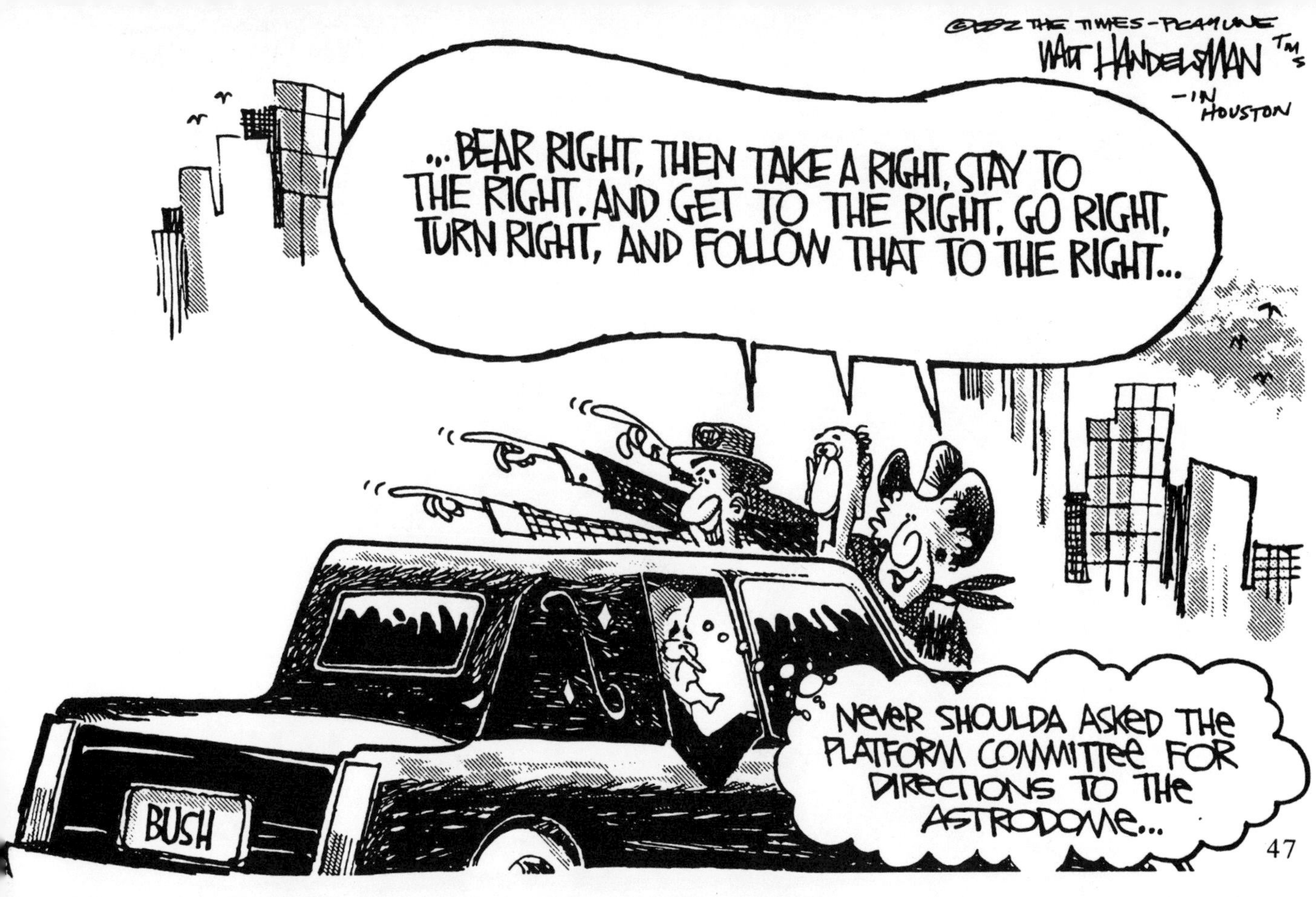
©1992 THE TIMES-PICAYUNE
WALT HANDELSMAN TMS
-IN HOUSTON
...BEAR RIGHT, THEN TAKE A RIGHT, STAY TO THE RIGHT, AND GET TO THE RIGHT, GO RIGHT, TURN RIGHT, AND FOLLOW THAT TO THE RIGHT...
BUSH
NEVER SHOULDA ASKED THE PLATFORM COMMITTEE FOR DIRECTIONS TO THE ASTRODOME...

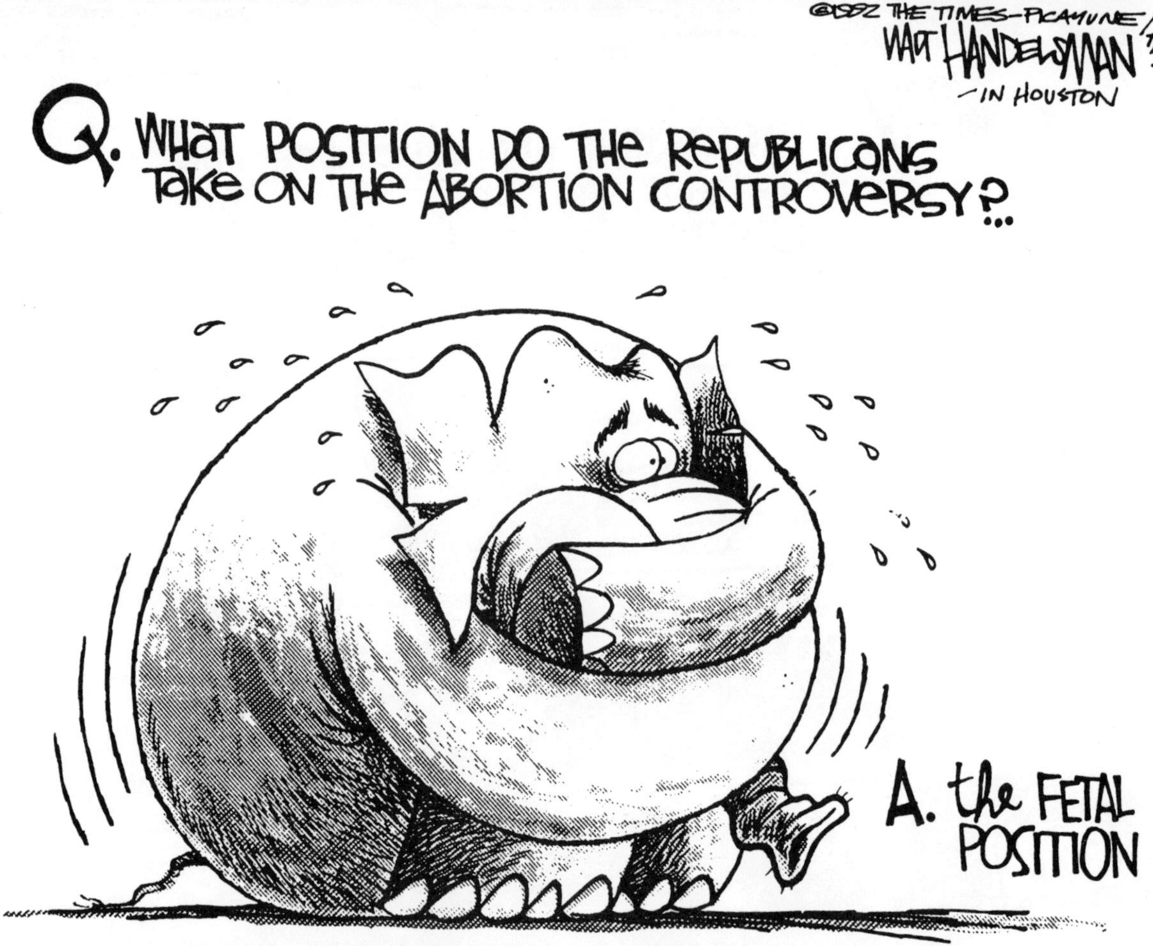
©1992 THE TIMES-PICAYUNE/
WALT HANDELSMAN TMS
-IN HOUSTON
Q. WHAT POSITION DO THE REPUBLICANS TAKE ON THE ABORTION CONTROVERSY?...
A. the FETAL POSITION

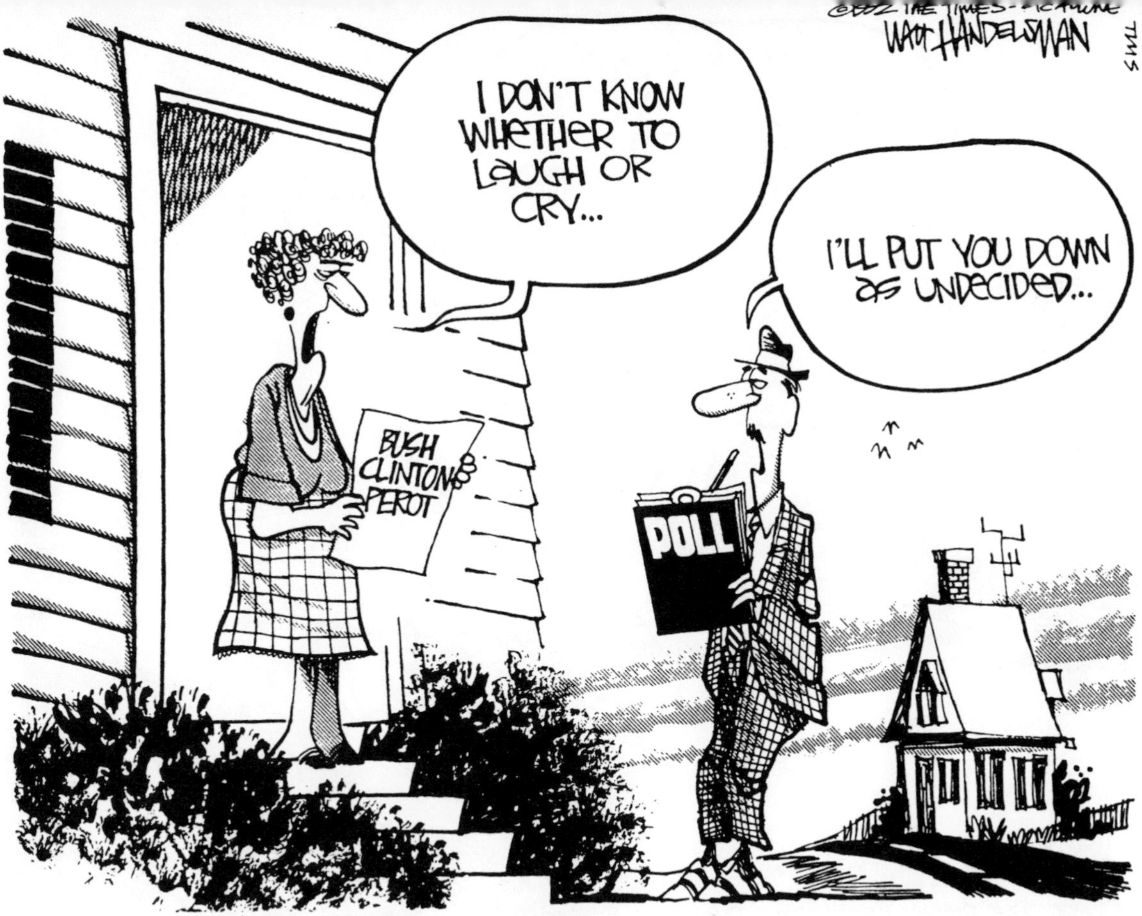
WALT HANDELSMAN
I DON'T KNOW WHETHER TO LAUGH OR CRY...
I'LL PUT YOU DOWN AS UNDECIDED...
BUSH
CLINTON
PEROT
POLL

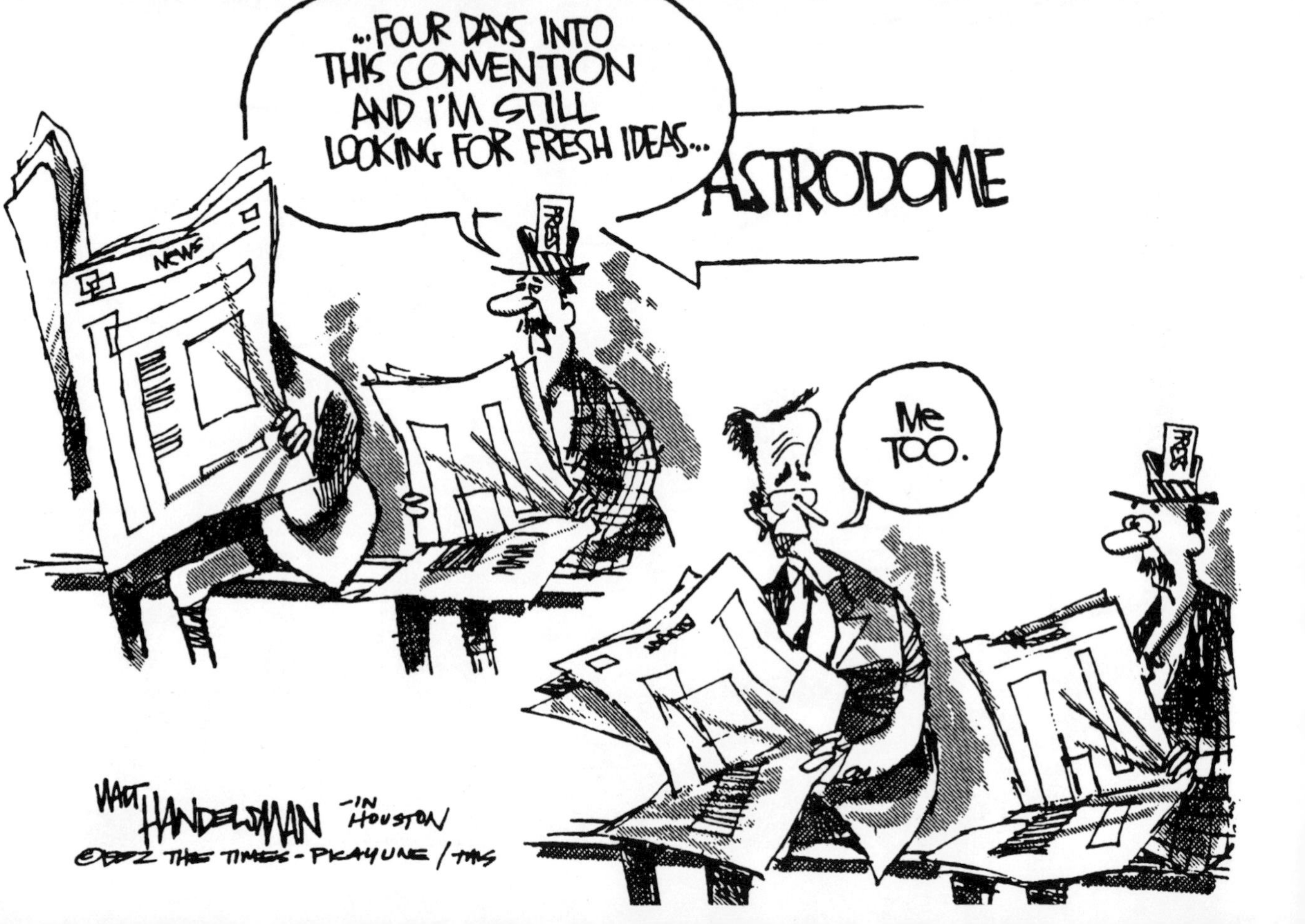
...FOUR DAYS INTO THIS CONVENTION AND I'M STILL LOOKING FOR FRESH IDEAS...
ASTRODOME
NEWS
PRESS
ME TOO.
WALT HANDELSMAN -IN HOUSTON
©1992 THE TIMES-PICAYUNE / TMS

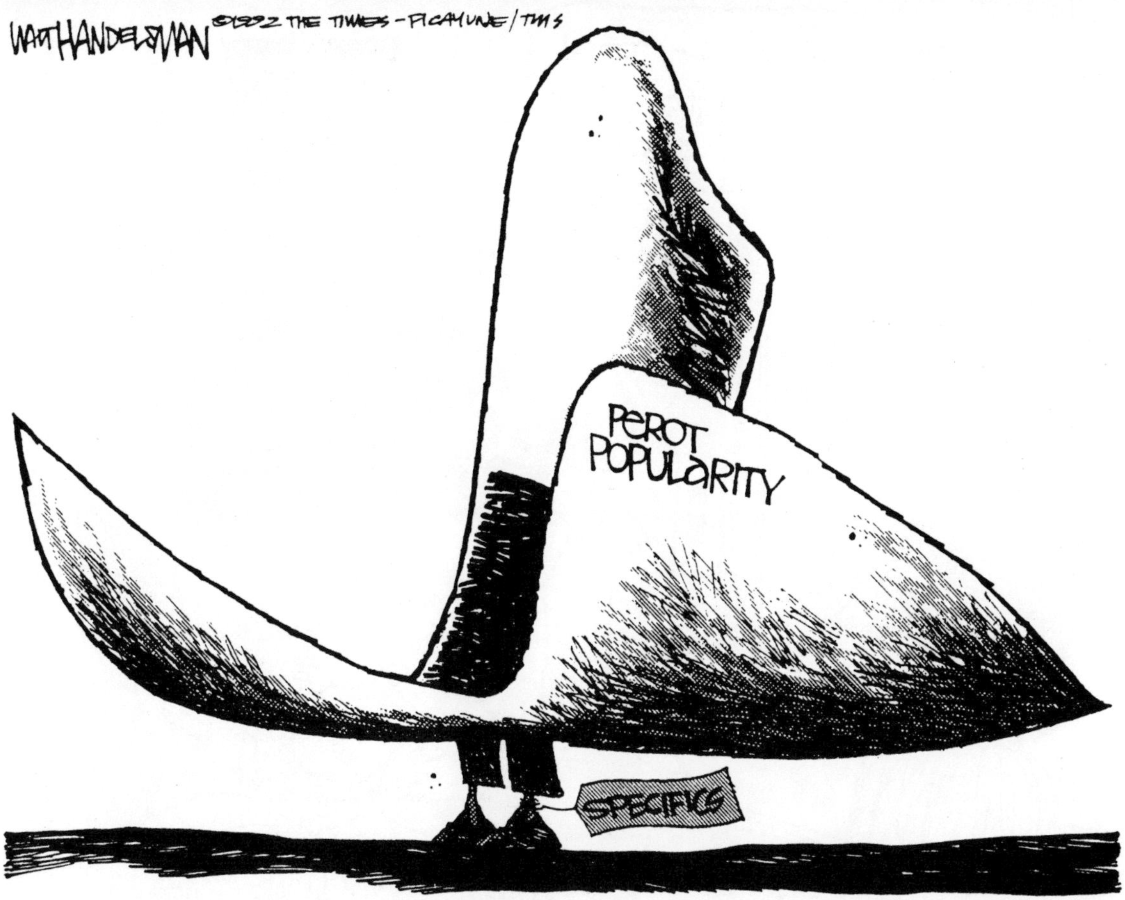

WALT HANDELSMAN ©1992 THE TIMES-PICAYUNE/TMS
PEROT POPULARITY
SPECIFICS

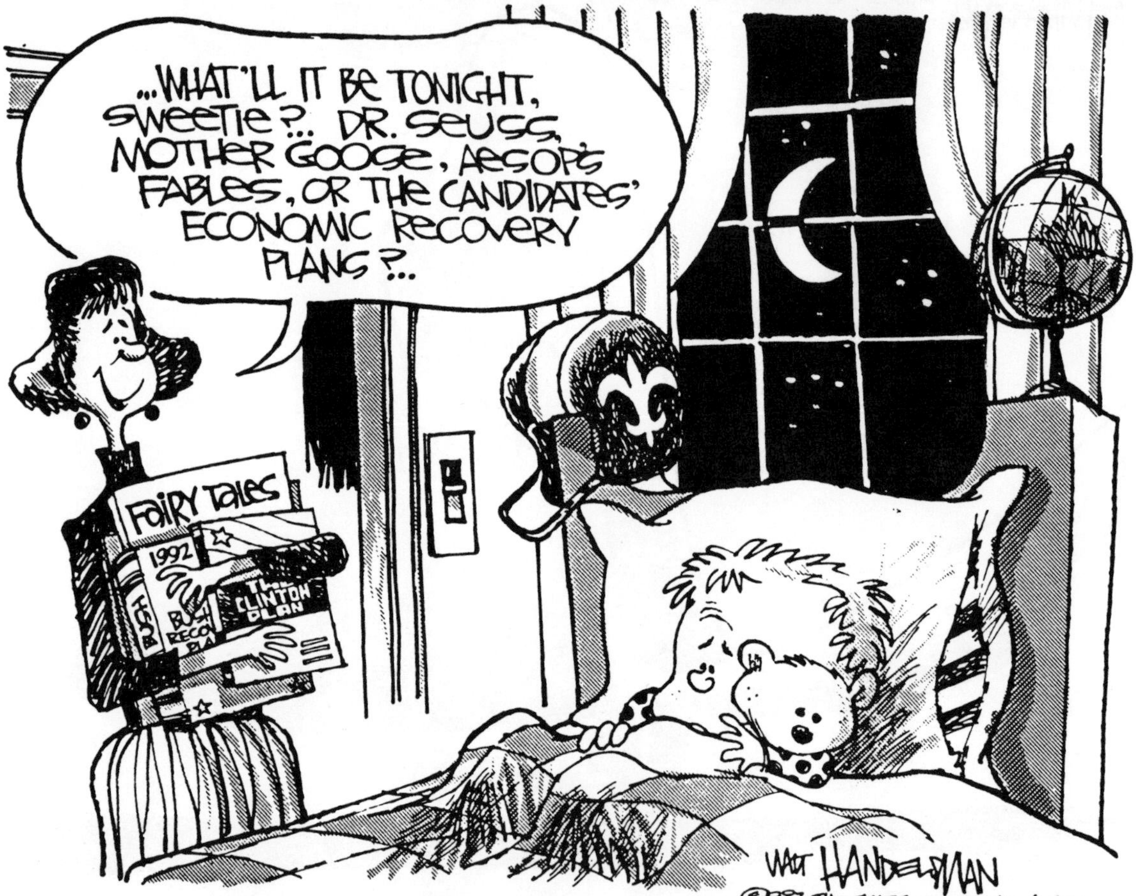
...WHAT'LL IT BE TONIGHT, SWEETIE?... DR. SEUSS, MOTHER GOOSE, AESOP'S FABLES, OR THE CANDIDATES' ECONOMIC RECOVERY PLANS?...
FAIRY TALES
1992
CLINTON PLAN
WALT HANDELSMAN
©1992 THE TIMES-PICAYUNE / TMS

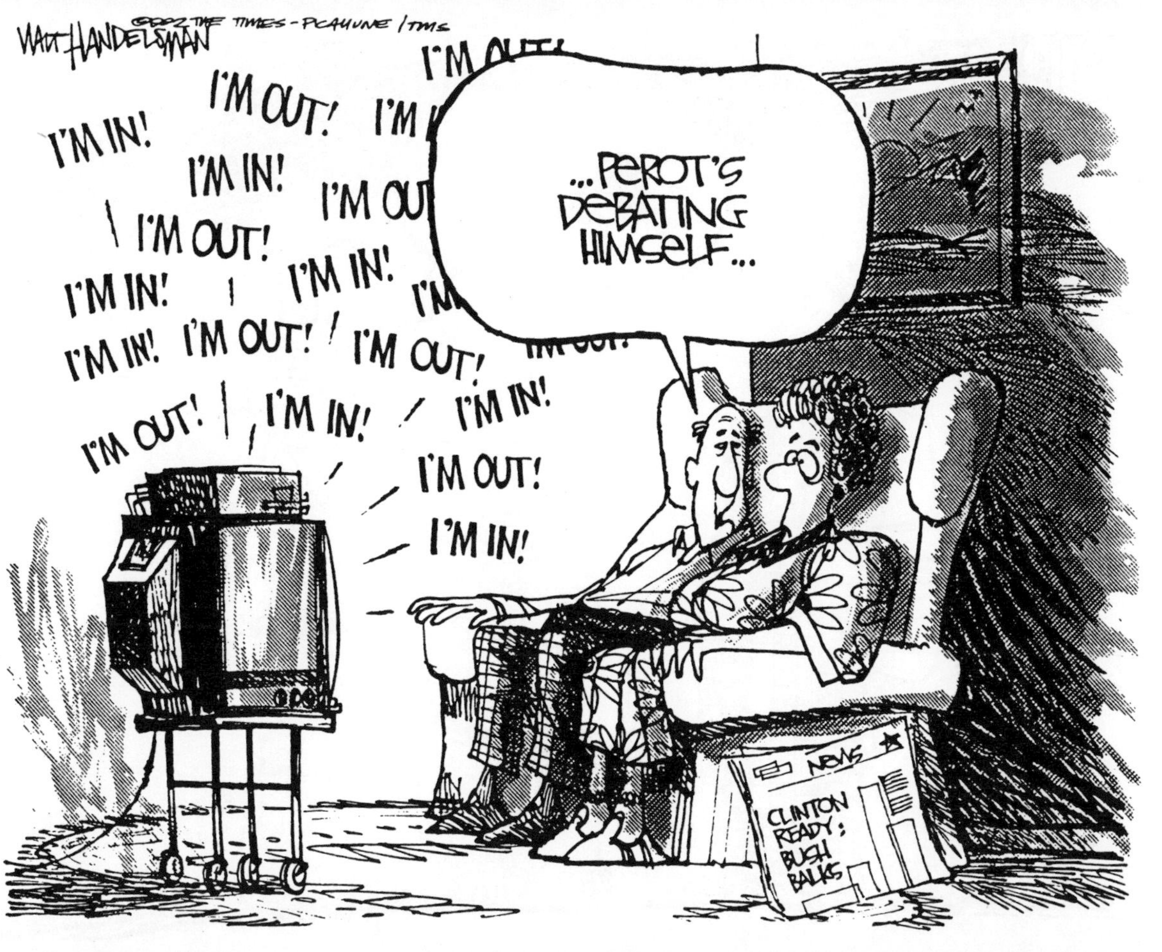
WALT HANDELSMAN
©1992 THE TIMES-PICAYUNE / TMS
I'M IN!
I'M OUT!
I'M IN!
I'M OUT!
I'M IN!
I'M IN!
I'M IN!
I'M OUT!
I'M OUT!
I'M OUT!
I'M IN!
I'M IN!
I'M OUT!
I'M IN!
...PEROT'S DEBATING HIMSELF...
NEWS
CLINTON READY; BUSH BALKS

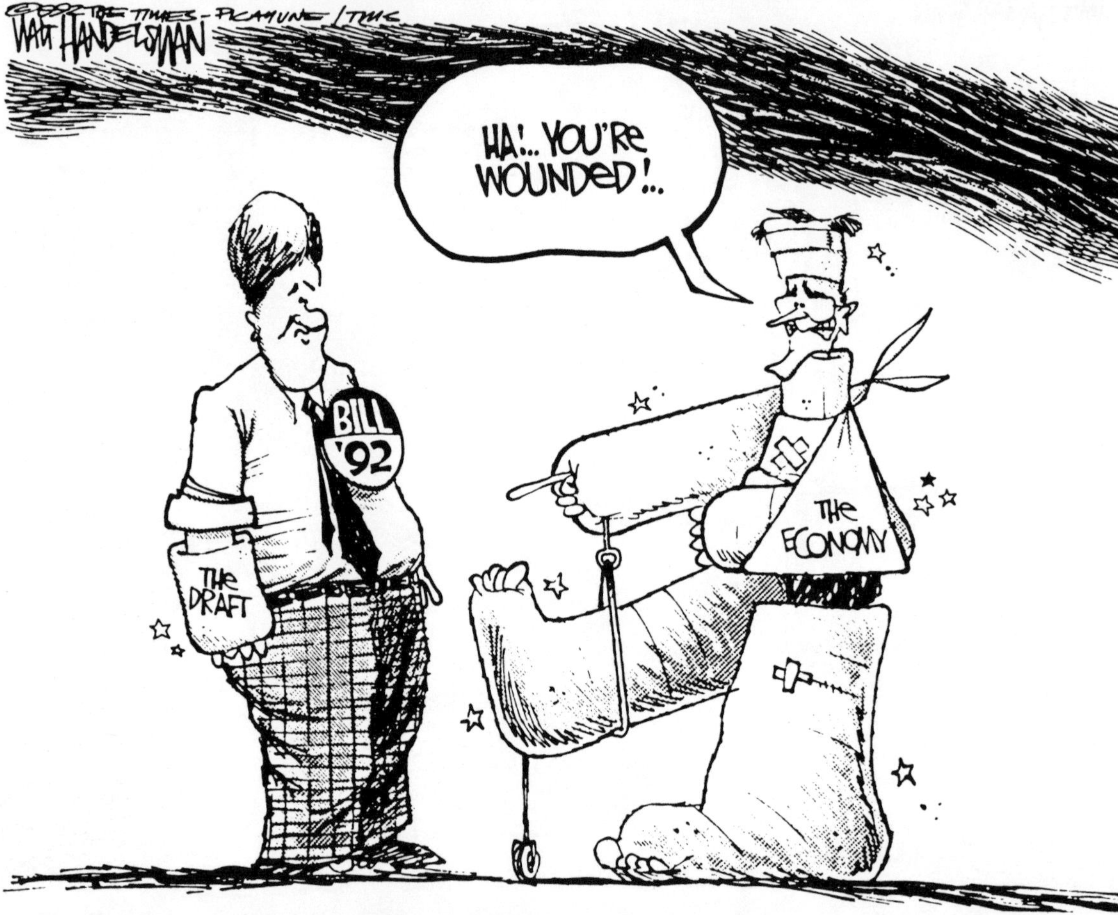
HA!... YOU'RE WOUNDED!...
BILL '92
THE DRAFT
THE ECONOMY

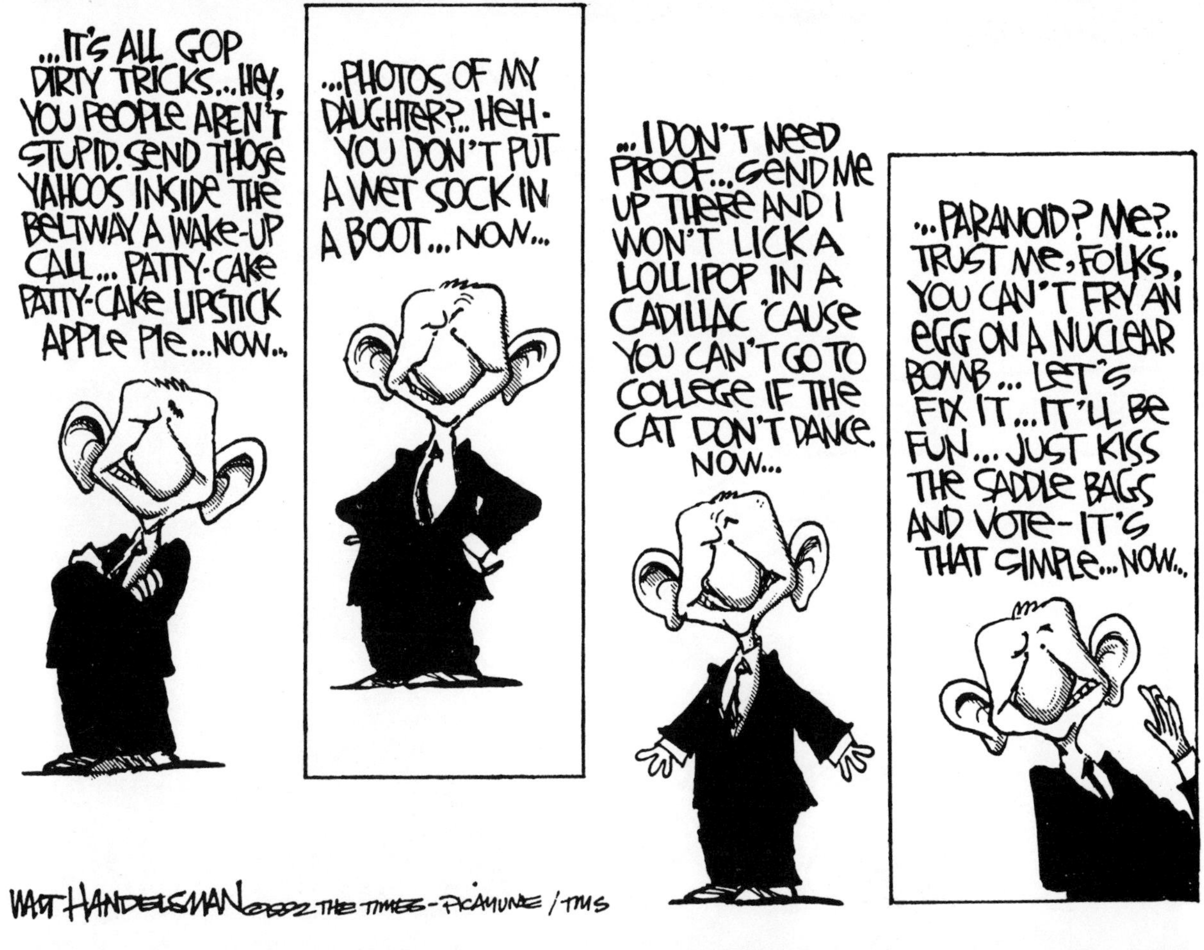
...IT'S ALL GOP DIRTY TRICKS...HEY, YOU PEOPLE AREN'T STUPID. SEND THOSE YAHOOS INSIDE THE BELTWAY A WAKE-UP CALL... PATTY-CAKE PATTY-CAKE LIPSTICK APPLE PIE...NOW...
...PHOTOS OF MY DAUGHTER?.. HEH- YOU DON'T PUT A WET SOCK IN A BOOT... NOW...
...I DON'T NEED PROOF...SEND ME UP THERE AND I WON'T LICK A LOLLIPOP IN A CADILLAC 'CAUSE YOU CAN'T GO TO COLLEGE IF THE CAT DON'T DANCE. NOW...
...PARANOID? ME?... TRUST ME, FOLKS, YOU CAN'T FRY AN EGG ON A NUCLEAR BOMB... LET'S FIX IT...IT'LL BE FUN... JUST KISS THE SADDLE BAGS AND VOTE- IT'S THAT SIMPLE...NOW...
WALT HANDELSMAN ©1992 THE TIMES-PICAYUNE / TMS

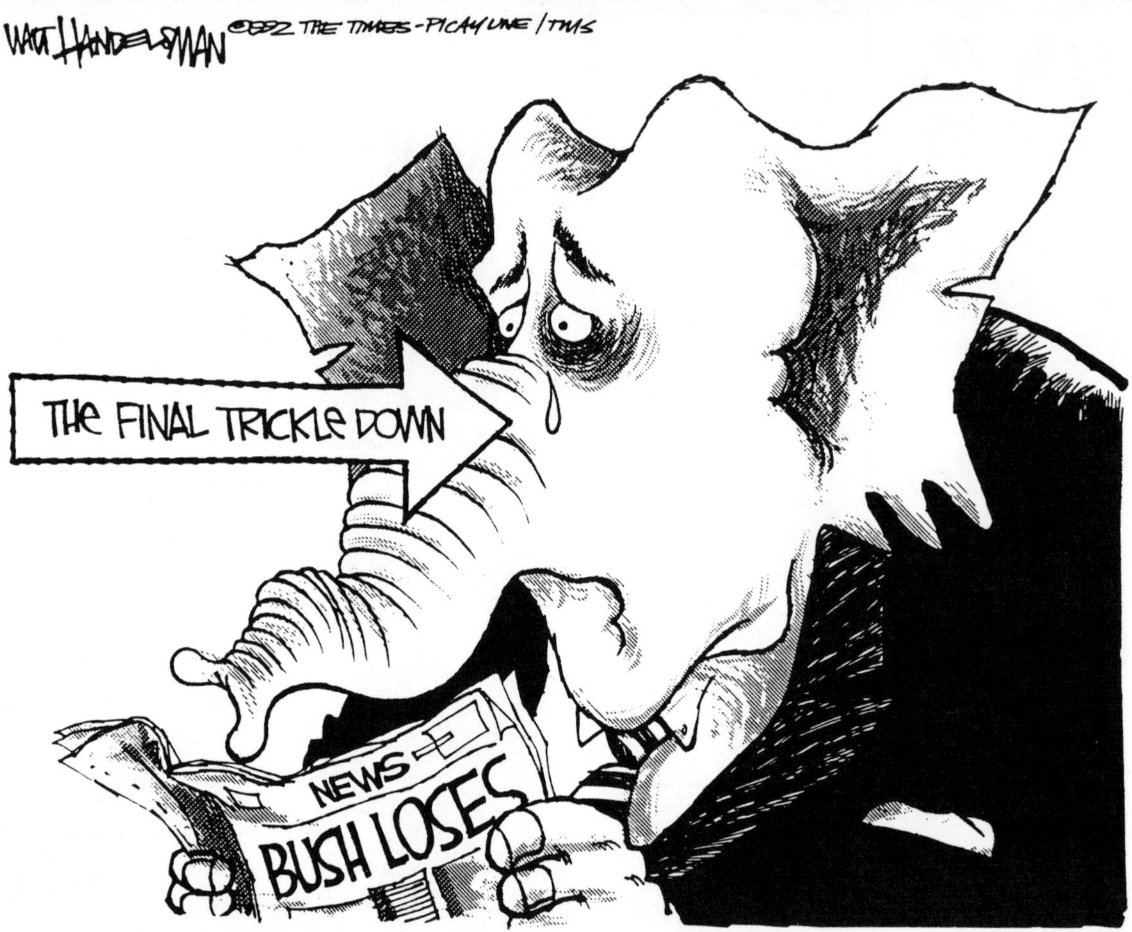
WALT HANDELSMAN ©1992 THE TIMES-PICAYUNE / TMS
THE FINAL TRICKLE DOWN
NEWS
BUSH LOSES

The Economy

We've fallen, and we can't get up.

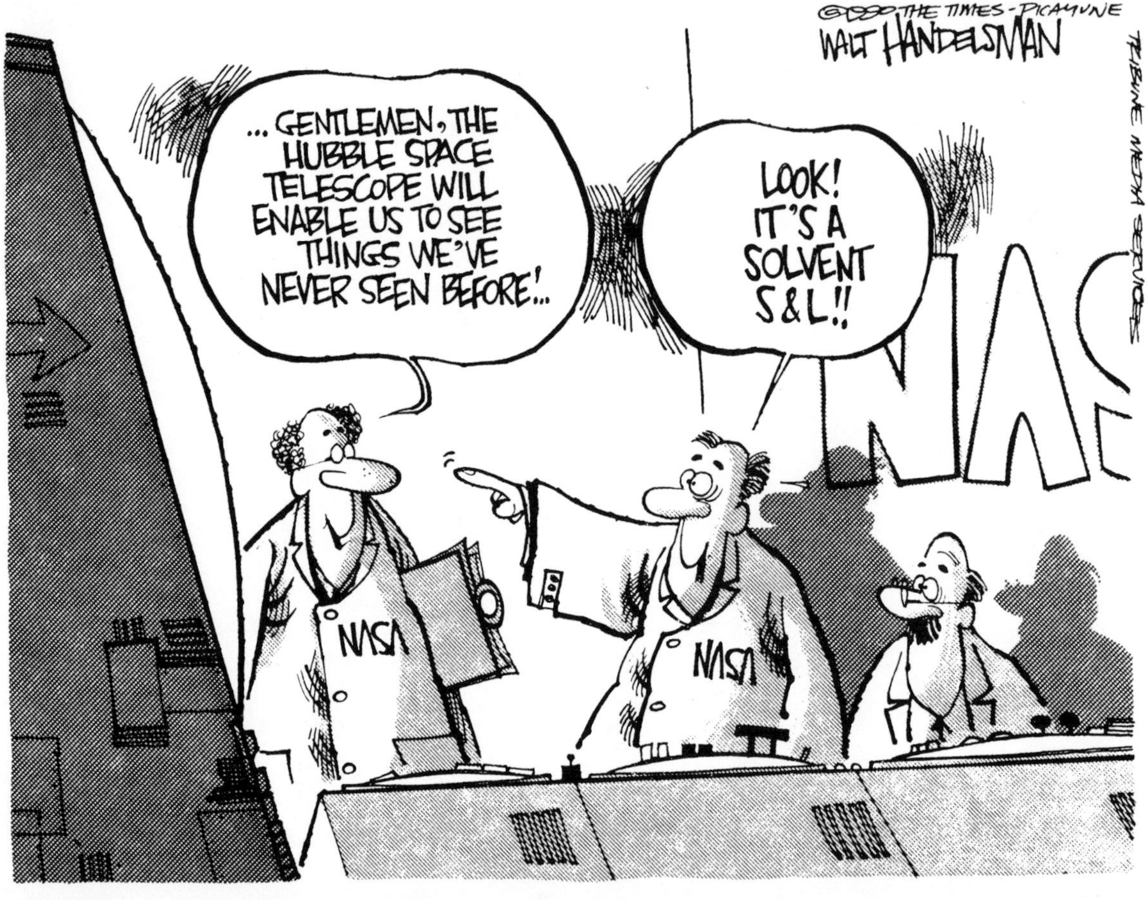
©1990 THE TIMES-PICAYUNE
WALT HANDELSMAN
TRIBUNE MEDIA SERVICES
... GENTLEMEN, THE HUBBLE SPACE TELESCOPE WILL ENABLE US TO SEE THINGS WE'VE NEVER SEEN BEFORE!...
LOOK! IT'S A SOLVENT S&L!!
NASA
NASA

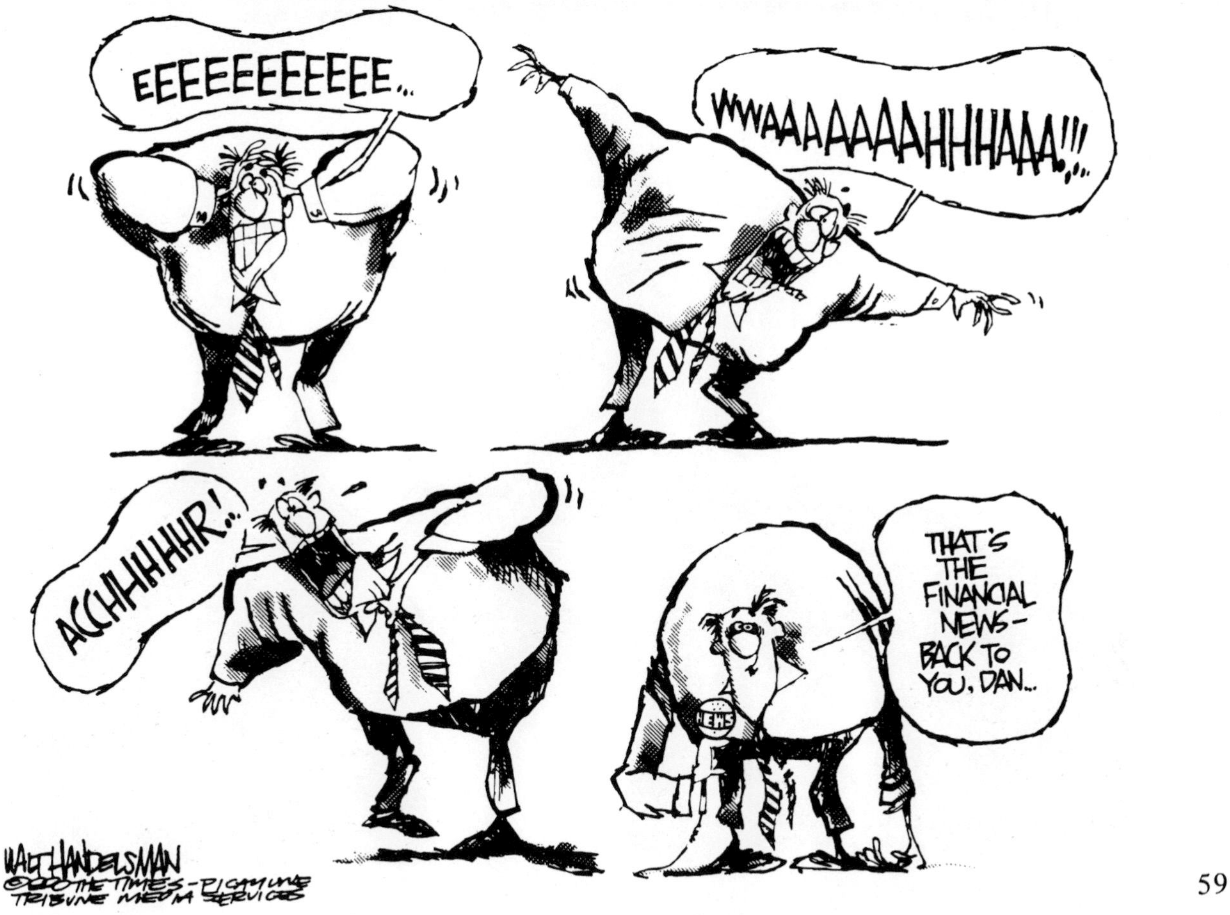
EEEEEEEEEEEE...
WWAAAAAAAHHHAAA!!!...
ACCHHHHHR!...
THAT'S THE FINANCIAL NEWS- BACK TO YOU, DAN...
NEWS
WALT HANDELSMAN
THE TIMES-PICAYUNE
TRIBUNE MEDIA SERVICES

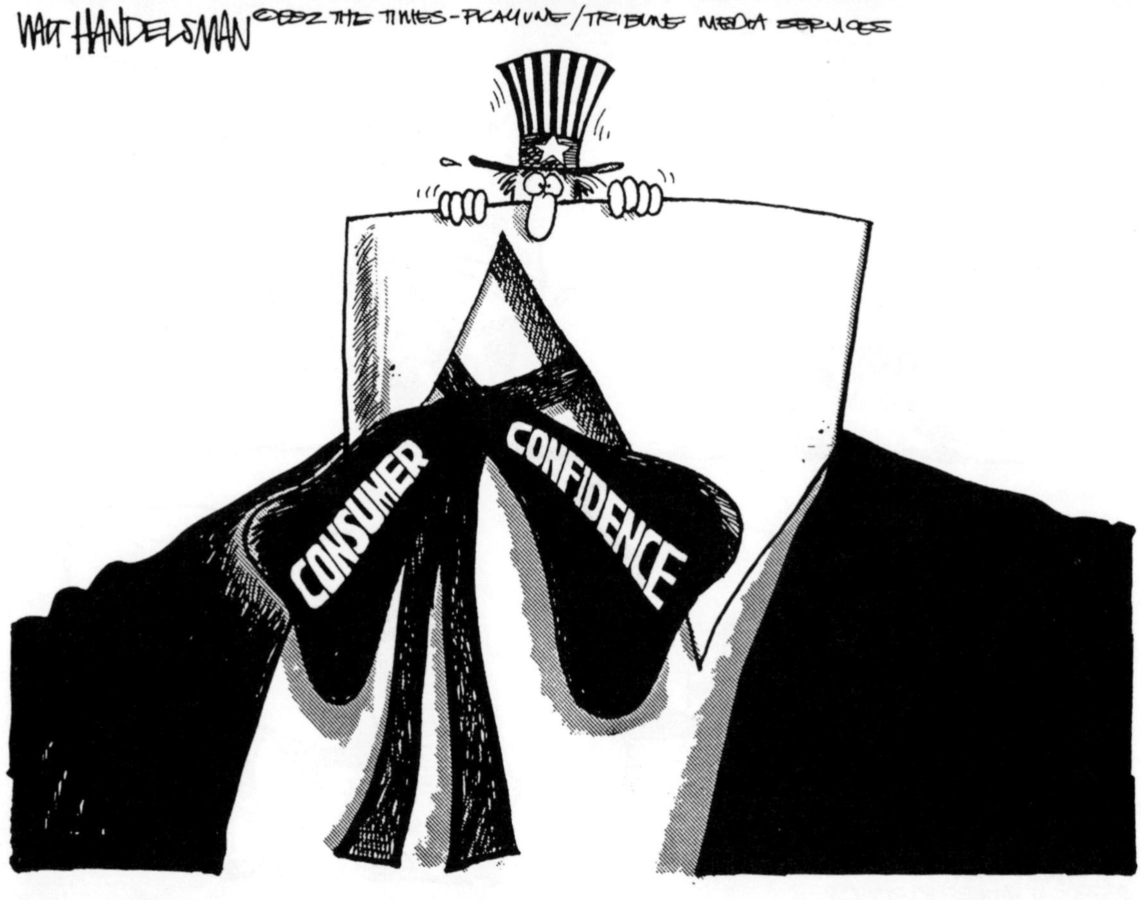
WALT HANDELSMAN ©2002 THE TIMES-PICAYUNE/TRIBUNE MEDIA SERVICES
CONSUMER
CONFIDENCE

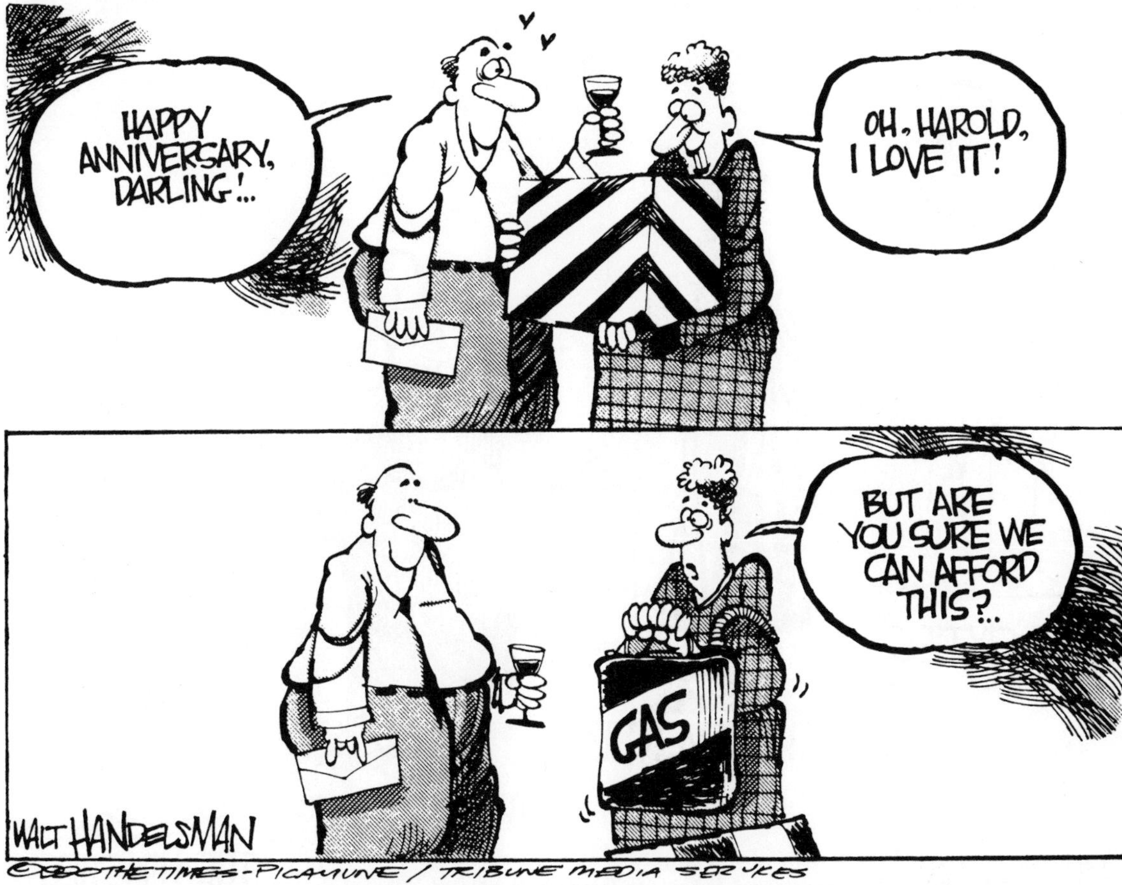
HAPPY ANNIVERSARY, DARLING!...
OH, HAROLD, I LOVE IT!
BUT ARE YOU SURE WE CAN AFFORD THIS?...
GAS
WALT HANDELSMAN
© THE TIMES-PICAYUNE / TRIBUNE MEDIA SERVICES

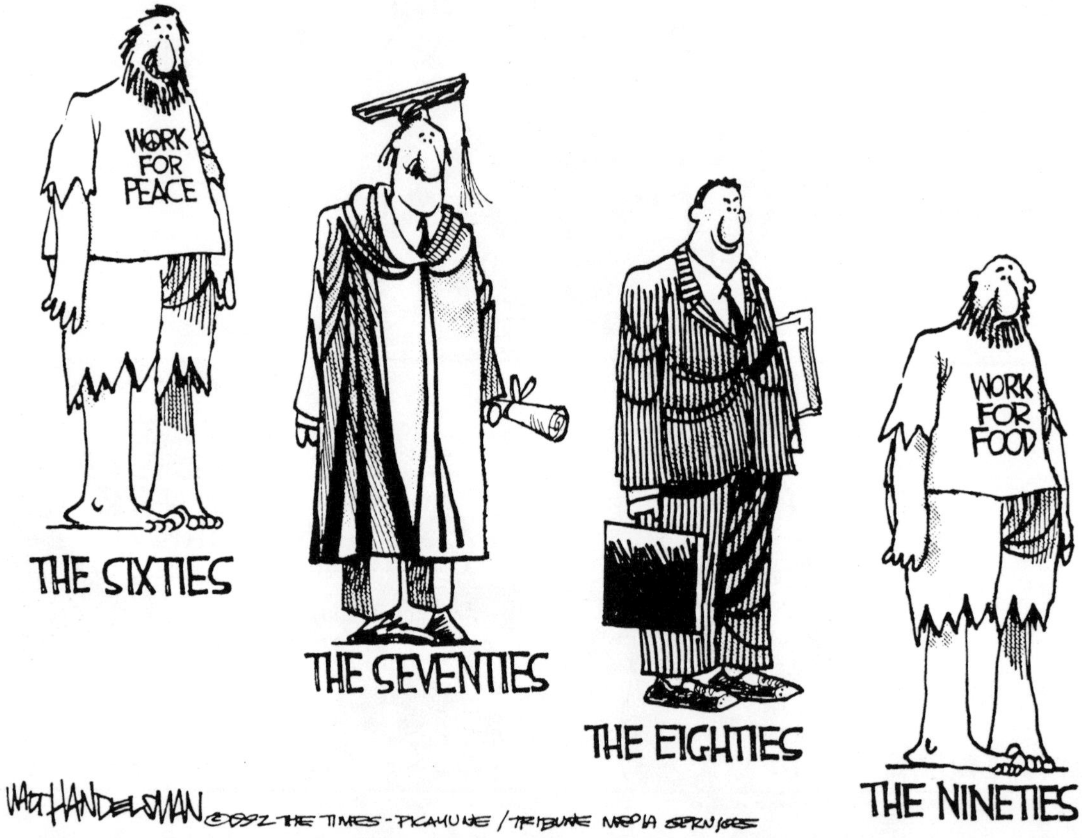
WORK FOR PEACE
THE SIXTIES
THE SEVENTIES
THE EIGHTIES
WORK FOR FOOD
THE NINETIES
HANDELSMAN

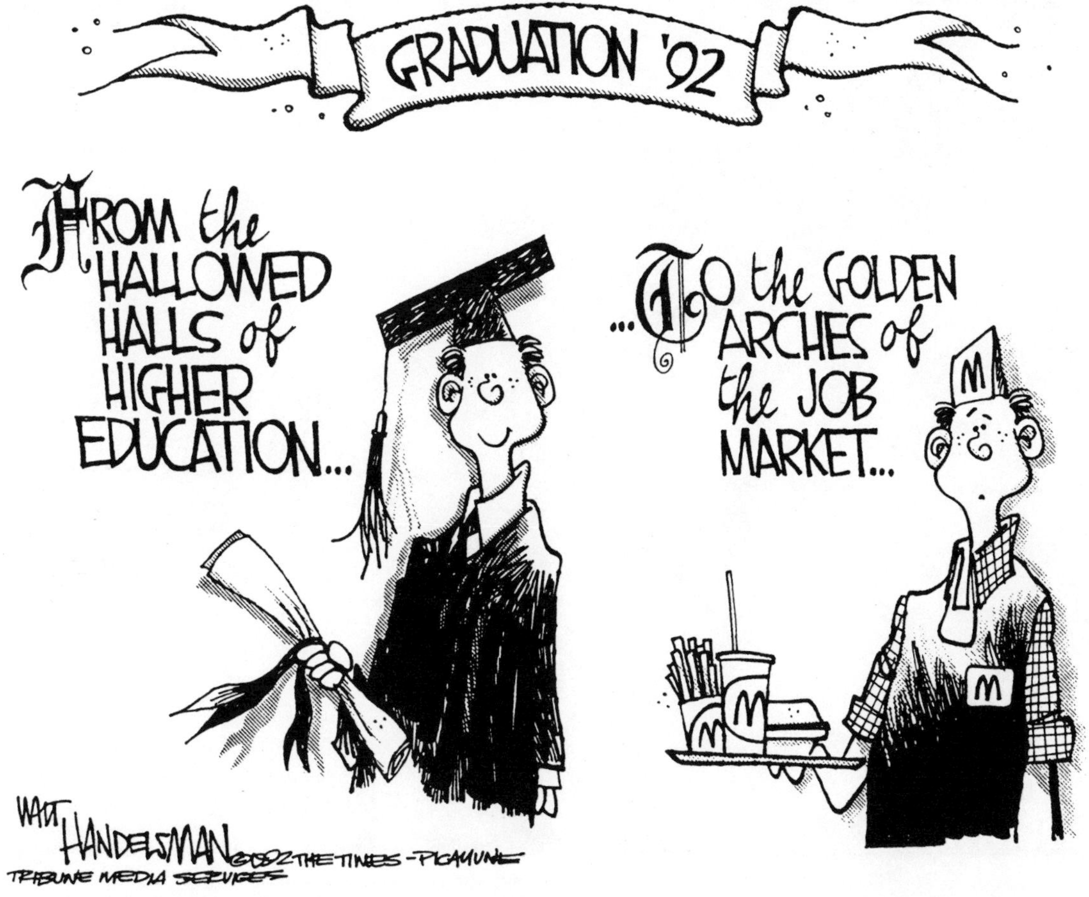
GRADUATION '92
FROM the HALLOWED HALLS of HIGHER EDUCATION...
...TO the GOLDEN ARCHES of the JOB MARKET...
M
M
M
M
WALT HANDELSMAN ©1992 THE TIMES-PICAYUNE
TRIBUNE MEDIA SERVICES

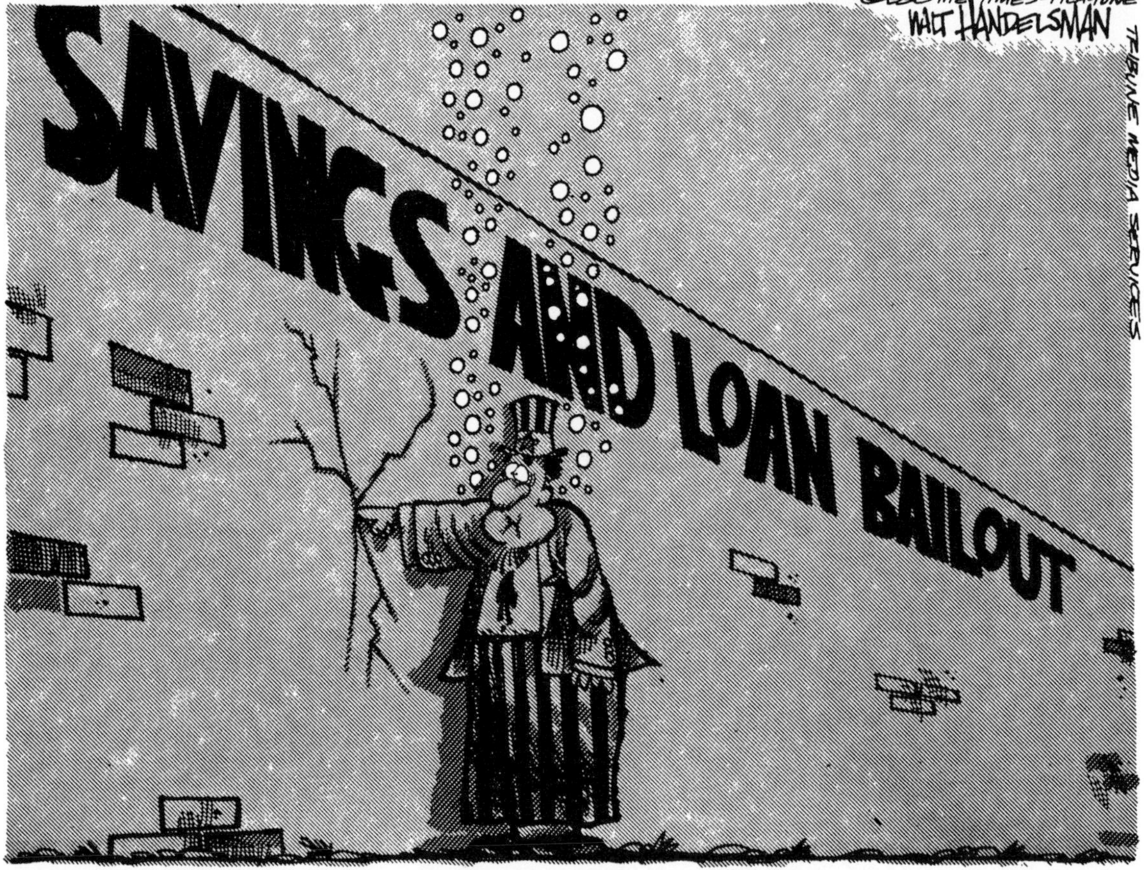
©1990 THE TIMES-PICAYUNE
WALT HANDELSMAN
TRIBUNE MEDIA SERVICES
SAVINGS AND LOAN BAILOUT

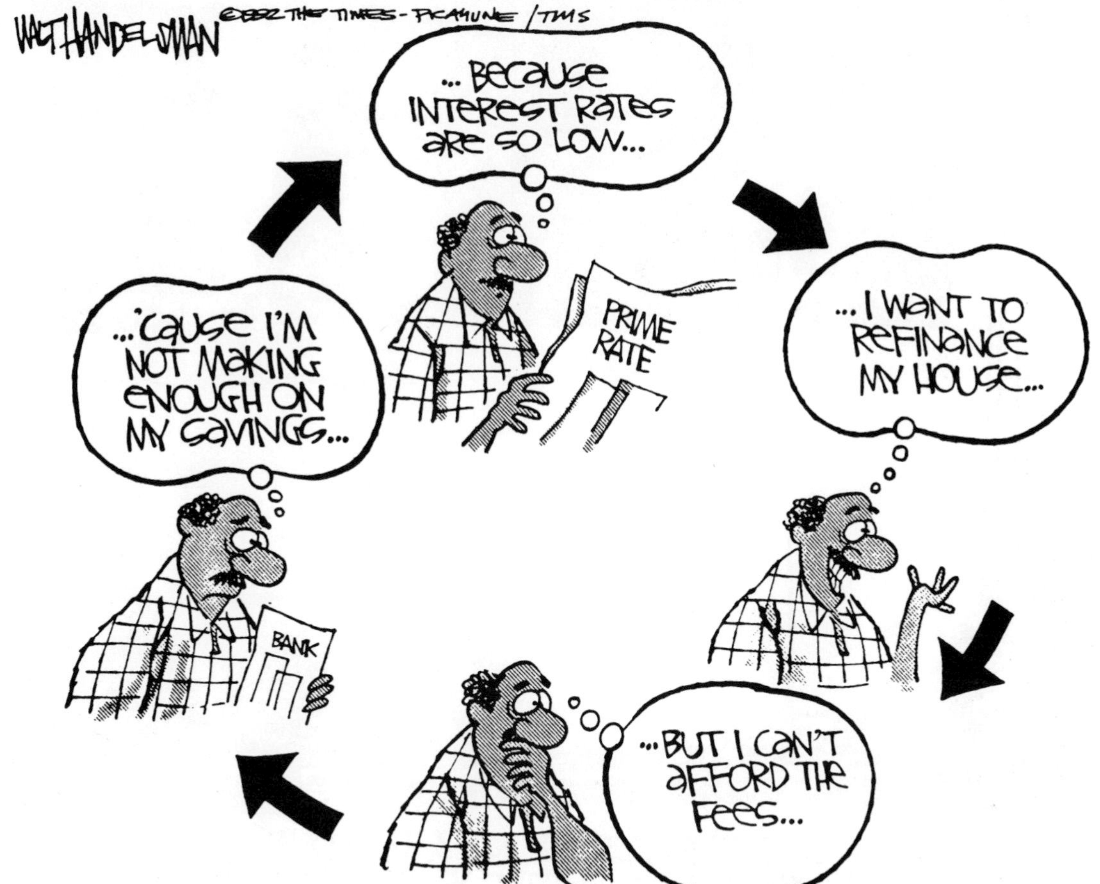
WALT HANDELSMAN
©1992 THE TIMES-PICAYUNE / TMS
...BECAUSE INTEREST RATES ARE SO LOW...
PRIME RATE
...I WANT TO REFINANCE MY HOUSE...
...BUT I CAN'T AFFORD THE FEES...
...'CAUSE I'M NOT MAKING ENOUGH ON MY SAVINGS...
BANK

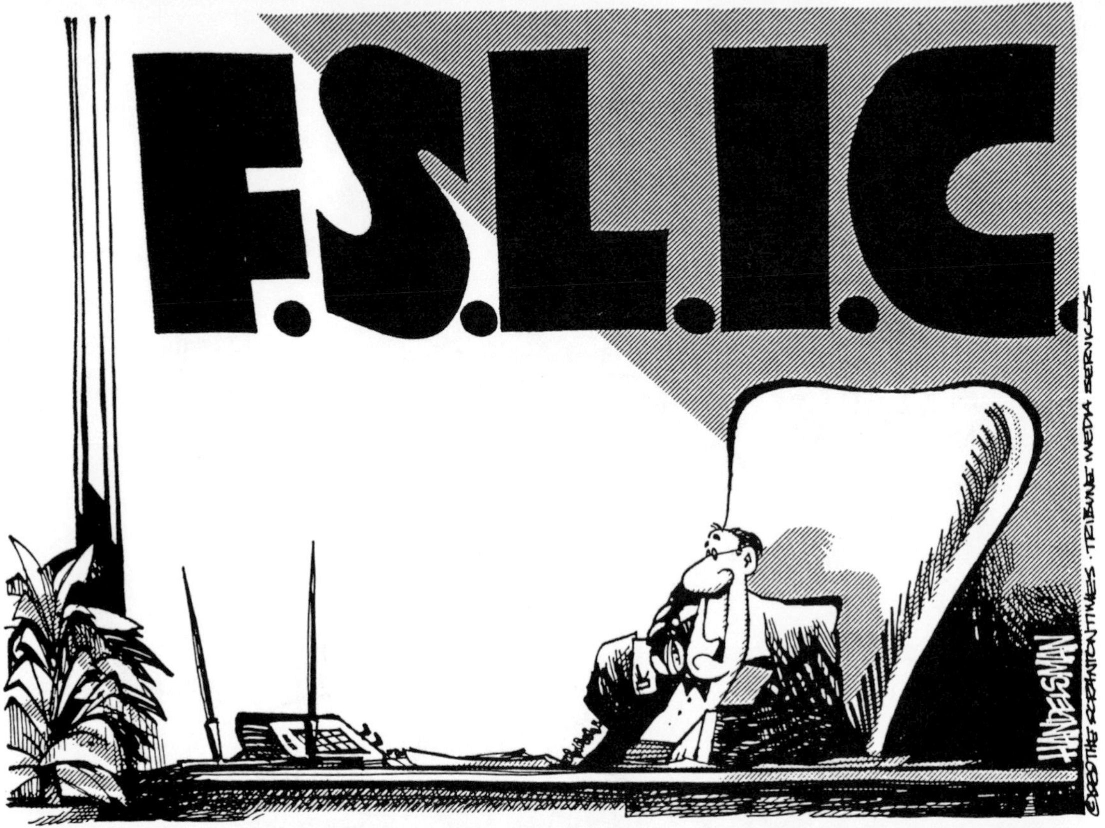
F.S.L.I.C.
HANDELSMAN
THE SCRANTON TIMES · TRIBUNE MEDIA SERVICES

...I'M SORRY, MA'AM, BUT EXPERIENCING A PERSONAL SAVINGS CRISIS AFTER THE HOLIDAYS DOES NOT ENTITLE YOU TO A FEDERAL BAILOUT...

The Environment

. . . or what's left of it.

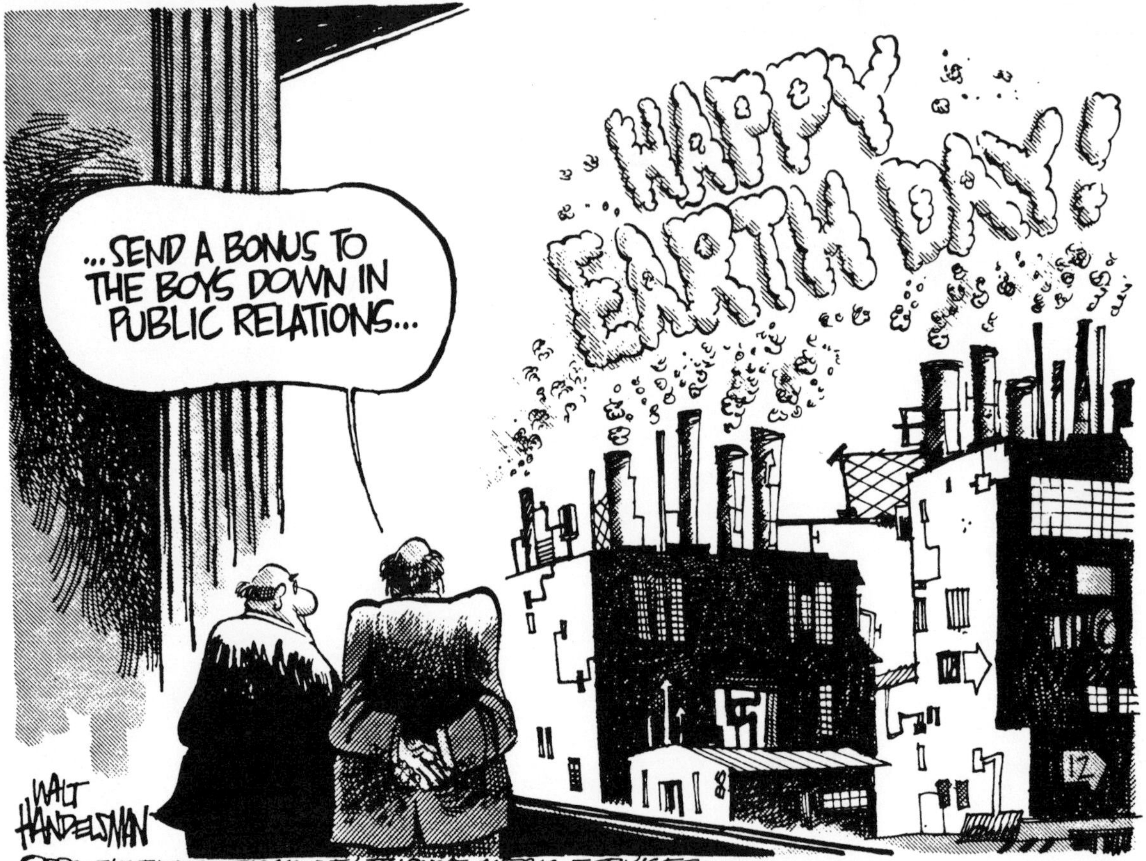

...SEND A BONUS TO THE BOYS DOWN IN PUBLIC RELATIONS...
HAPPY EARTH DAY!
WALT HANDELSMAN
©1990 THE TIMES - PICAYUNE / TRIBUNE MEDIA SERVICES

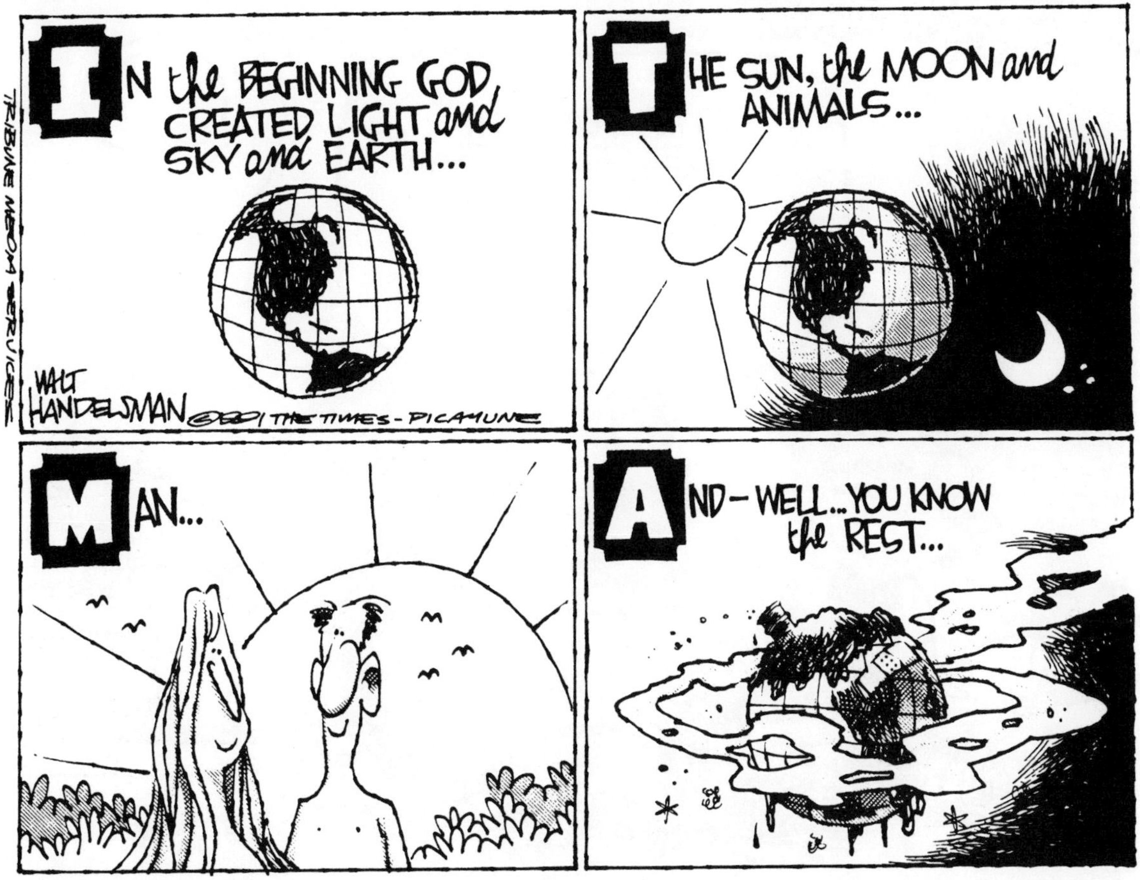
TRIBUNE MEDIA SERVICES
IN the BEGINNING GOD CREATED LIGHT and SKY and EARTH...
WALT HANDELSMAN ©1991 THE TIMES-PICAYUNE
THE SUN, the MOON and ANIMALS...
MAN...
AND - WELL... YOU KNOW the REST...

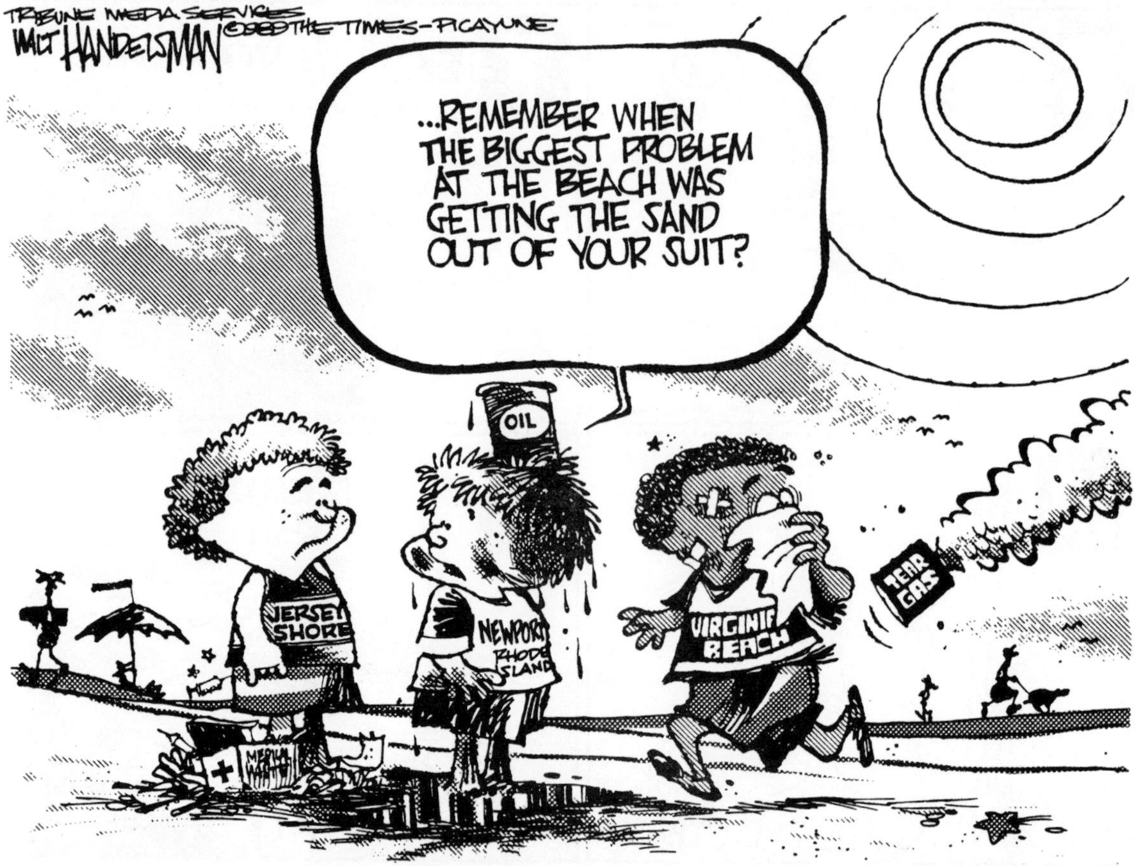
TRIBUNE MEDIA SERVICES
WALT HANDELSMAN ©1989 THE TIMES-PICAYUNE
...REMEMBER WHEN THE BIGGEST PROBLEM AT THE BEACH WAS GETTING THE SAND OUT OF YOUR SUIT?
OIL
JERSEY SHORE
NEWPORT RHODE ISLAND
VIRGINIA BEACH
TEAR GAS
MEDICAL WASTE

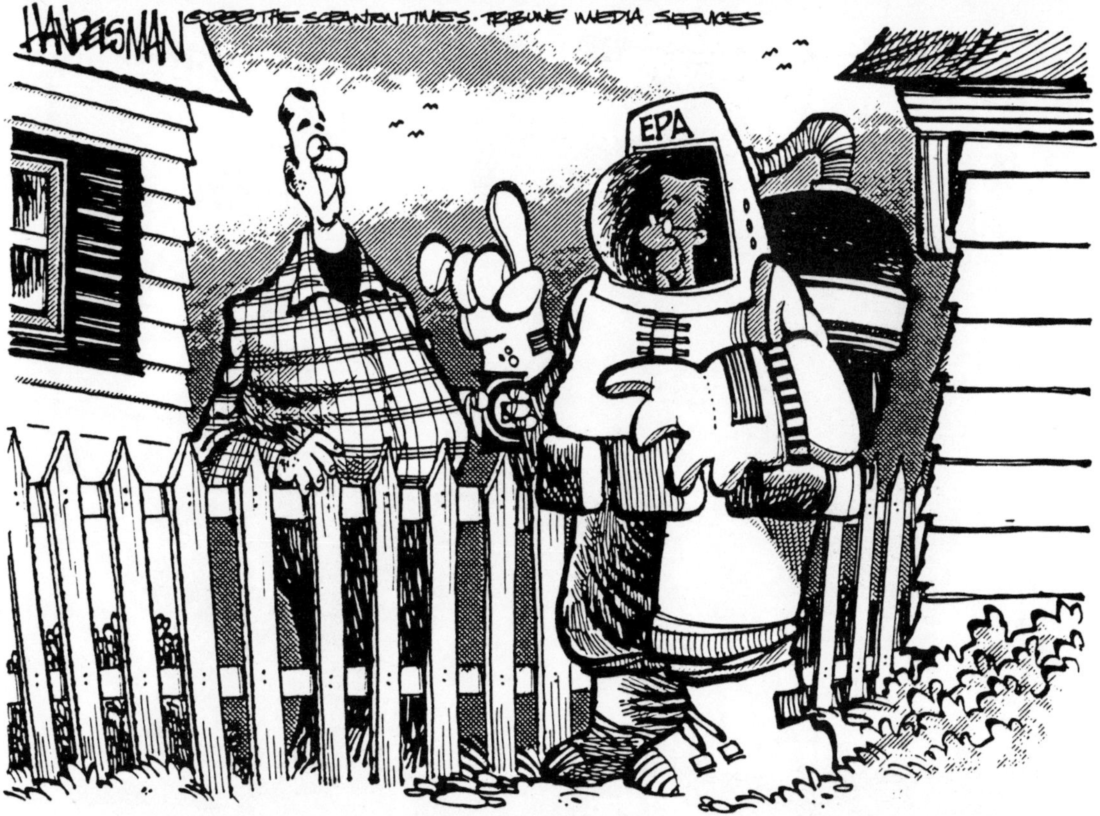
HANDELSMAN ©1988 THE SCRANTON TIMES · TRIBUNE MEDIA SERVICES
EPA

GOOD NEWS!.. THE LEAD IN YOUR WATER IS SHIELDING YOU FROM THE RADON GAS IN YOUR HOUSE!...

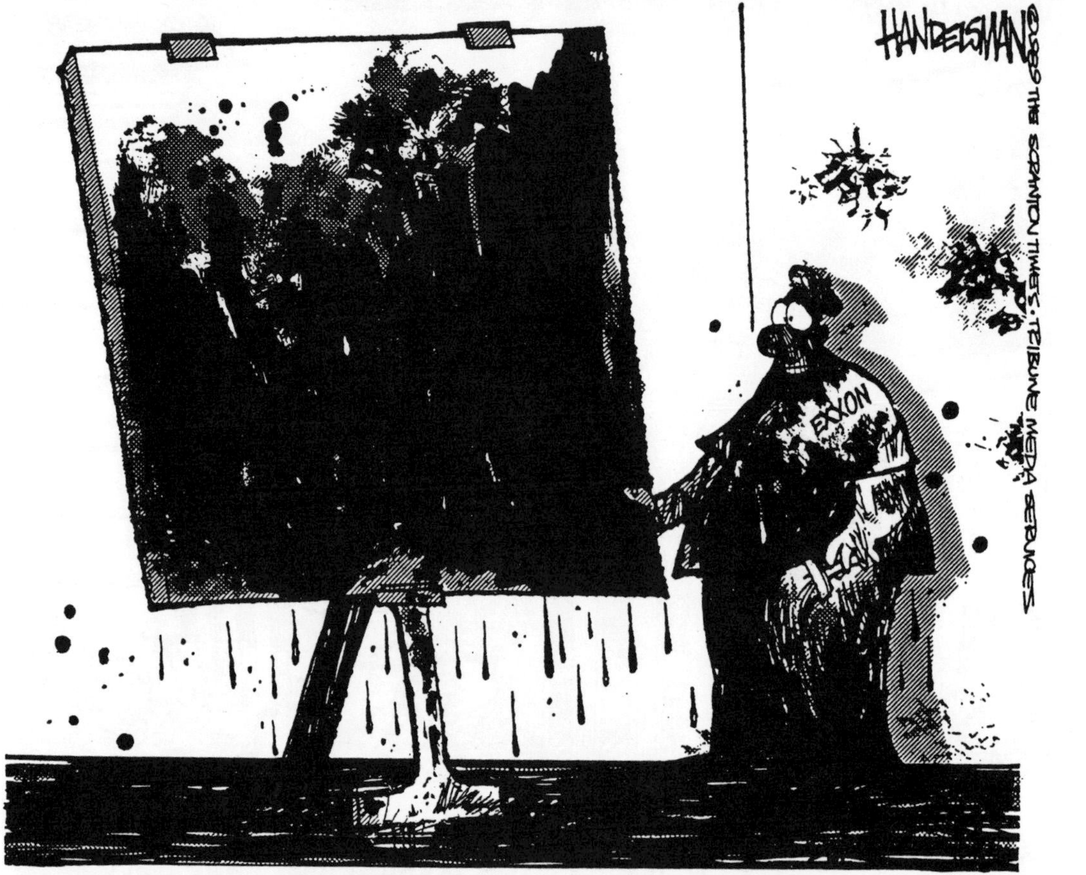
HANDELSMAN
©1989 THE SCRANTON TIMES-TRIBUNE MEDIA SERVICES
EXXON

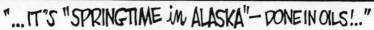

"...IT'S "SPRINGTIME in ALASKA"– DONE IN OILS!..."

Crime

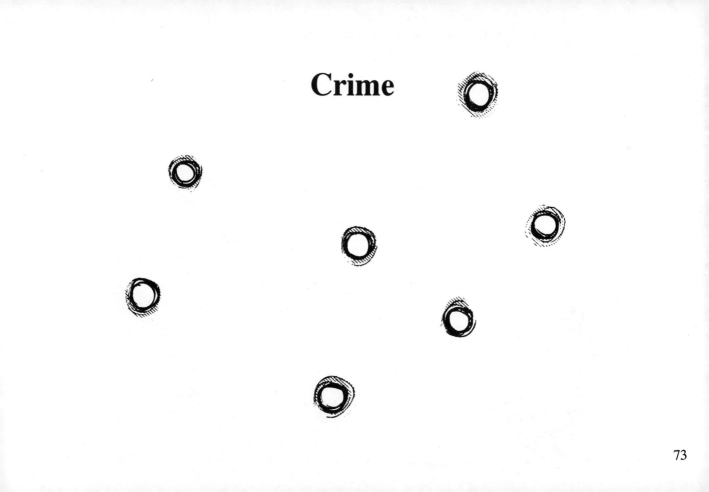

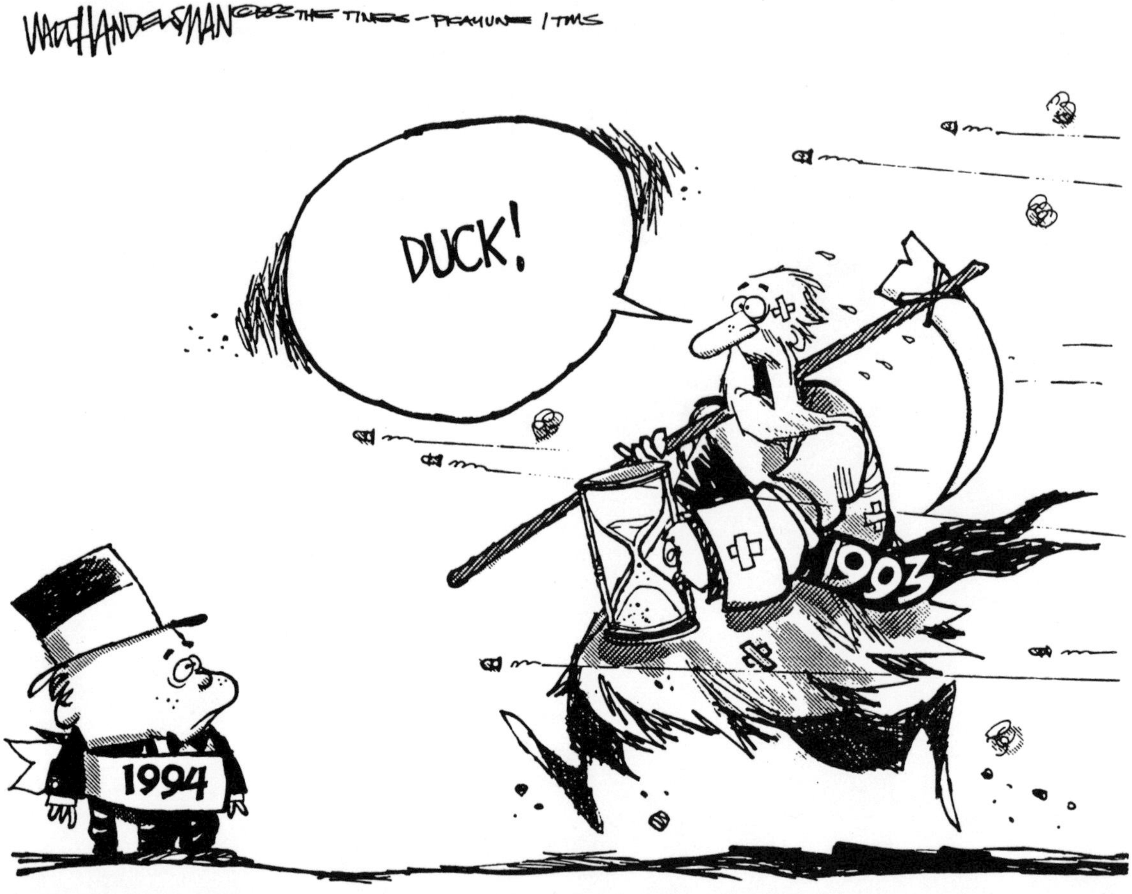
DUCK!
1993
1994

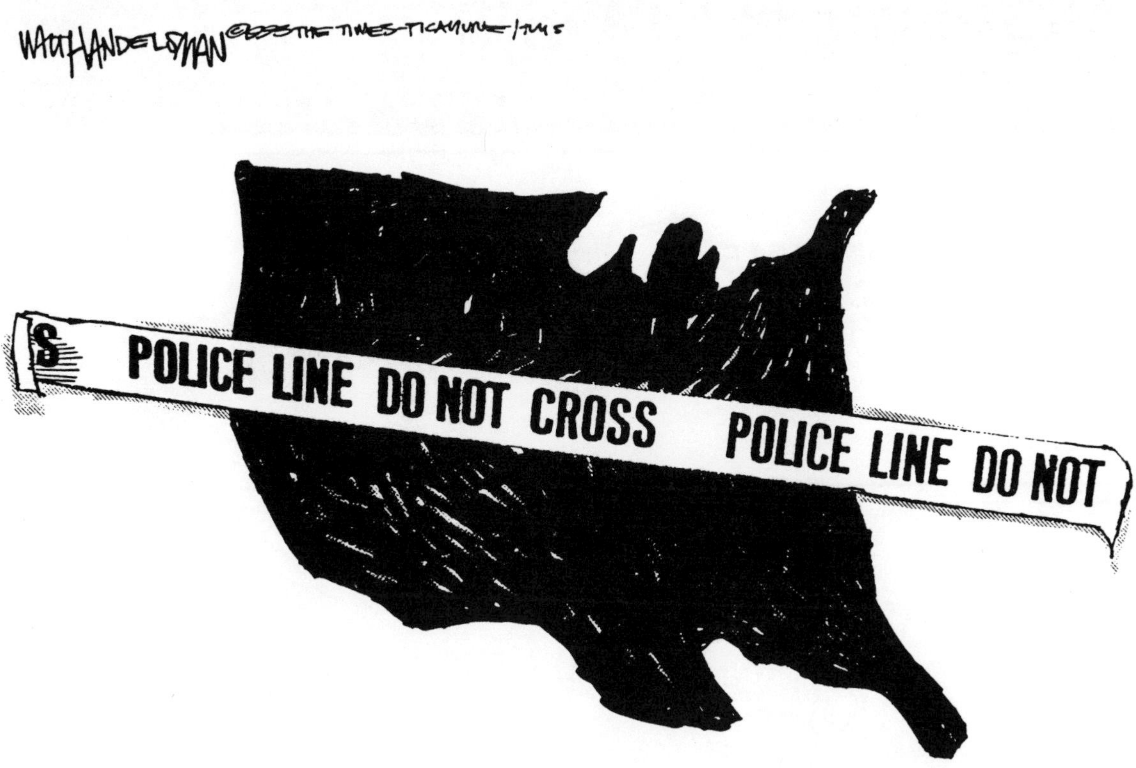
WALT HANDELSMAN
POLICE LINE DO NOT CROSS POLICE LINE DO NOT

THE UNITED STATE OF ANXIETY...

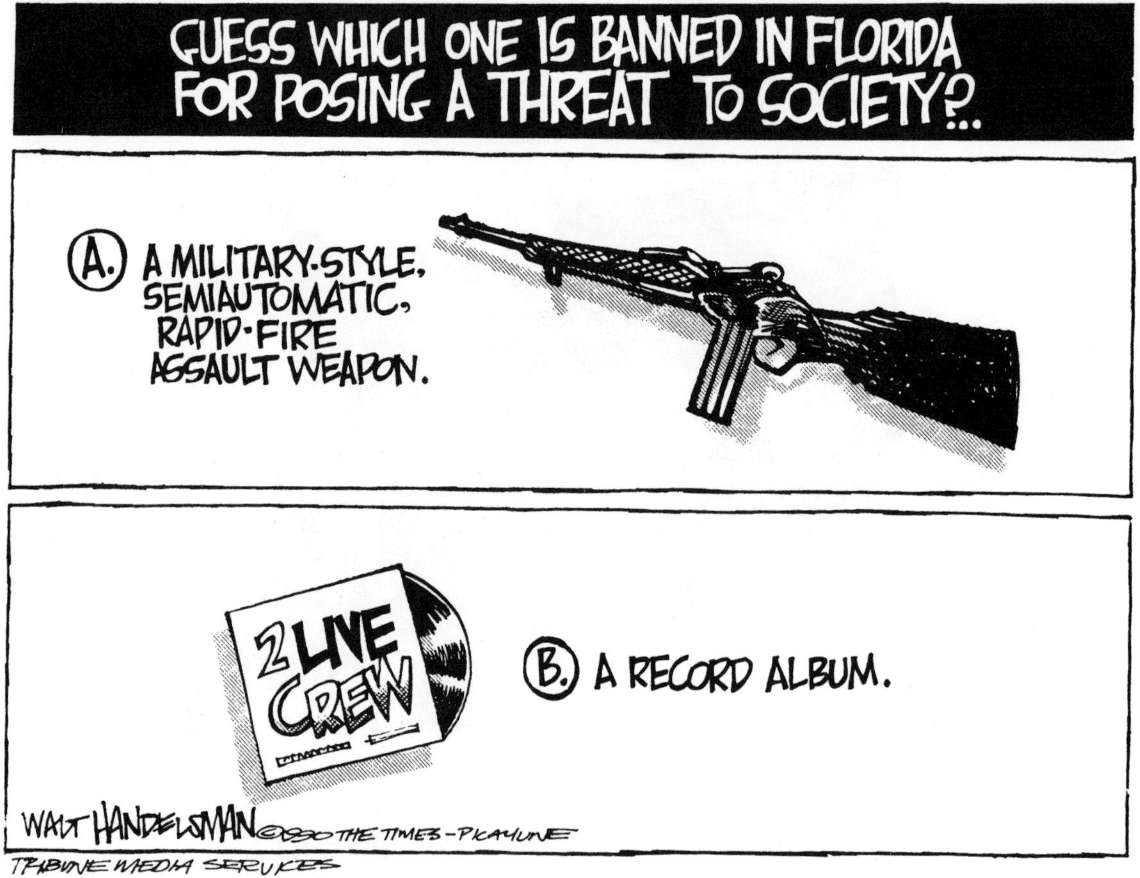
GUESS WHICH ONE IS BANNED IN FLORIDA FOR POSING A THREAT TO SOCIETY?...
A.) A MILITARY-STYLE, SEMIAUTOMATIC, RAPID-FIRE ASSAULT WEAPON.
2 LIVE CREW
B.) A RECORD ALBUM.
WALT HANDELSMAN ©1990 THE TIMES-PICAYUNE
TRIBUNE MEDIA SERVICES

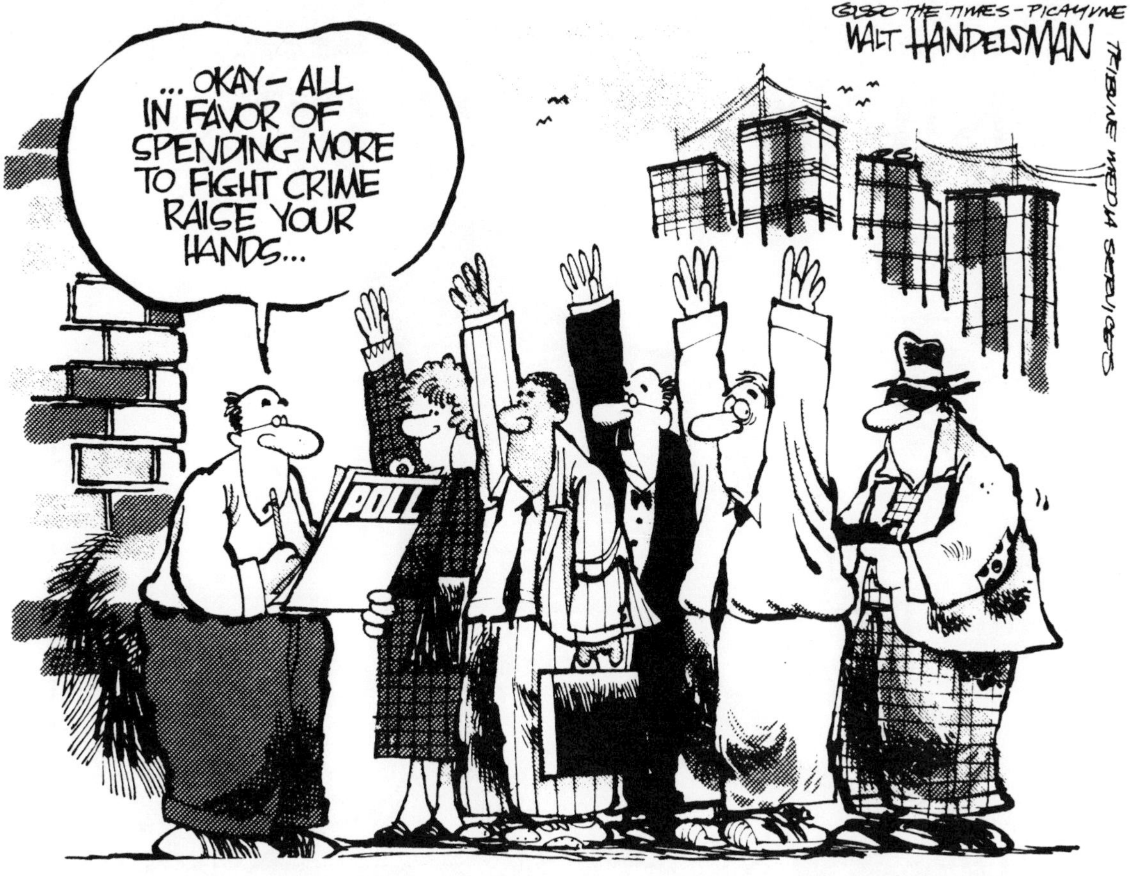
©1990 THE TIMES - PICAYUNE
WALT HANDELSMAN
TRIBUNE MEDIA SERVICES
... OKAY - ALL IN FAVOR OF SPENDING MORE TO FIGHT CRIME RAISE YOUR HANDS...
POLL

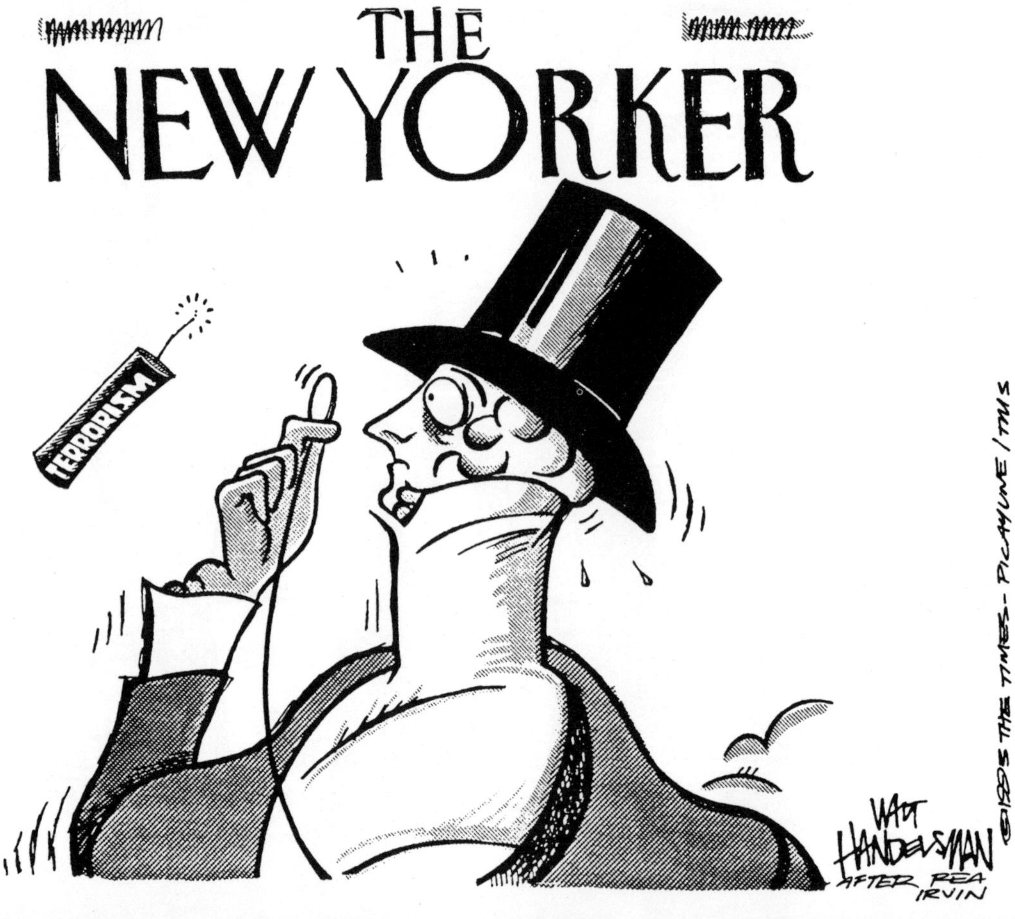
THE NEW YORKER
TERRORISM
WALT HANDELSMAN
AFTER REA IRVIN
©1995 THE TIMES-PICAYUNE / TMS

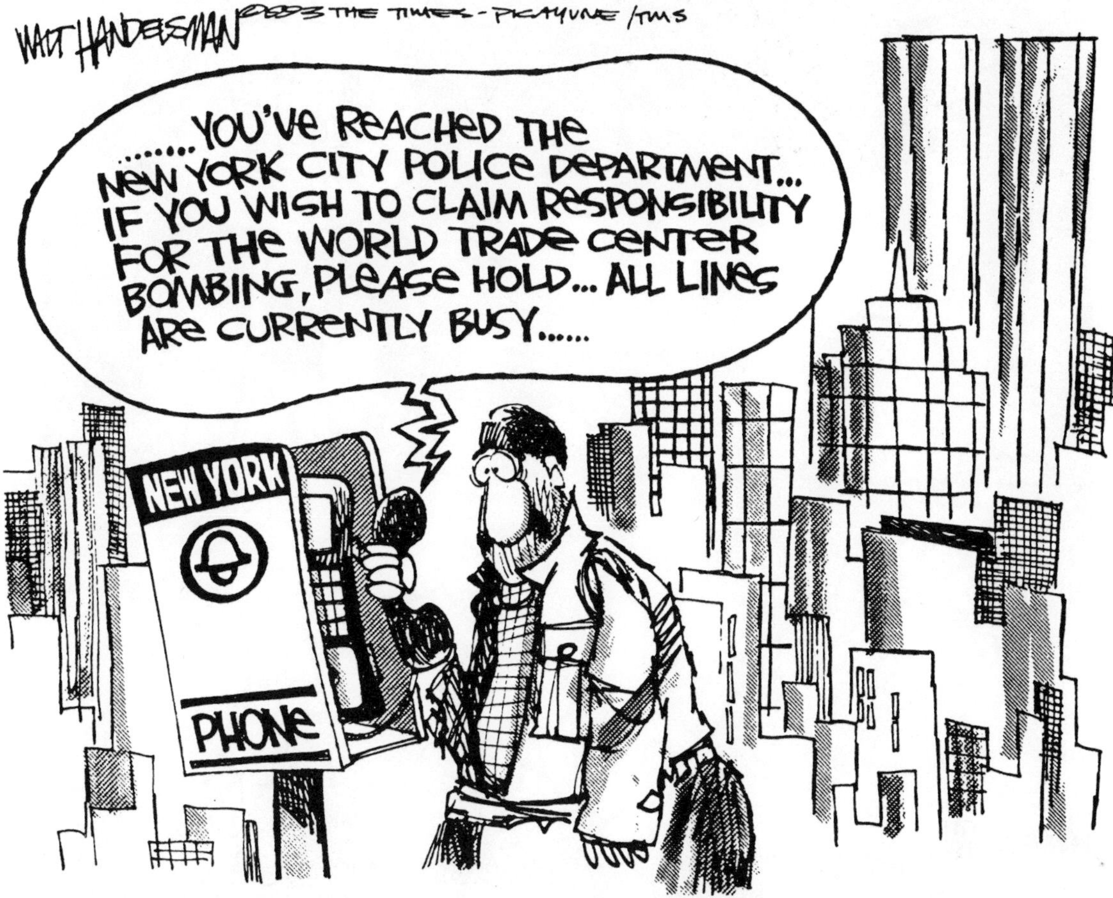
WALT HANDELSMAN ©1993 THE TIMES-PICAYUNE /TMS
.......YOU'VE REACHED THE NEW YORK CITY POLICE DEPARTMENT... IF YOU WISH TO CLAIM RESPONSIBILITY FOR THE WORLD TRADE CENTER BOMBING, PLEASE HOLD... ALL LINES ARE CURRENTLY BUSY......
NEW YORK
PHONE

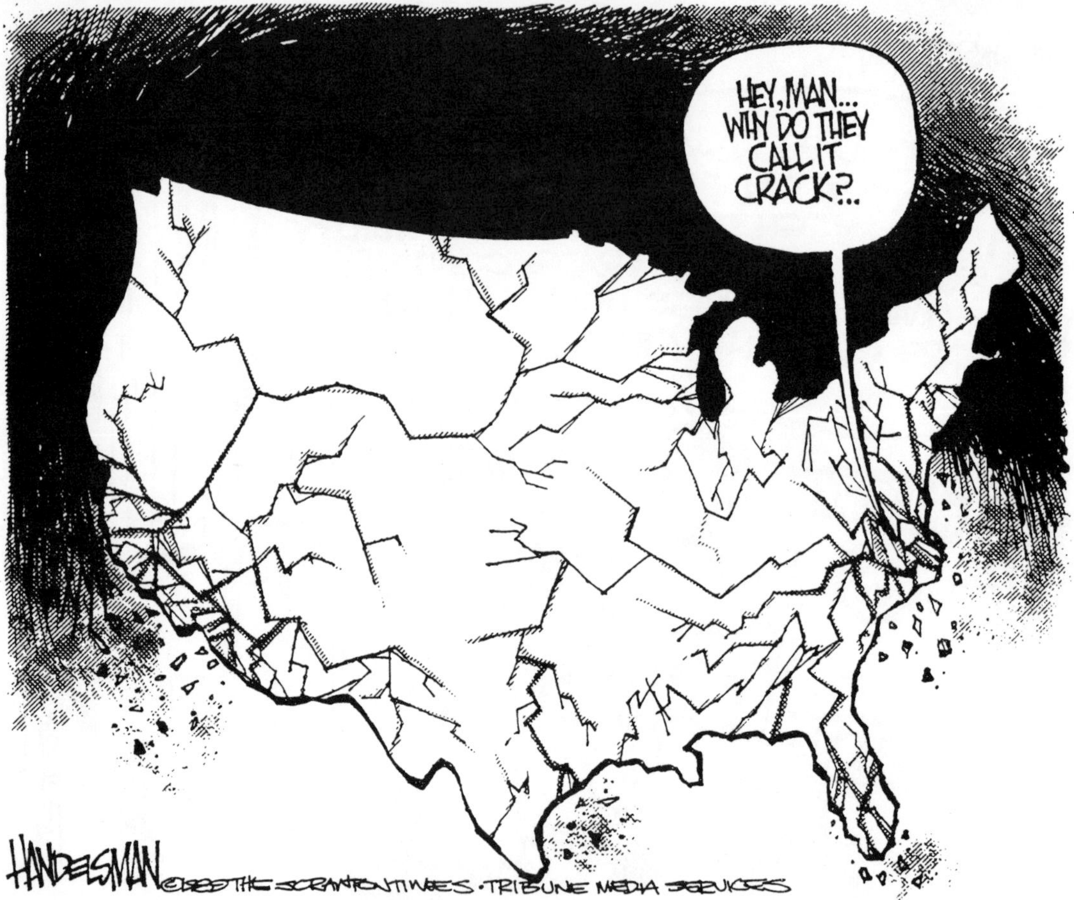
HEY, MAN... WHY DO THEY CALL IT CRACK?..
HANDELSMAN
© THE SCRANTON TIMES · TRIBUNE MEDIA SERVICES

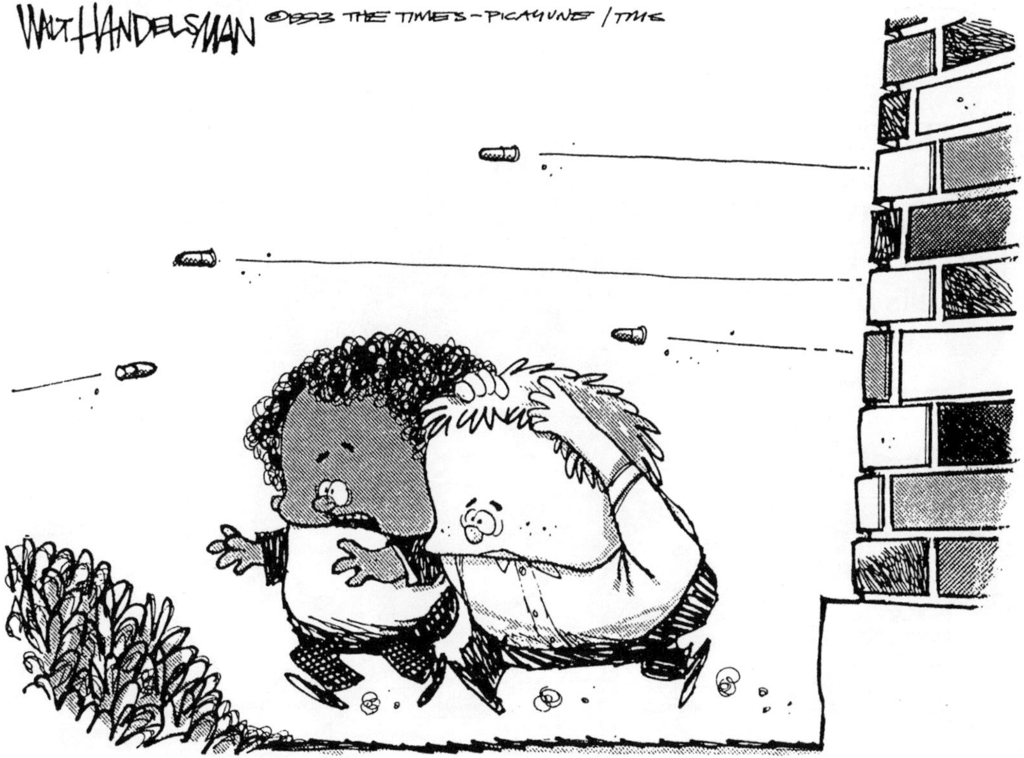
WALT HANDELSMAN ©1993 THE TIMES-PICAYUNE / TMS

"....WHO NEEDS A CASINO WHEN JUST *LIVING* HERE'S A GAMBLE?...."

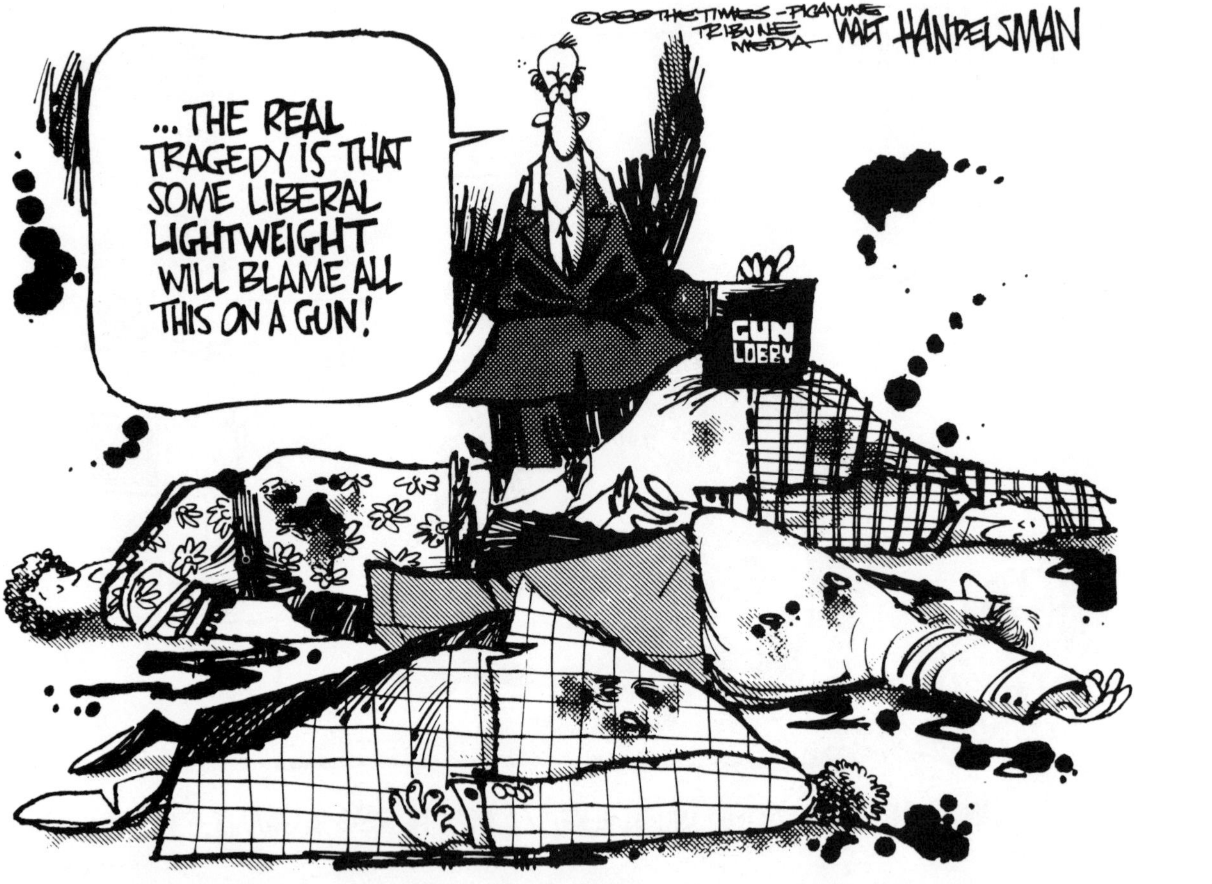
THE TIMES-PICAYUNE TRIBUNE MEDIA
WALT HANDELSMAN
...THE REAL TRAGEDY IS THAT SOME LIBERAL LIGHTWEIGHT WILL BLAME ALL THIS ON A GUN!
GUN LOBBY

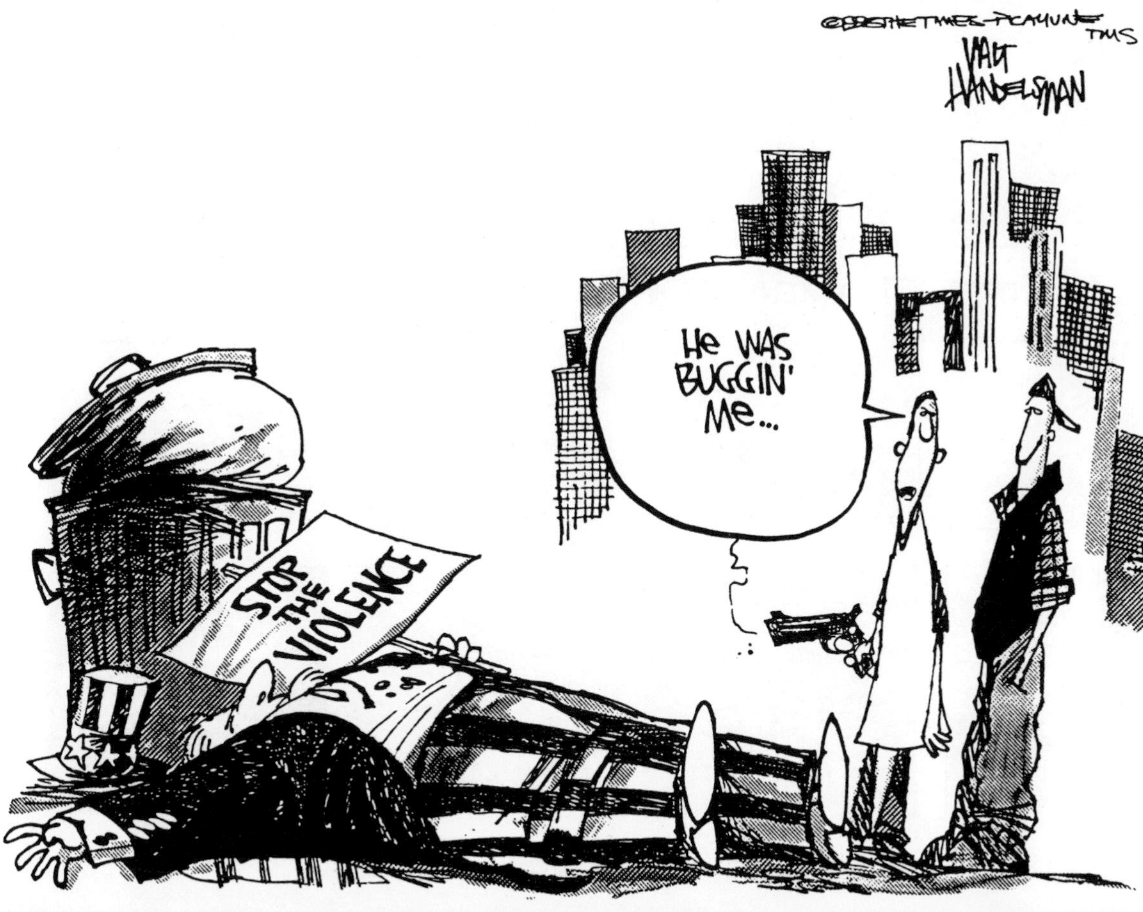
WALT HANDELSMAN
STOP THE VIOLENCE
He WAS BUGGIN' Me...

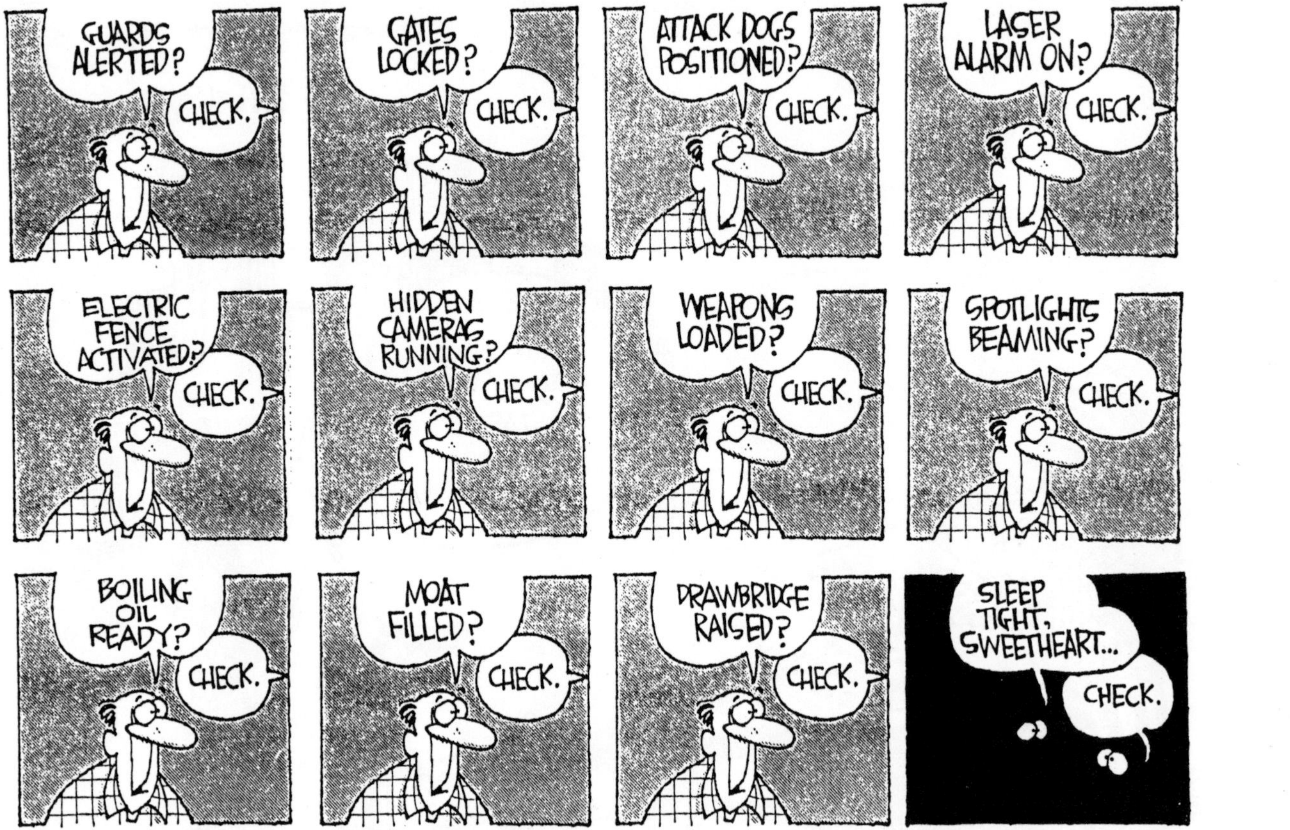
GUARDS ALERTED?
CHECK.
GATES LOCKED?
CHECK.
ATTACK DOGS POSITIONED?
CHECK.
LASER ALARM ON?
CHECK.
ELECTRIC FENCE ACTIVATED?
CHECK.
HIDDEN CAMERAS RUNNING?
CHECK.
WEAPONS LOADED?
CHECK.
SPOTLIGHTS BEAMING?
CHECK.
BOILING OIL READY?
CHECK.
MOAT FILLED?
CHECK.
DRAWBRIDGE RAISED?
CHECK.
SLEEP TIGHT, SWEETHEART...
CHECK.

WALT HANDELSMAN

Race Relations

When South Central L.A. erupted, Washington didn't have a clue.

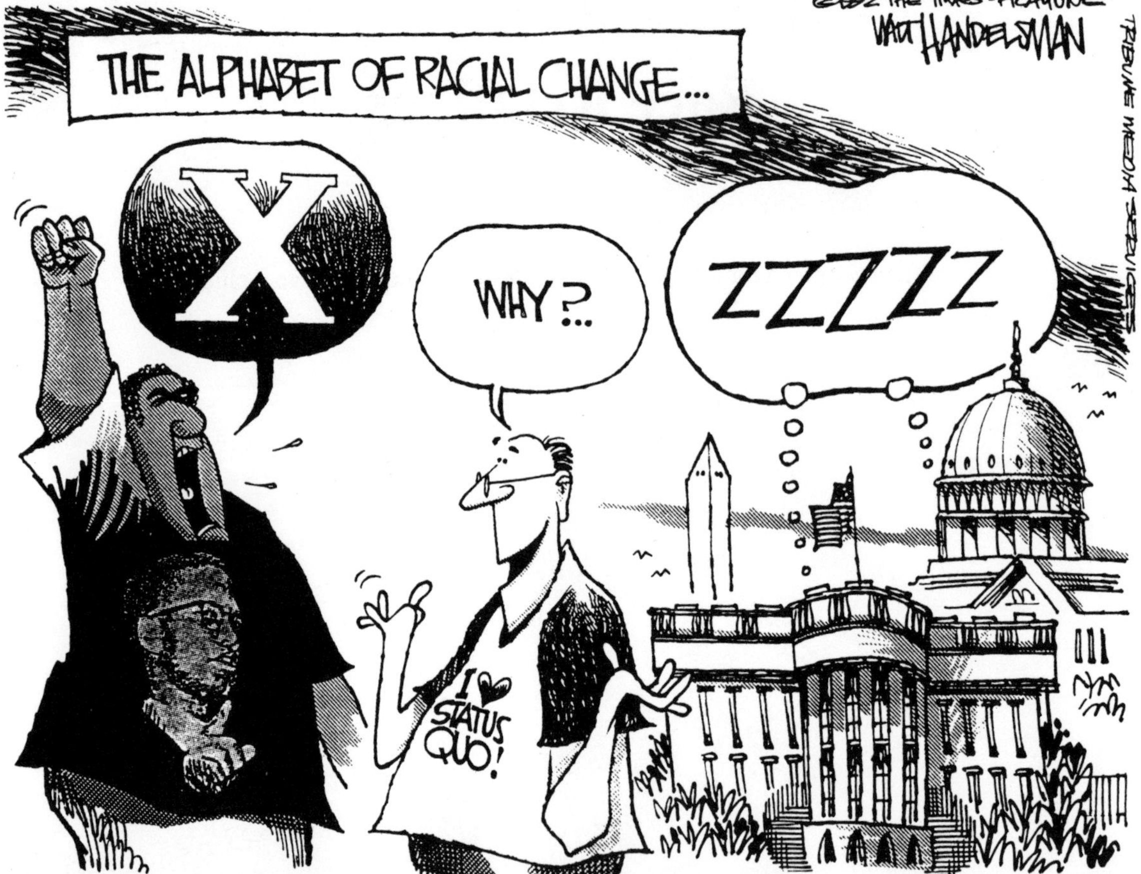
THE ALPHABET OF RACIAL CHANGE...
©1992 THE TIMES-PICAYUNE
WALT HANDELSMAN
TRIBUNE MEDIA SERVICES
X
WHY?...
ZZZZZ
I ♥ STATUS QUO!

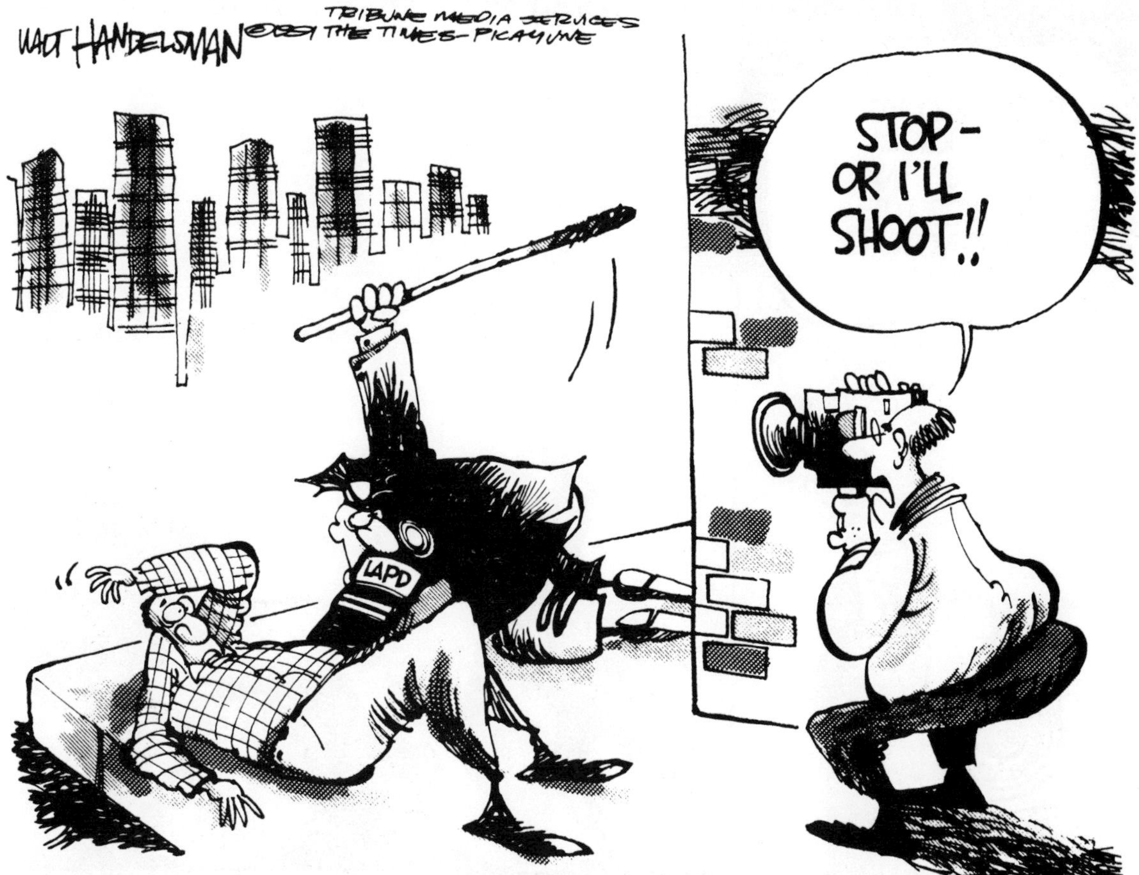
WALT HANDELSMAN ©1991 TRIBUNE MEDIA SERVICES THE TIMES-PICAYUNE
STOP-
OR I'LL
SHOOT!!
LAPD

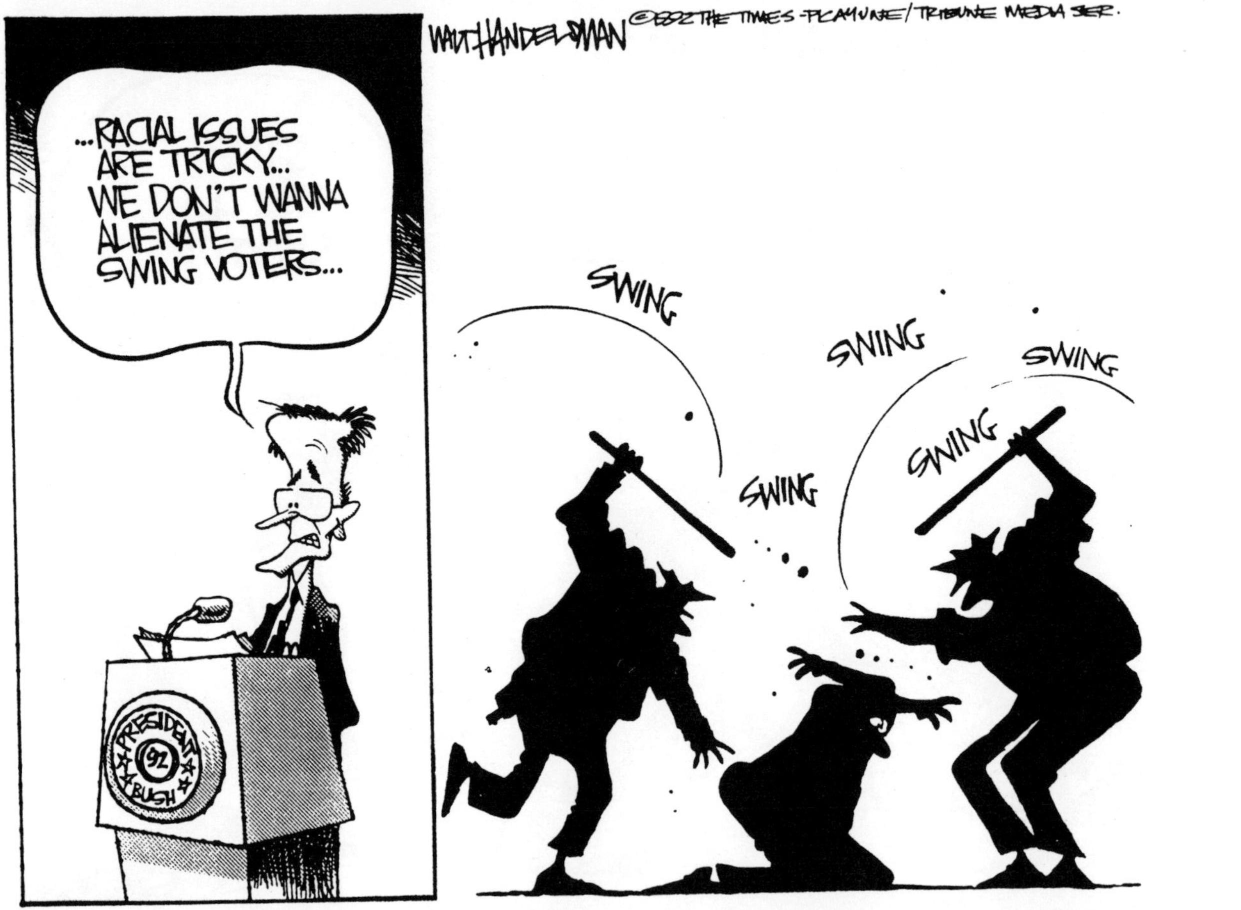
WALT HANDELSMAN ©1992 THE TIMES-PICAYUNE/TRIBUNE MEDIA SER.
...RACIAL ISSUES ARE TRICKY... WE DON'T WANNA ALIENATE THE SWING VOTERS...
PRESIDENT 92 BUSH
SWING
SWING
SWING
SWING
SWING

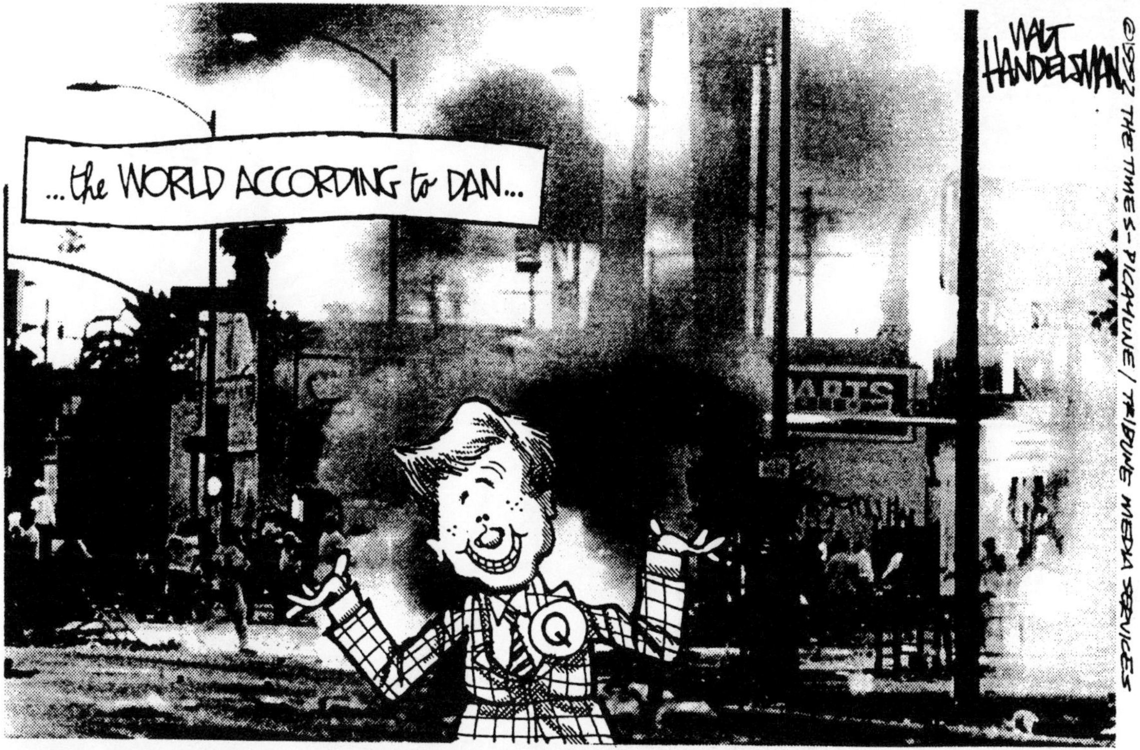
...the WORLD ACCORDING to DAN...
WALT HANDELSMAN
©1992 THE TIMES-PICAYUNE / TRIBUNE MEDIA SERVICES

"...IF THESE PEOPLE WOULD JUST GET MARRIED AND STOP WATCHING 'MURPHY BROWN', THIS KINDA JUNK WOULD NEVER HAPPEN..."

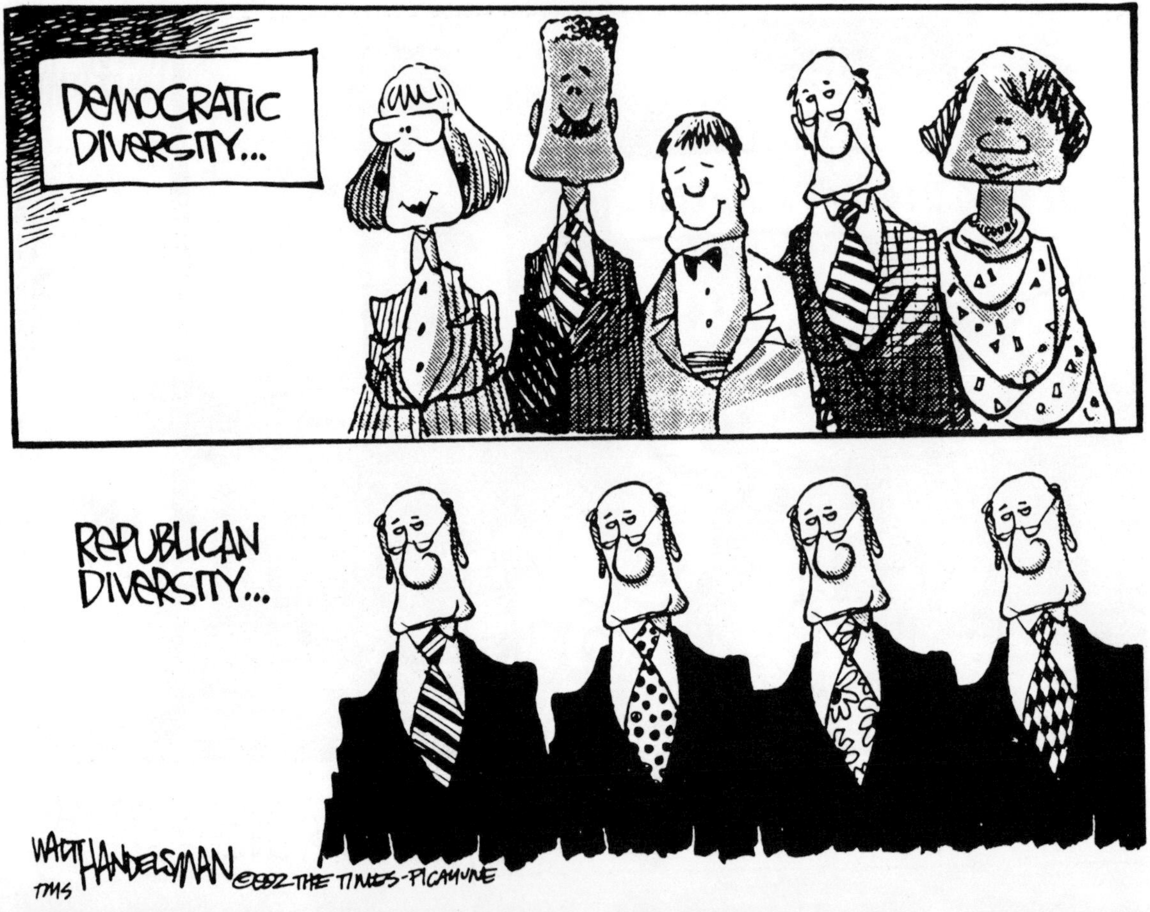
DEMOCRATIC DIVERSITY...
REPUBLICAN DIVERSITY...
WALT HANDELSMAN
TMS
©1992 THE TIMES-PICAYUNE

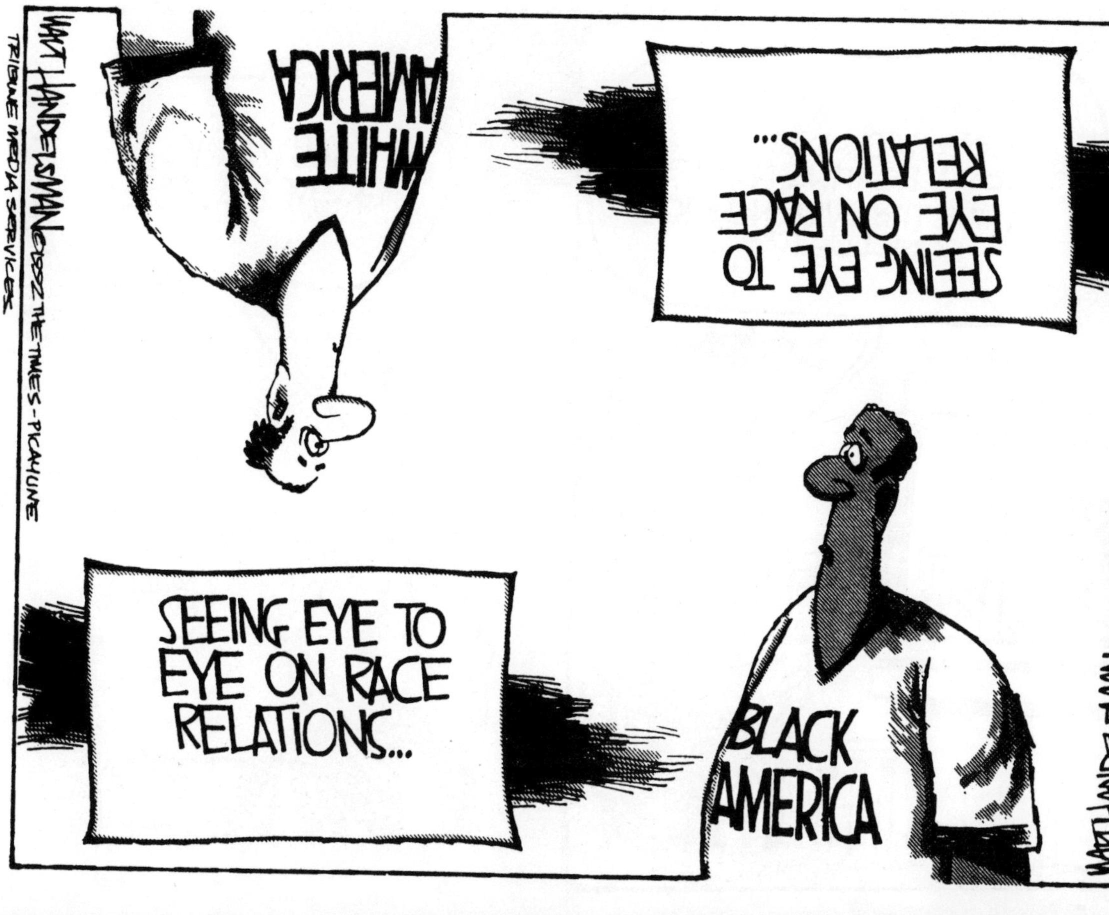

SEEING EYE TO EYE ON RACE RELATIONS...
BLACK AMERICA
WALT HANDELSMAN ©1992 THE TIMES-PICAYUNE
TRIBUNE MEDIA SERVICES
SEEING EYE TO EYE ON RACE RELATIONS...
WHITE AMERICA
WALT HANDELSMAN ©1992 THE TIMES-PICAYUNE
TRIBUNE MEDIA SERVICES

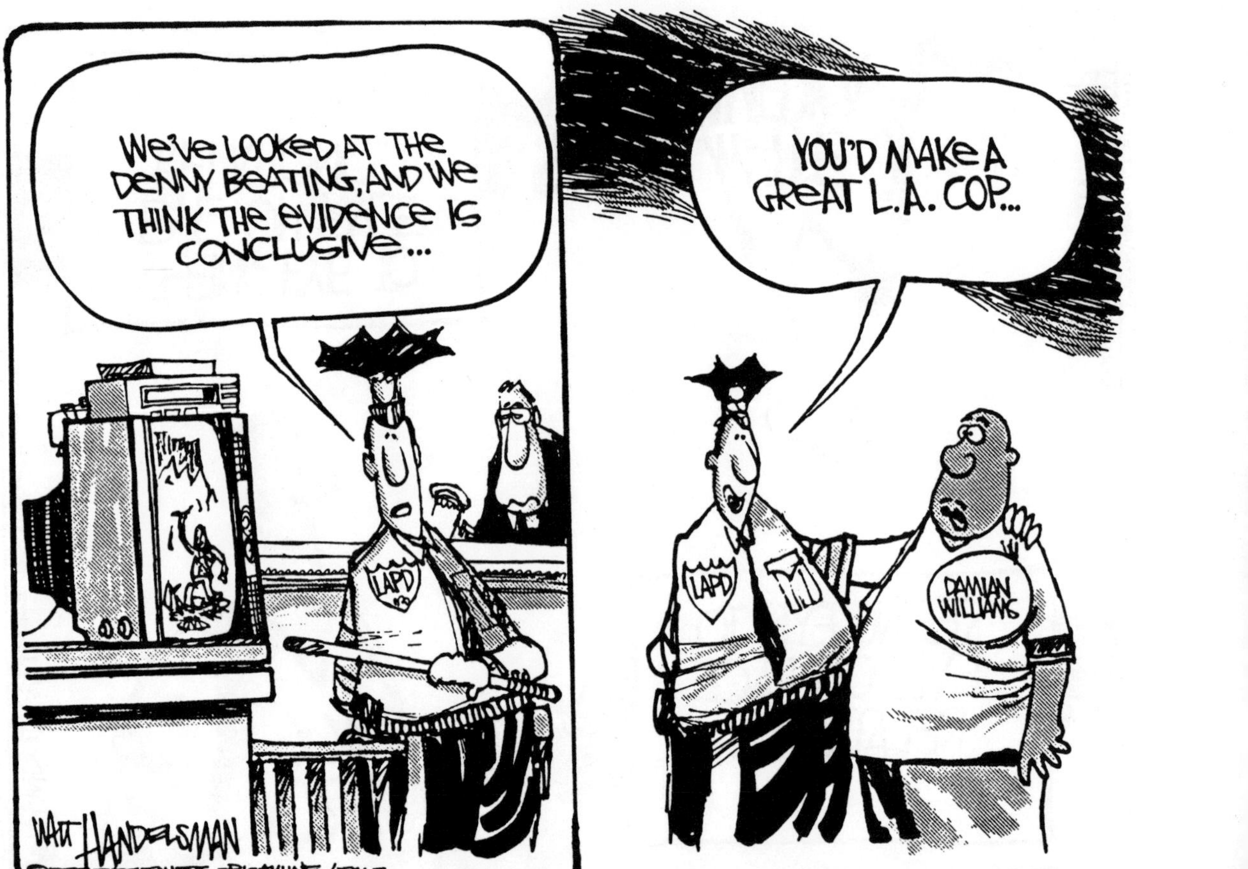

WE'VE LOOKED AT THE DENNY BEATING, AND WE THINK THE EVIDENCE IS CONCLUSIVE...
LAPD
LAPD
YOU'D MAKE A GREAT L.A. COP...
DAMIAN WILLIAMS
WALT HANDELSMAN
©1993 THE TIMES-PICAYUNE / TMS

The New World Order

Russians line up for Big Macs. A dove tries to land in the Middle East. The Berlin Wall collapses. . . . Unfortunately, so does Yugoslavia.

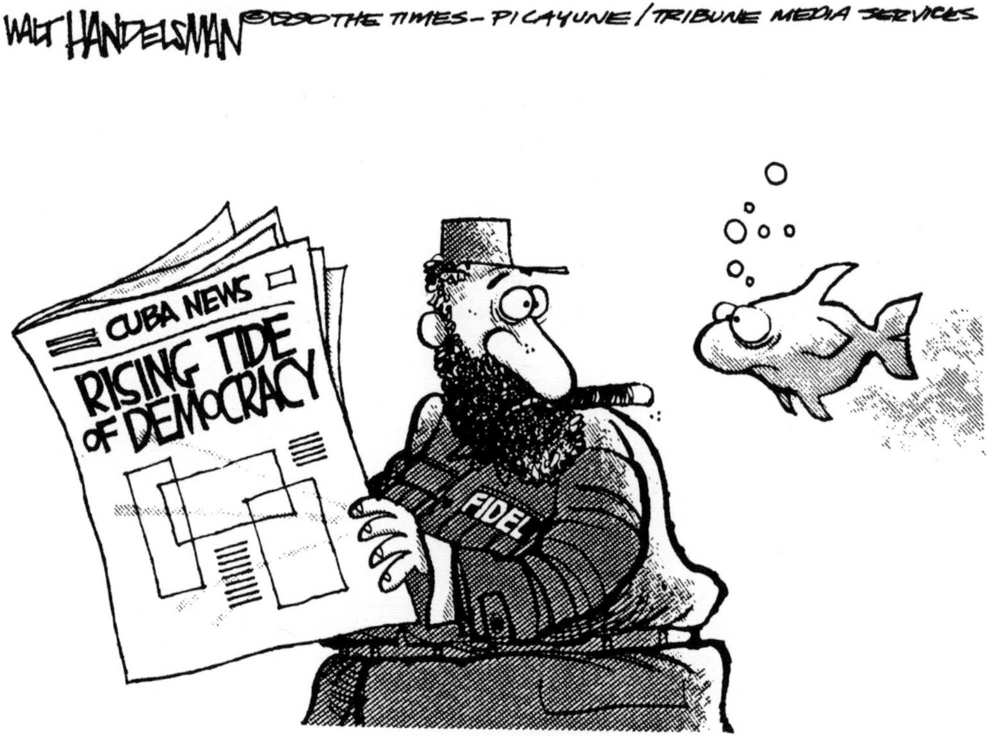
WALT HANDELSMAN ©1990 THE TIMES-PICAYUNE / TRIBUNE MEDIA SERVICES
CUBA NEWS
RISING TIDE OF DEMOCRACY
FIDEL

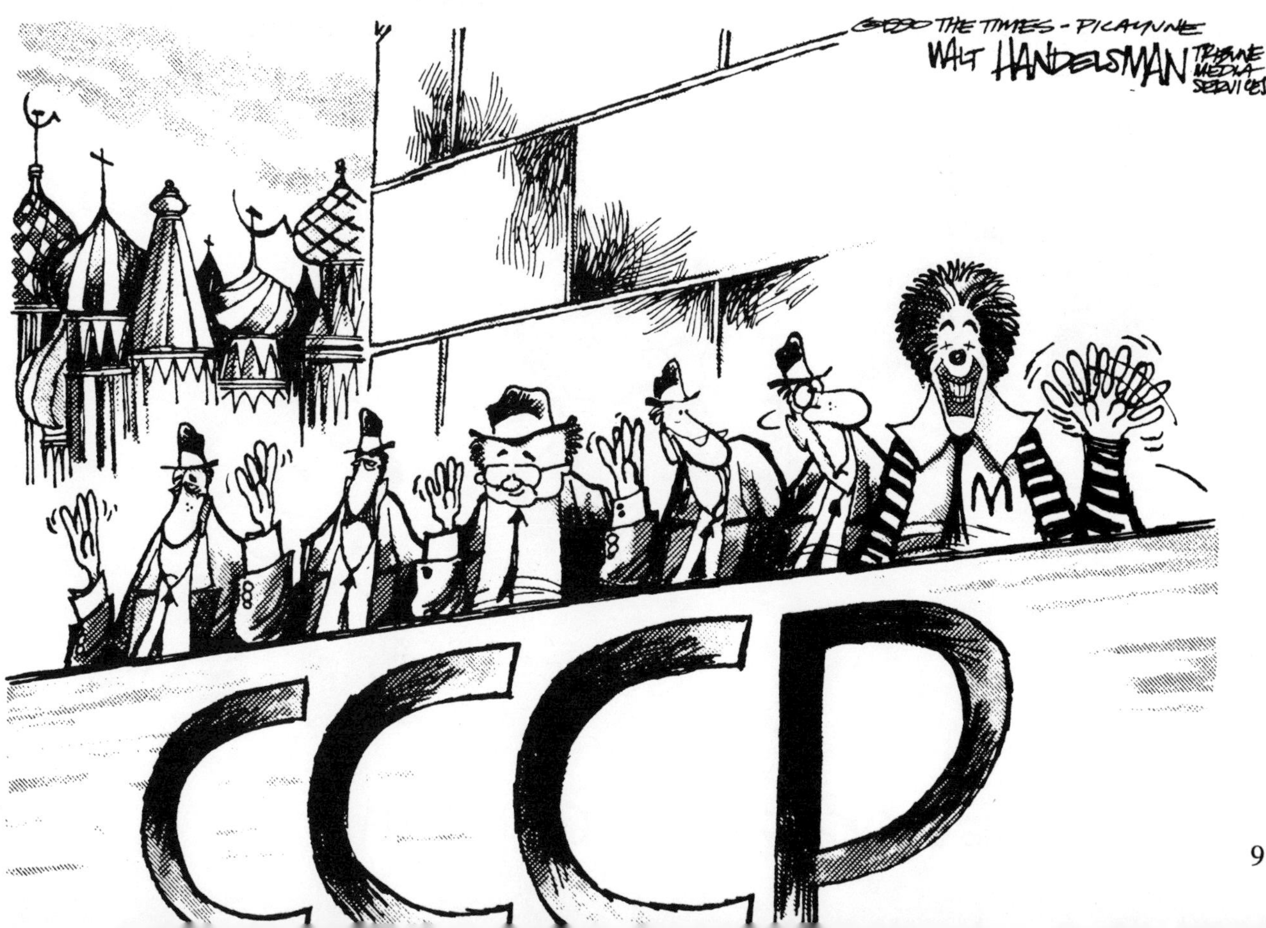
©1990 THE TIMES - PICAYUNE
WALT HANDELSMAN
TRIBUNE MEDIA SERVICES
M
CCCP

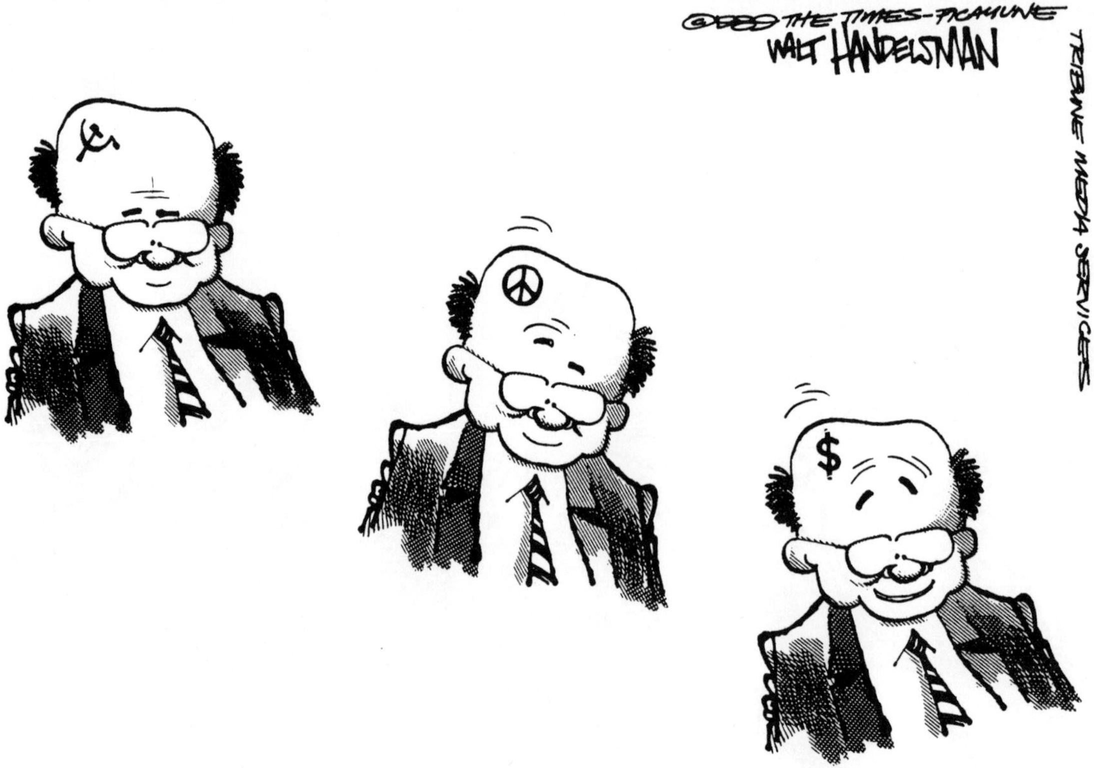
THE TIMES-PICAYUNE
WALT HANDELSMAN
TRIBUNE MEDIA SERVICES

THE CHANGING FACE of COMMUNISM...

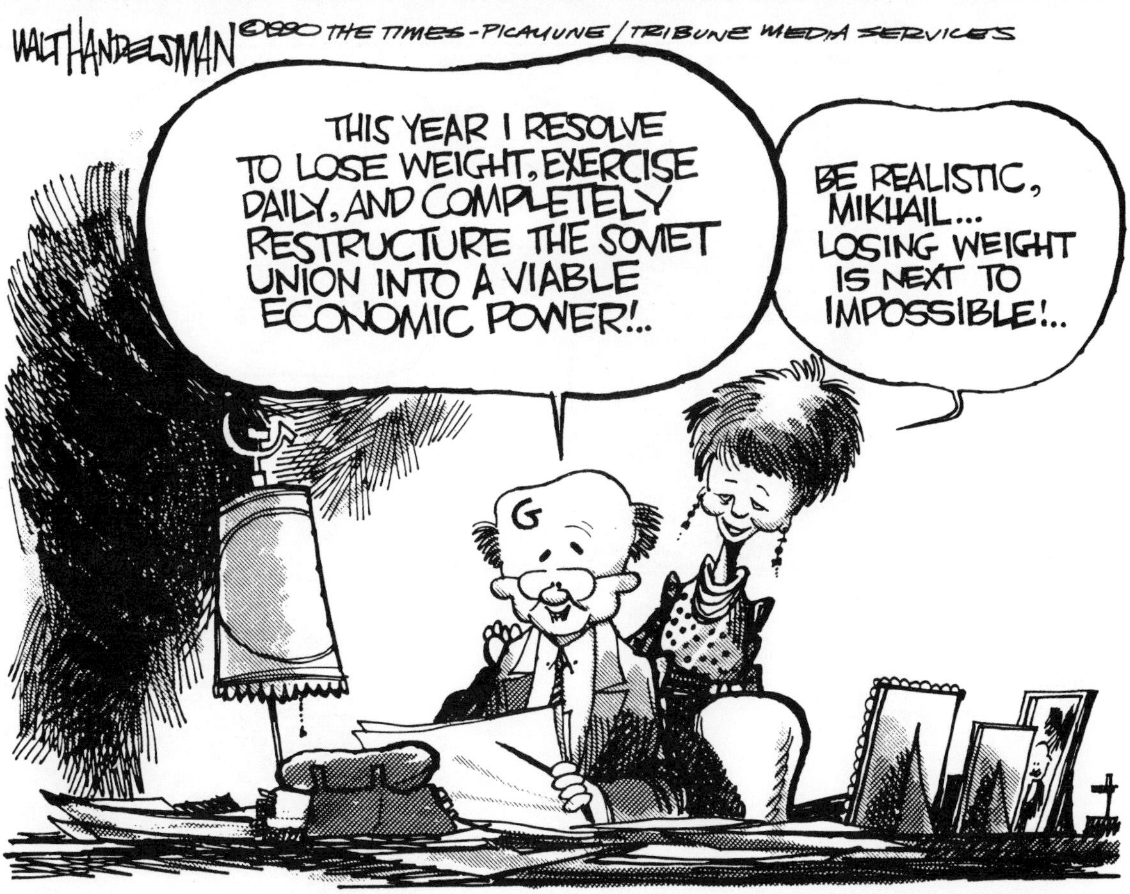
WALT HANDELSMAN ©1990 THE TIMES-PICAYUNE / TRIBUNE MEDIA SERVICES
THIS YEAR I RESOLVE TO LOSE WEIGHT, EXERCISE DAILY, AND COMPLETELY RESTRUCTURE THE SOVIET UNION INTO A VIABLE ECONOMIC POWER!..
BE REALISTIC, MIKHAIL... LOSING WEIGHT IS NEXT TO IMPOSSIBLE!..
G

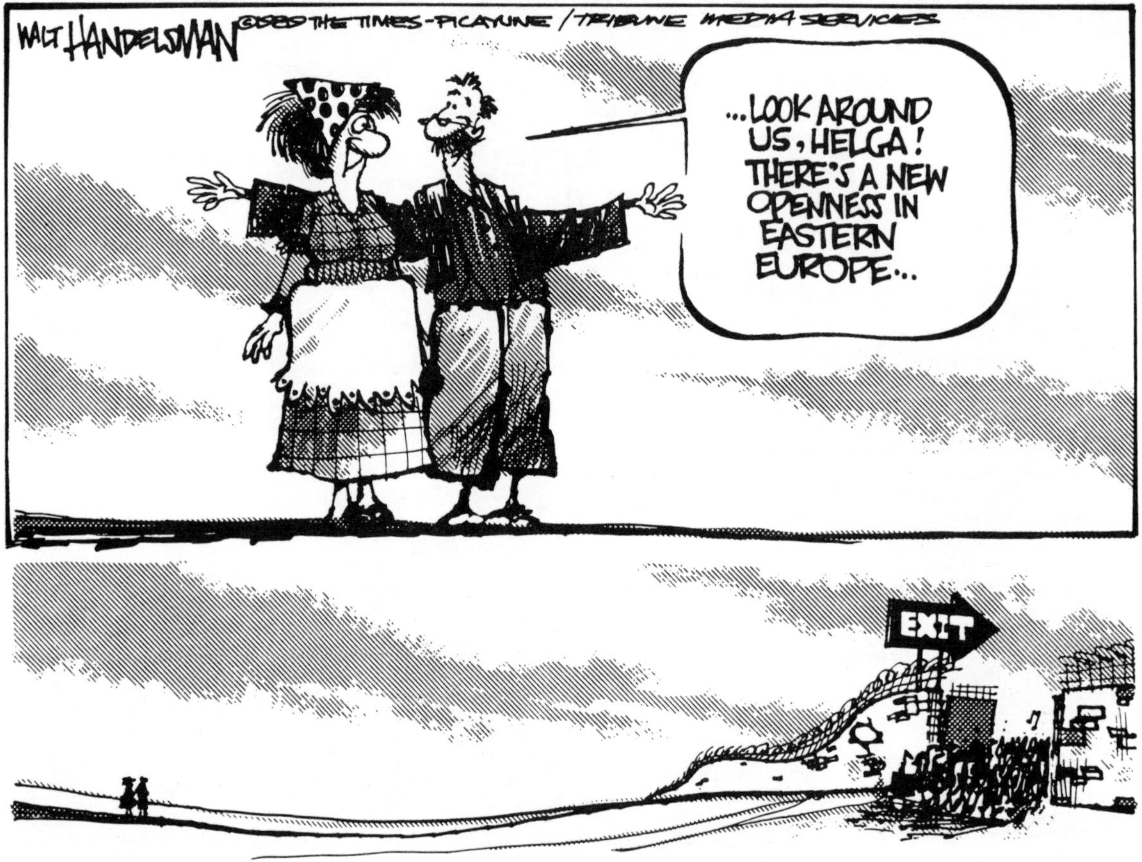

WALT HANDELSMAN ©1989 THE TIMES-PICAYUNE / TRIBUNE MEDIA SERVICES
...LOOK AROUND US, HELGA! THERE'S A NEW OPENNESS IN EASTERN EUROPE...
EXIT

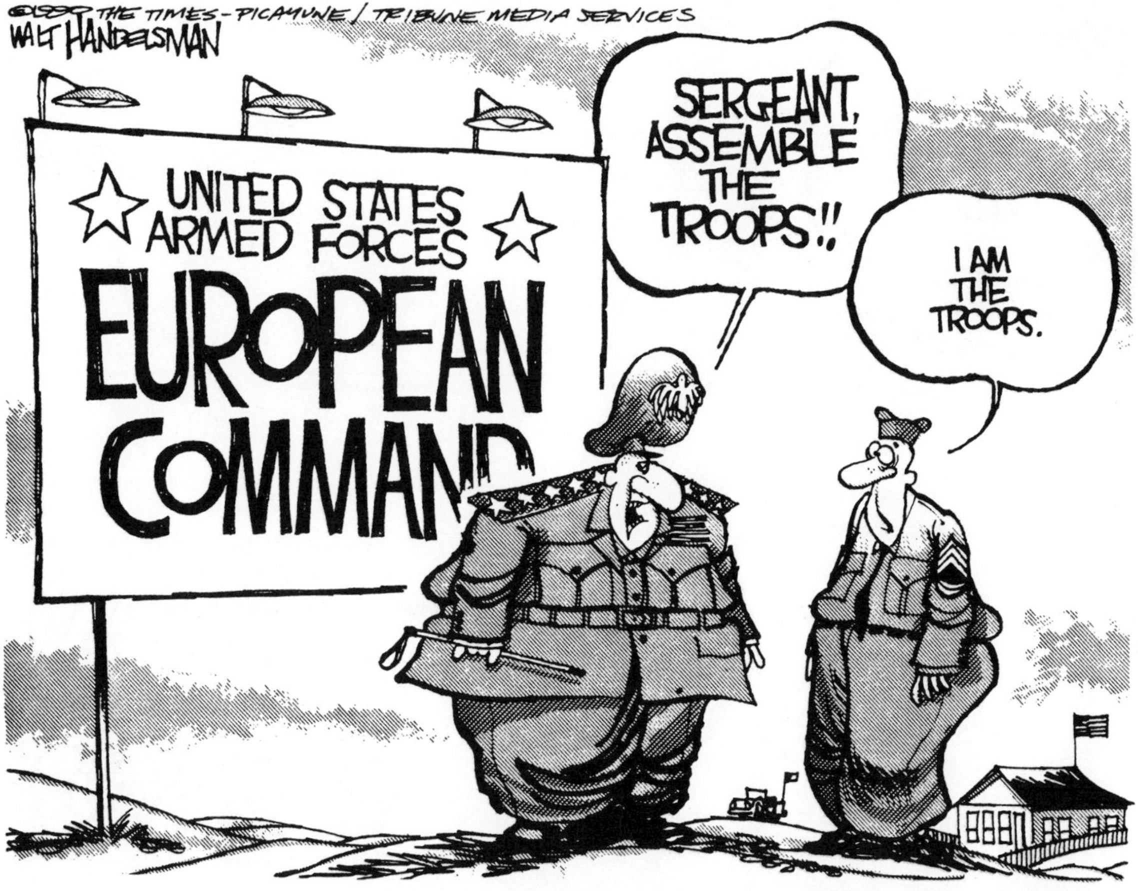
©1999 THE TIMES-PICAYUNE / TRIBUNE MEDIA SERVICES
WALT HANDELSMAN
UNITED STATES ARMED FORCES
EUROPEAN COMMAND
SERGEANT, ASSEMBLE THE TROOPS!!
I AM THE TROOPS.

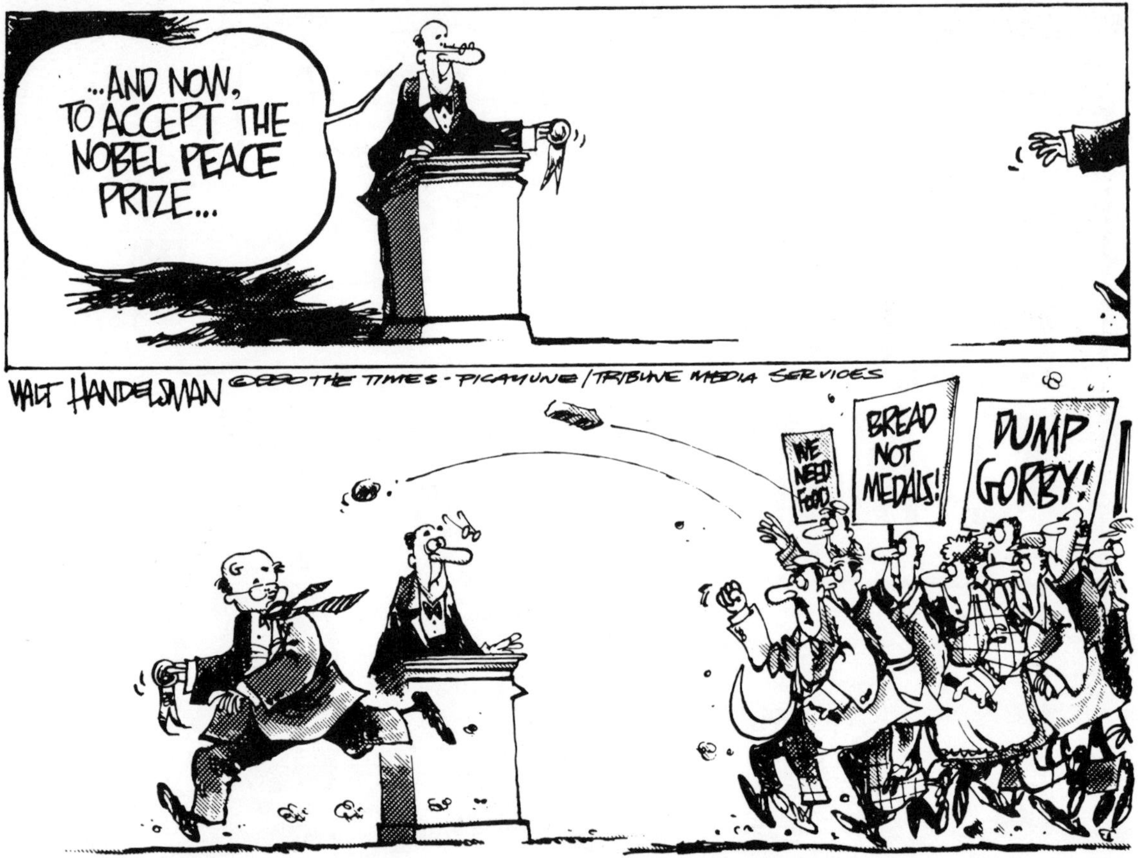
...AND NOW, TO ACCEPT THE NOBEL PEACE PRIZE...
WALT HANDELSMAN ©1990 THE TIMES-PICAYUNE / TRIBUNE MEDIA SERVICES
WE NEED FOOD
BREAD NOT MEDALS!
DUMP GORBY!

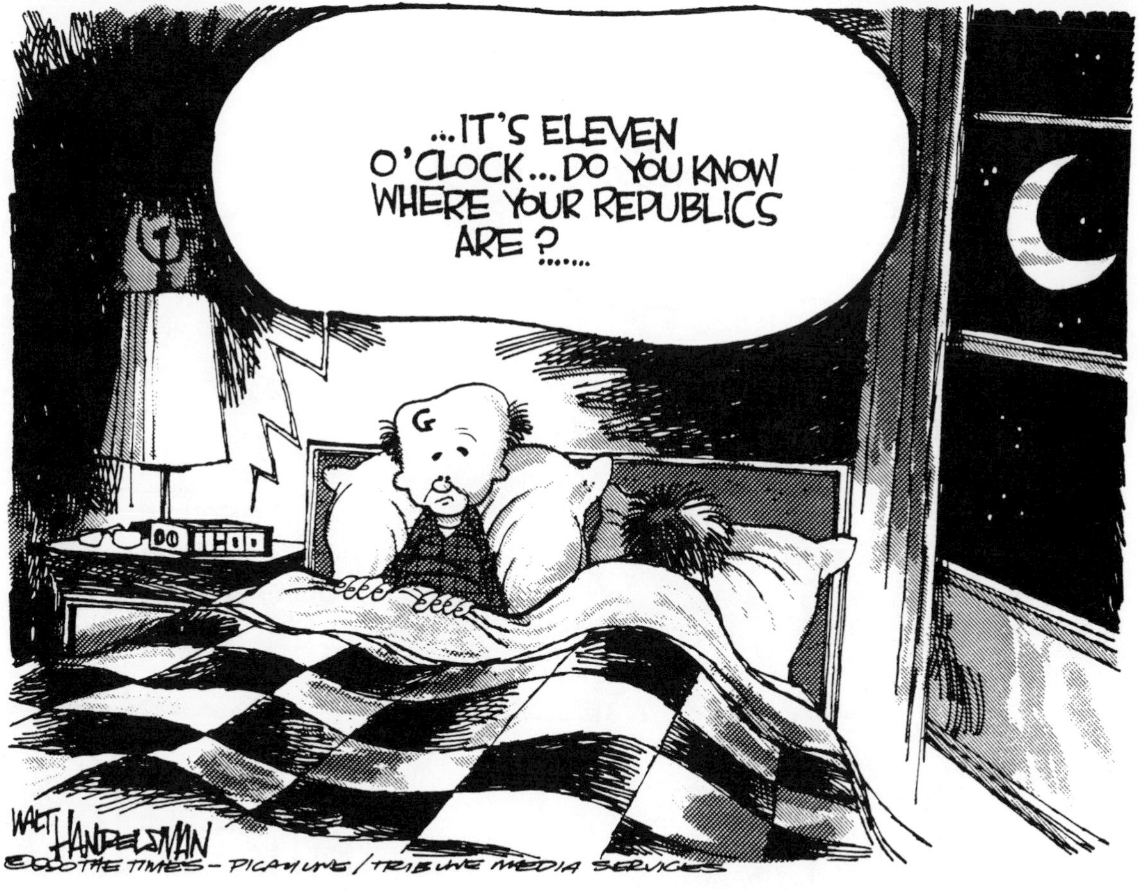
...IT'S ELEVEN O'CLOCK...DO YOU KNOW WHERE YOUR REPUBLICS ARE ?......
G
WALT HANDELSMAN
©1990 THE TIMES-PICAYUNE/TRIBUNE MEDIA SERVICES

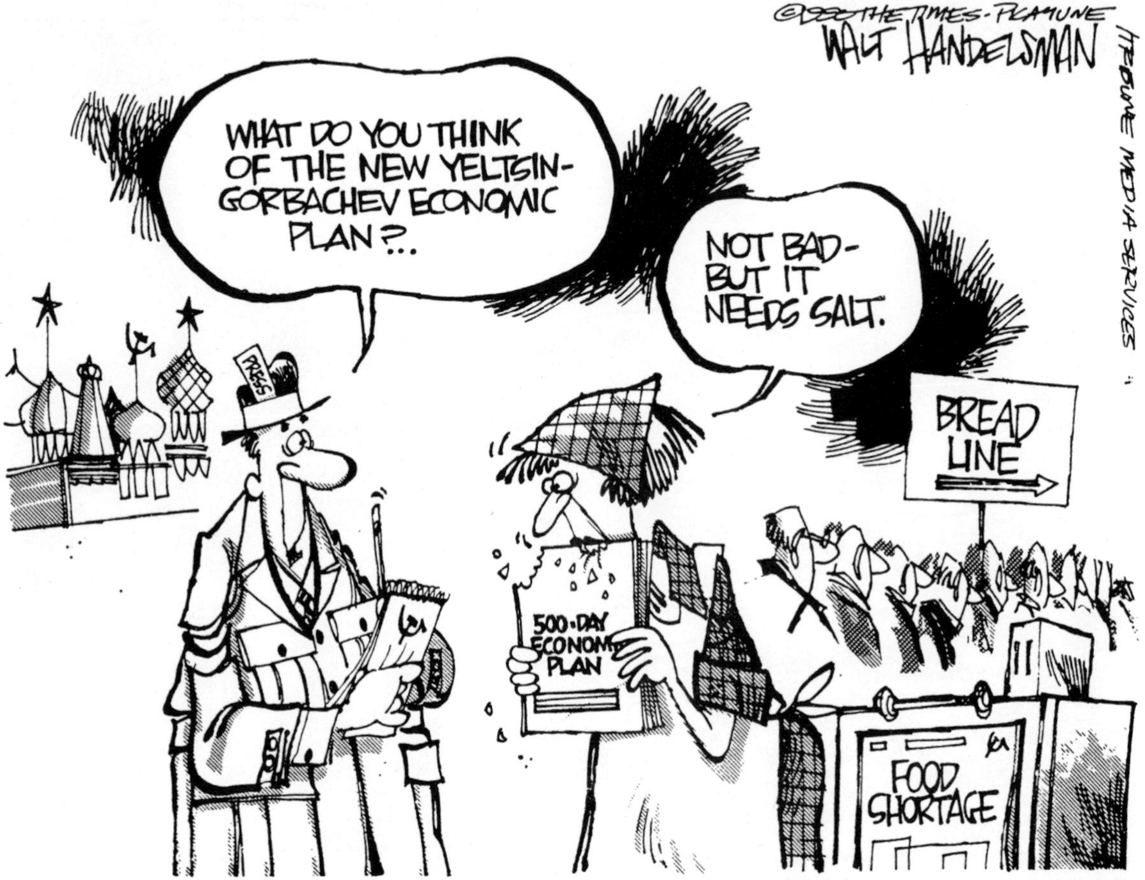
©1990 THE TIMES-PICAYUNE
WALT HANDELSMAN
TRIBUNE MEDIA SERVICES
WHAT DO YOU THINK OF THE NEW YELTSIN-GORBACHEV ECONOMIC PLAN?...
NOT BAD- BUT IT NEEDS SALT.
PRESS
500-DAY ECONOMIC PLAN
BREAD LINE
FOOD SHORTAGE

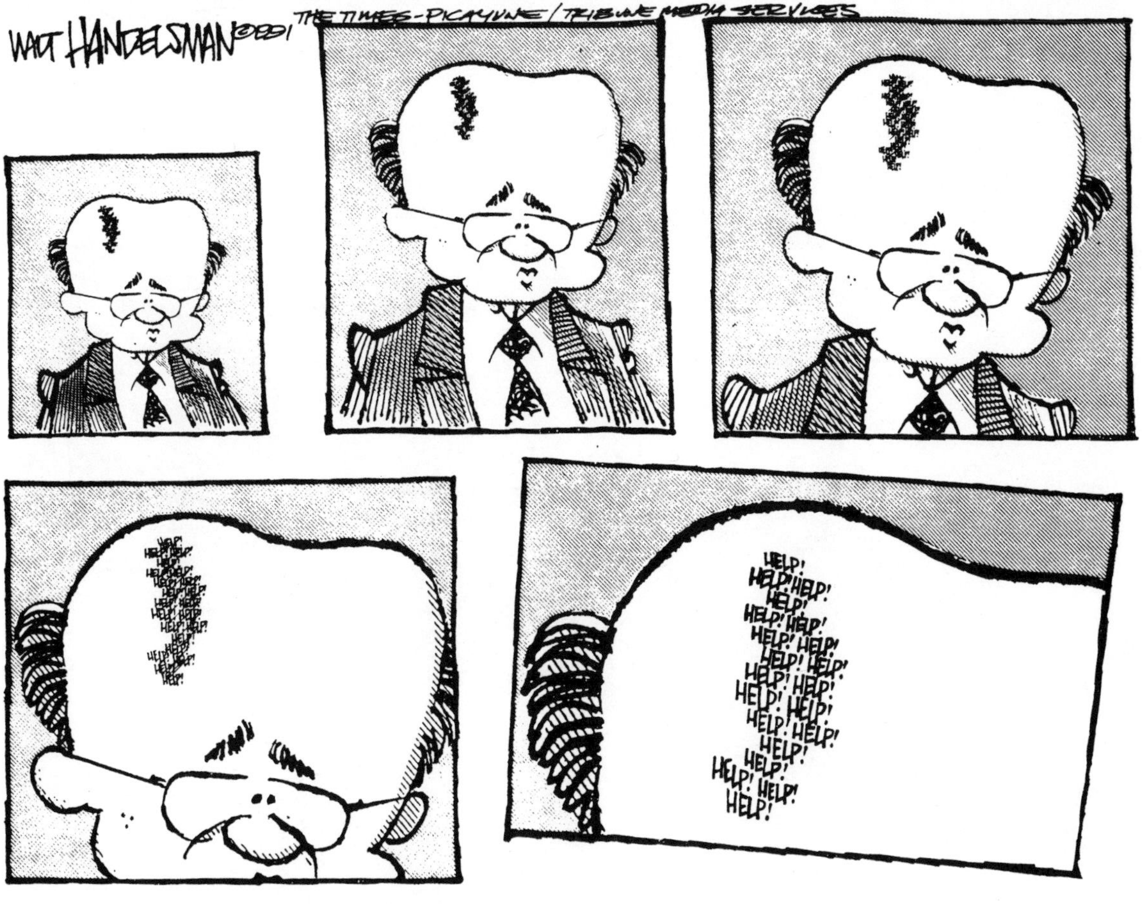
WALT HANDELSMAN ©1991 THE TIMES-PICAYUNE / TRIBUNE MEDIA SERVICES
HELP!
HELP! HELP!
HELP!
HELP! HELP!
HELP! HELP!
HELP! HELP!
HELP! HELP!
HELP! HELP!
HELP! HELP!
HELP!
HELP!
HELP! HELP!
HELP!

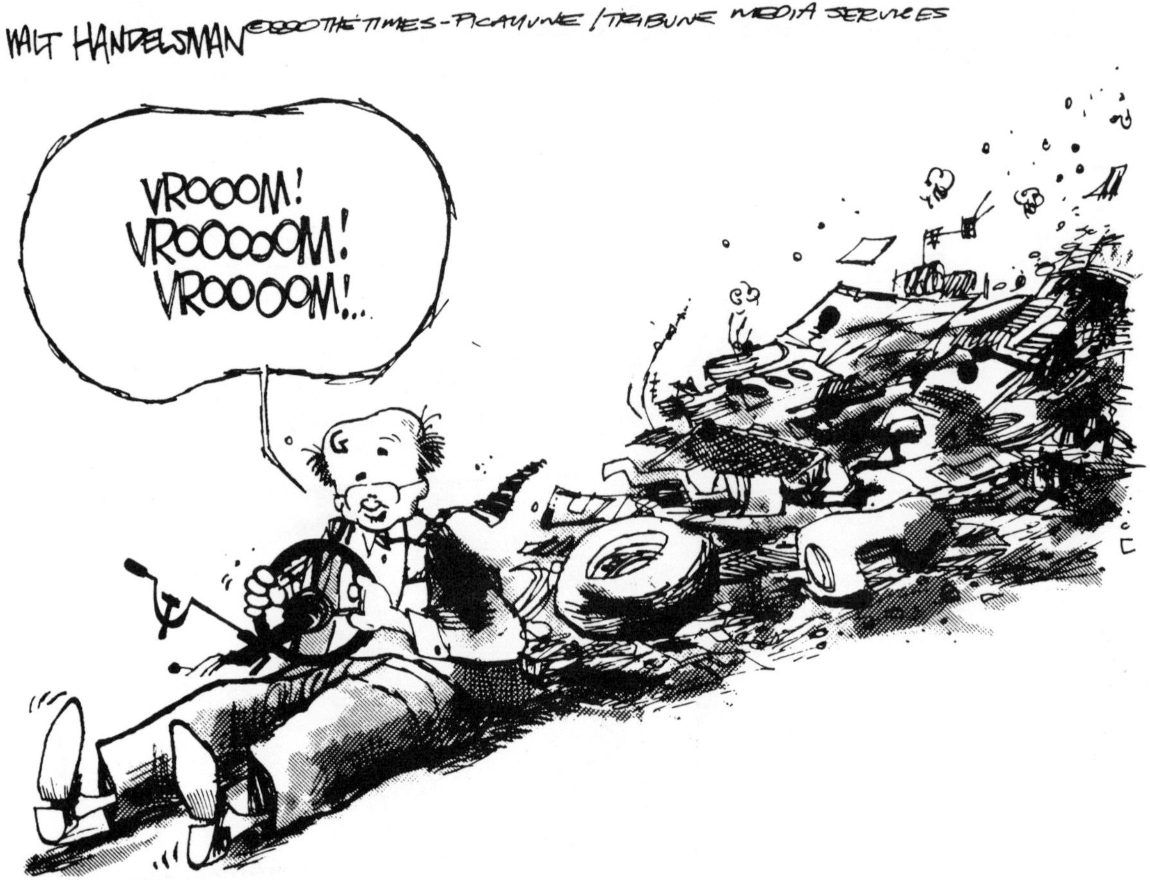
WALT HANDELSMAN
THE TIMES-PICAYUNE / TRIBUNE MEDIA SERVICES
VROOOM! VROOOOOOM! VROOOOM!...

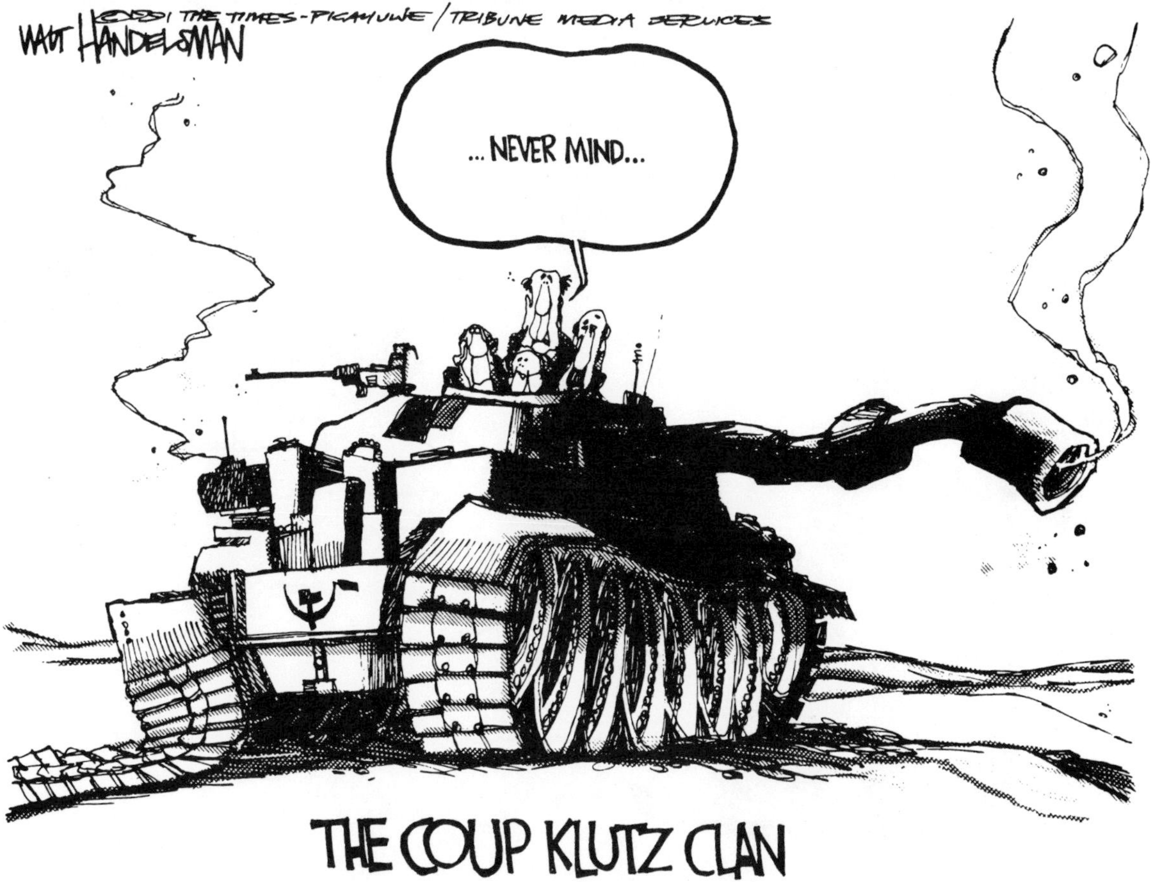
WALT HANDELSMAN
THE TIMES-PICAYUNE / TRIBUNE MEDIA SERVICES
...NEVER MIND...

THE COUP KLUTZ CLAN

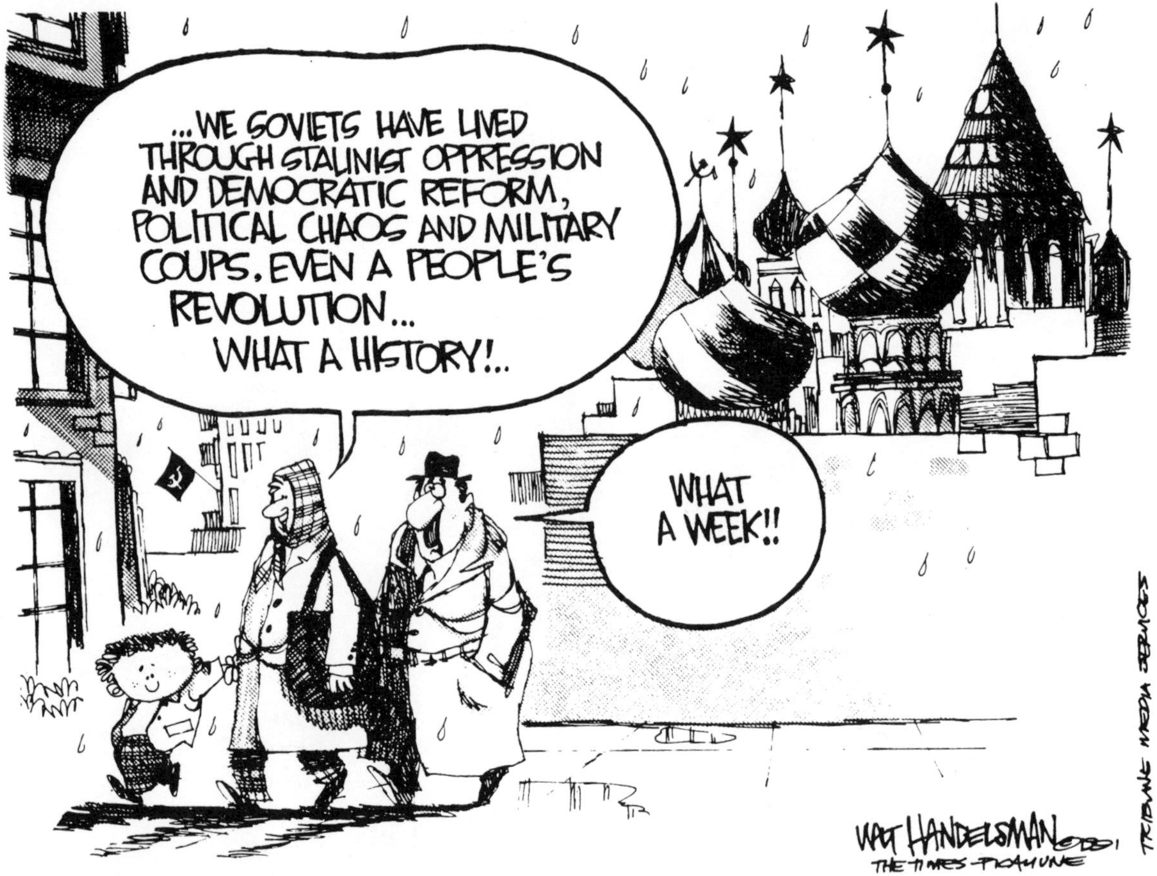
...WE SOVIETS HAVE LIVED THROUGH STALINIST OPPRESSION AND DEMOCRATIC REFORM, POLITICAL CHAOS AND MILITARY COUPS, EVEN A PEOPLE'S REVOLUTION... WHAT A HISTORY!..
WHAT A WEEK!!
WALT HANDELSMAN
THE TIMES-PICAYUNE
TRIBUNE MEDIA SERVICES

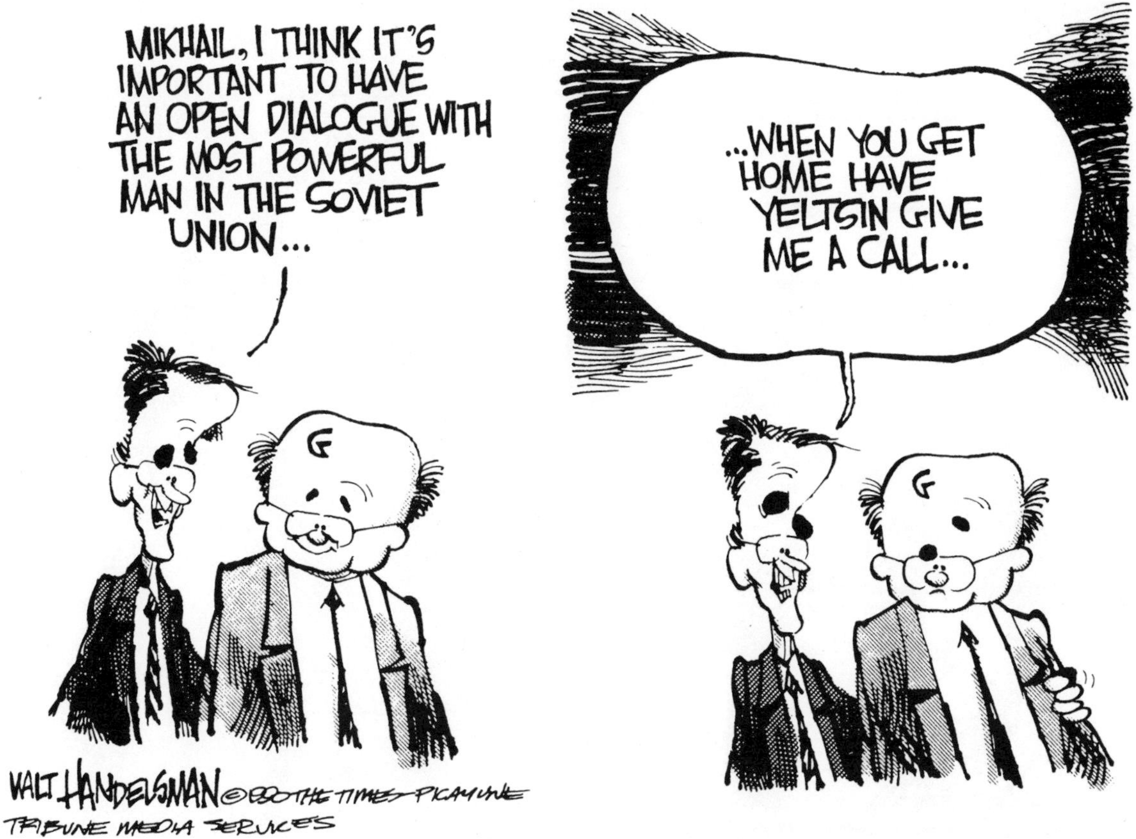
MIKHAIL, I THINK IT'S IMPORTANT TO HAVE AN OPEN DIALOGUE WITH THE MOST POWERFUL MAN IN THE SOVIET UNION...
...WHEN YOU GET HOME HAVE YELTSIN GIVE ME A CALL...
WALT HANDELSMAN © THE TIMES-PICAYUNE
TRIBUNE MEDIA SERVICES

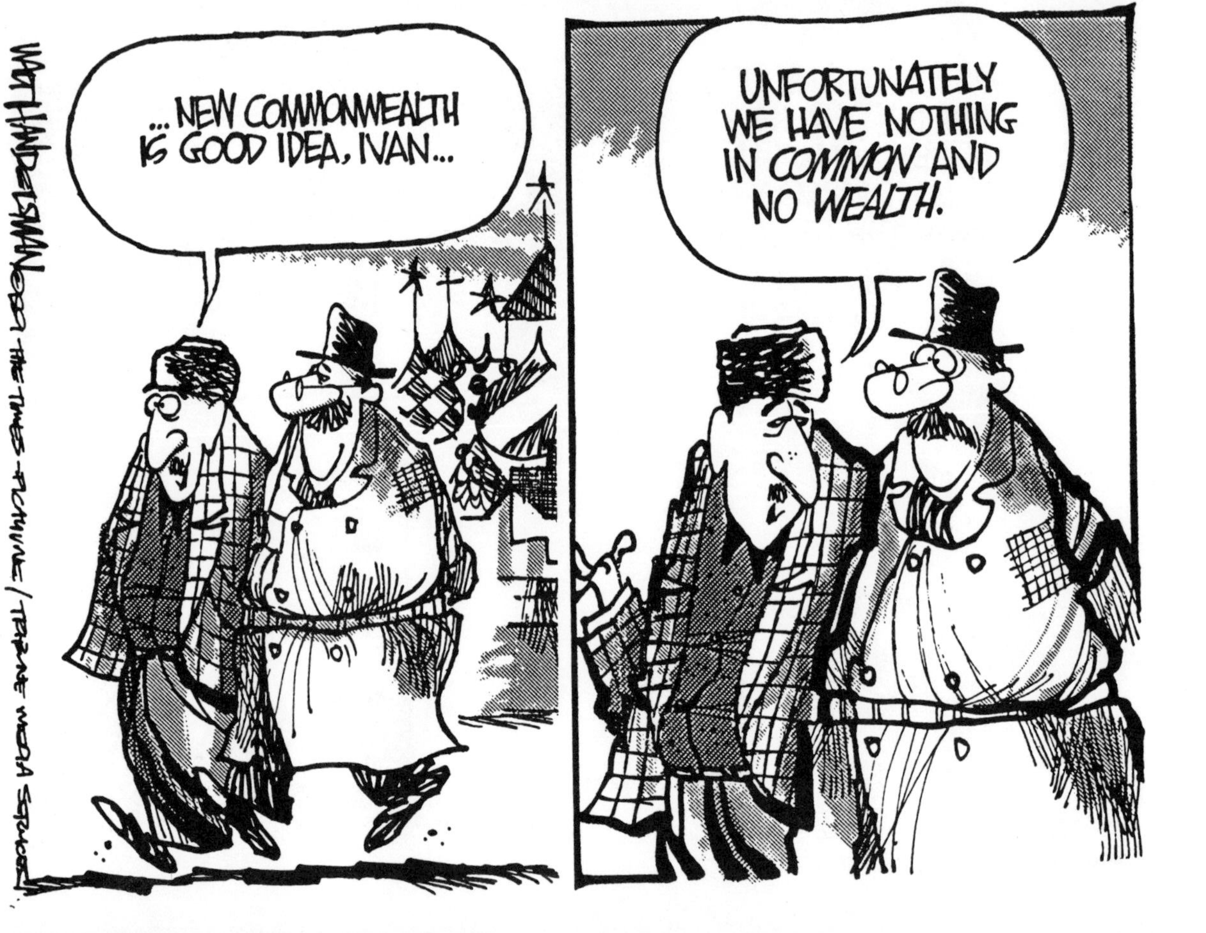
...NEW COMMONWEALTH IS GOOD IDEA, IVAN...
UNFORTUNATELY WE HAVE NOTHING IN COMMON AND NO WEALTH.

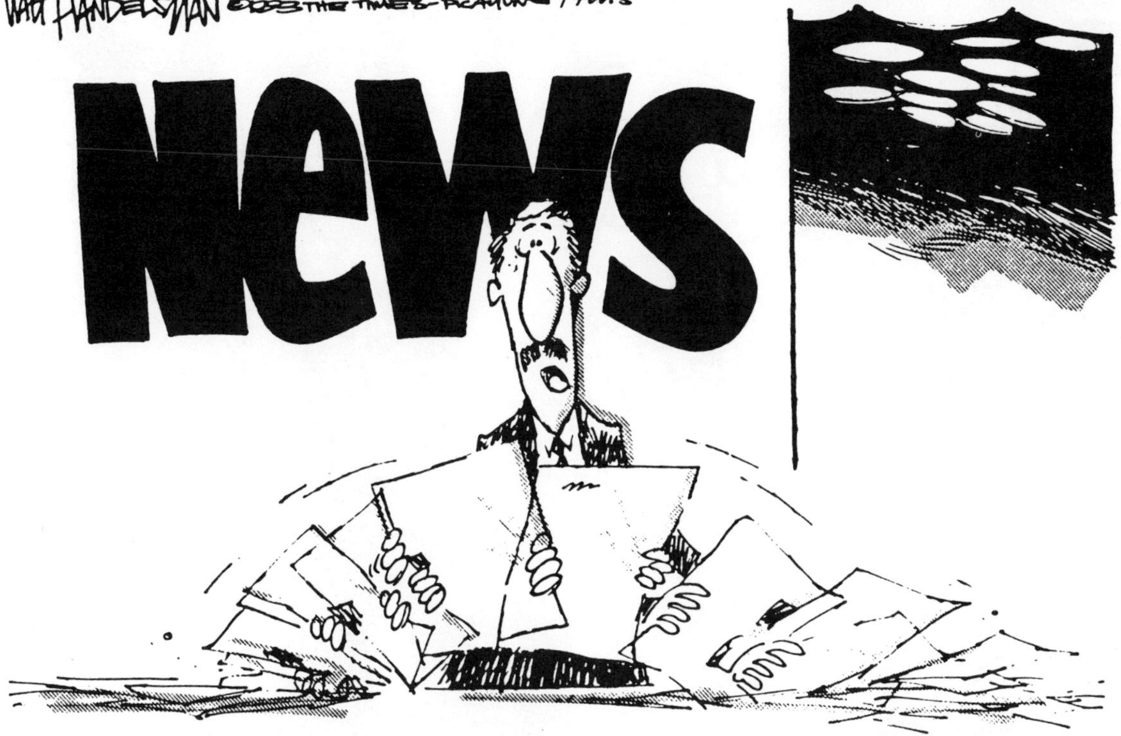
WALT HANDELSMAN
THE TIMES-PICAYUNE / TMS
NEWS

"..... AN ISRAELI MAN WAS STABBED TO DEATH TODAY IN RETALIATION FOR AN ARAB MAN'S DEATH YESTERDAY IN RETALIATION FOR AN ISRAELI'S DEATH MONDAY IN RET..."

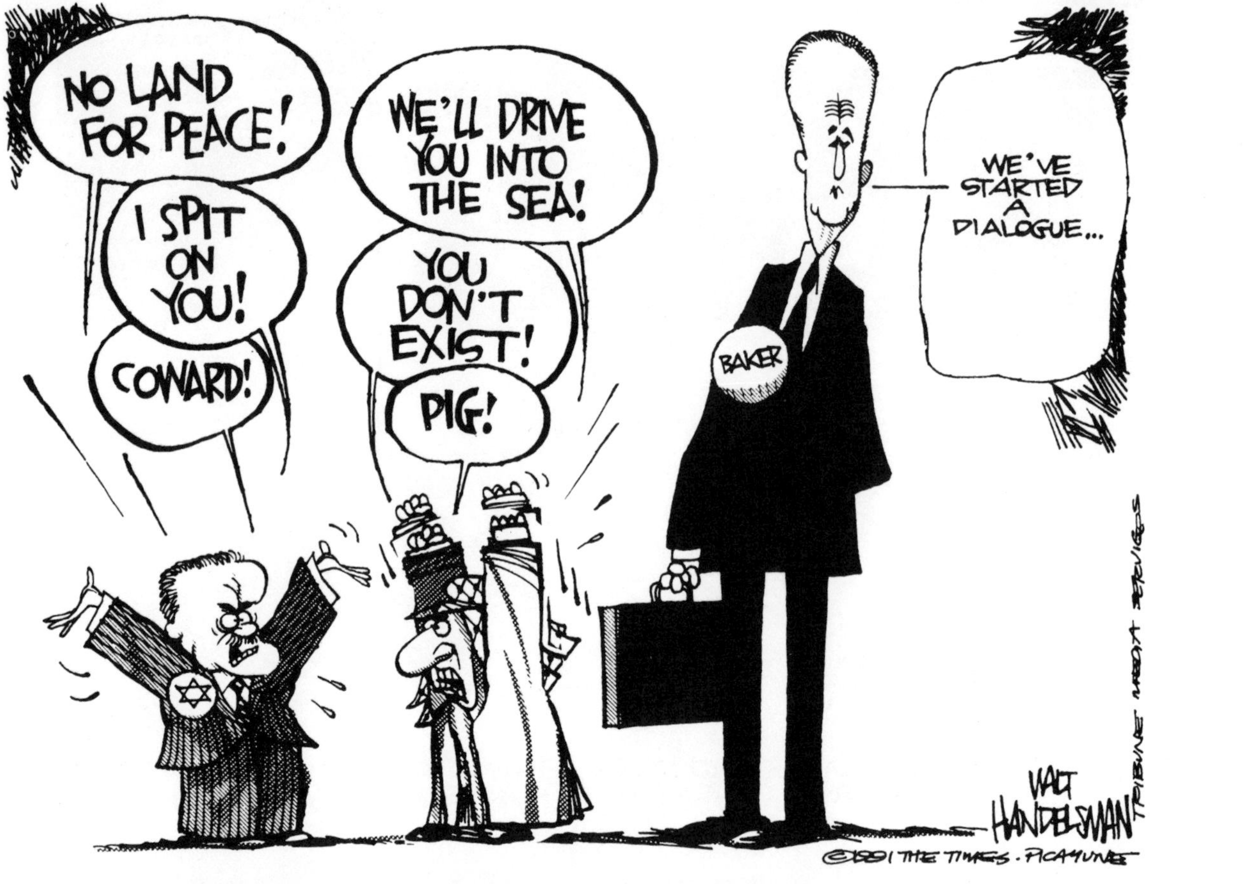
NO LAND FOR PEACE!
I SPIT ON YOU!
COWARD!
WE'LL DRIVE YOU INTO THE SEA!
YOU DON'T EXIST!
PIG!
BAKER
WE'VE STARTED A DIALOGUE...
WALT HANDELSMAN
TRIBUNE MEDIA SERVICES
©1991 THE TIMES-PICAYUNE

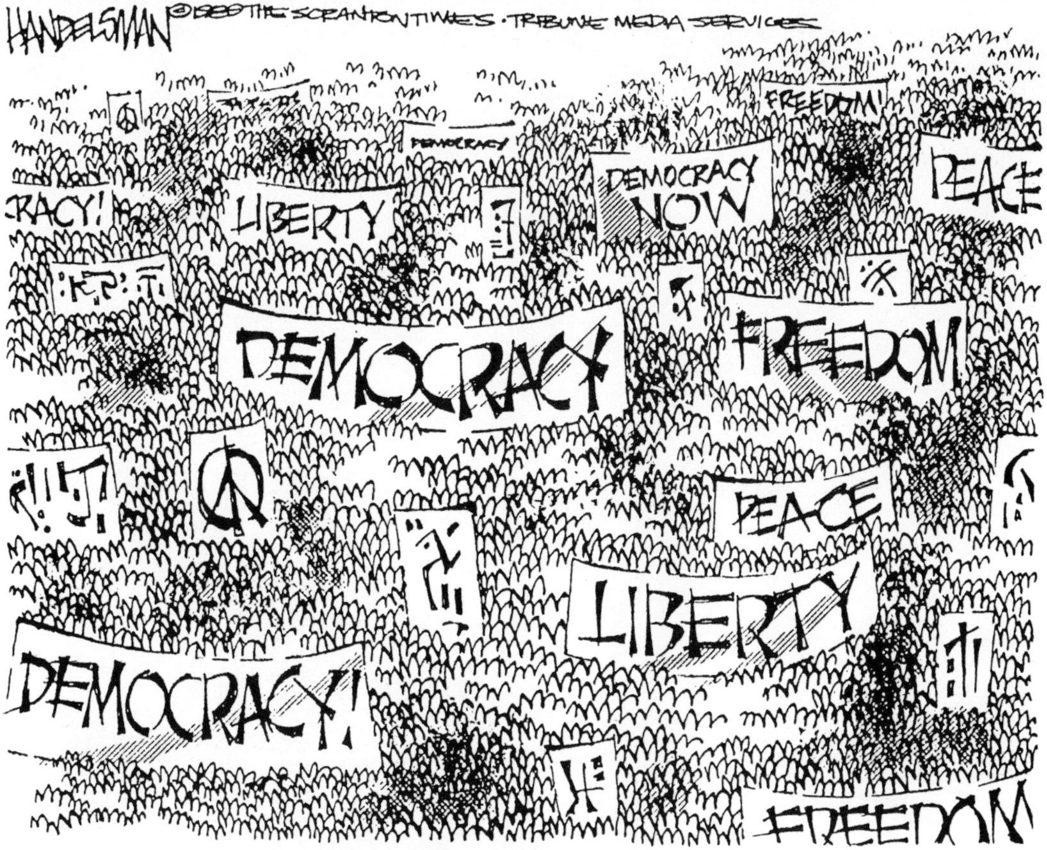
HANDELSMAN
THE SCRANTON TIMES · TRIBUNE MEDIA SERVICES
FREEDOM!
DEMOCRACY
DEMOCRACY NOW
PEACE
LIBERTY
DEMOCRACY
FREEDOM
PEACE
LIBERTY
DEMOCRACY!

A BILLION POINTS OF LIGHT

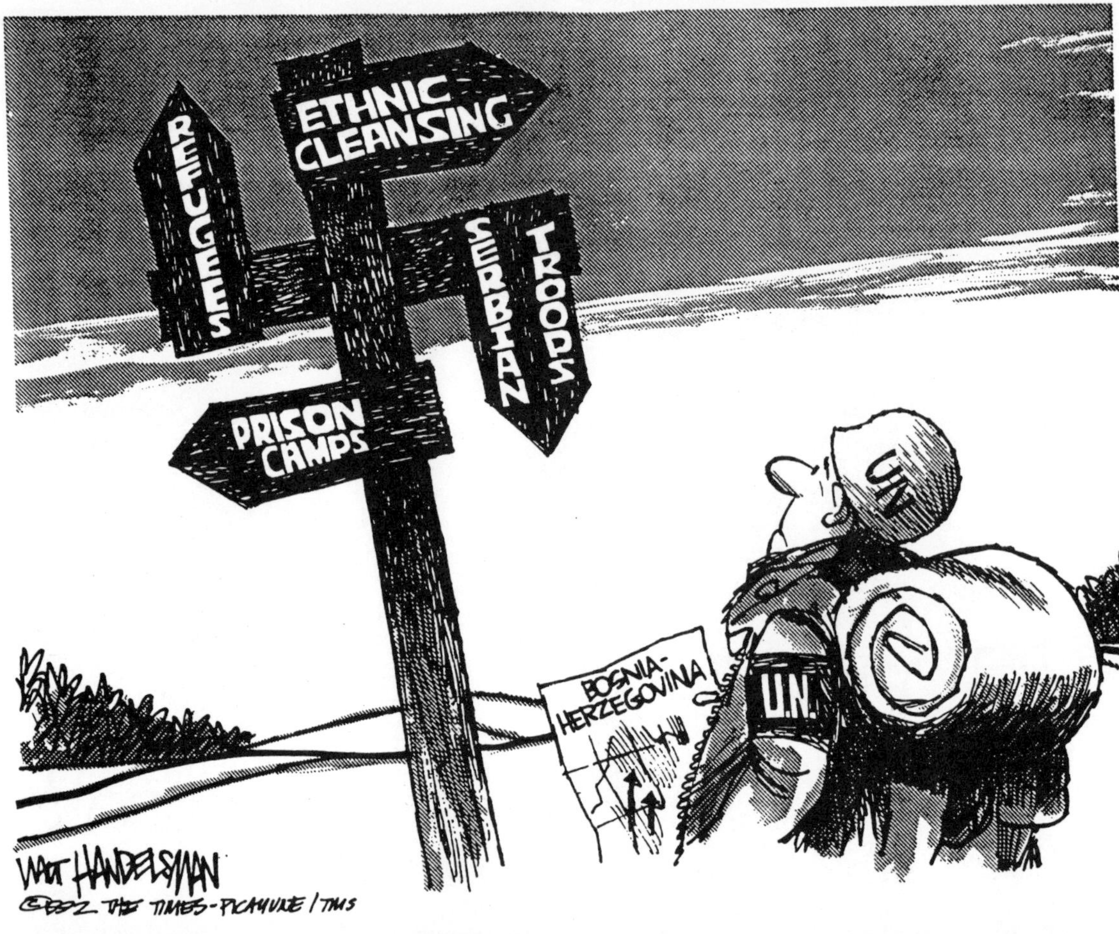
ETHNIC CLEANSING
REFUGEES
SERBIAN TROOPS
PRISON CAMPS
UN
U.N.
BOSNIA-HERZEGOVINA
WALT HANDELSMAN
©1992 THE TIMES-PICAYUNE / TMS

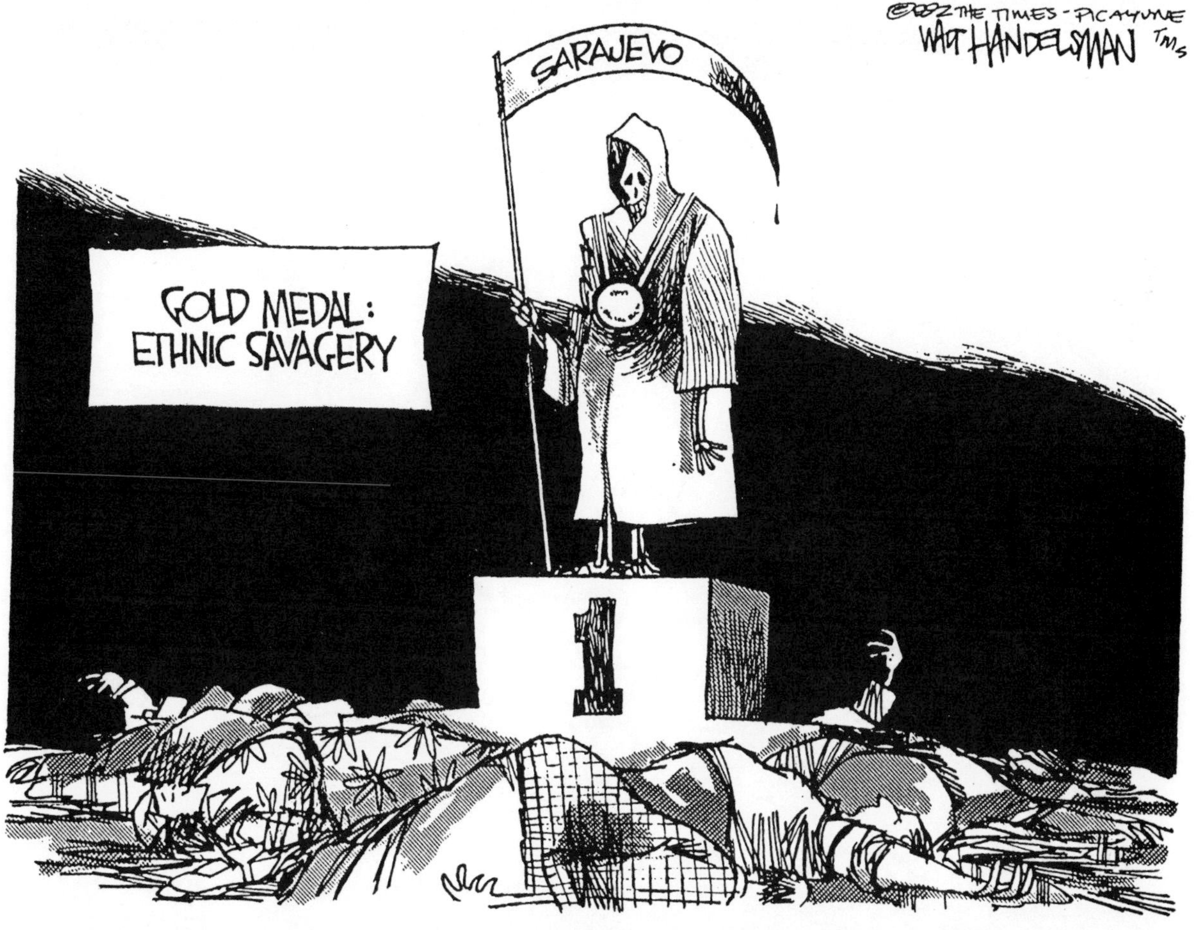
©1992 THE TIMES-PICAYUNE
WALT HANDELSMAN
TMS
SARAJEVO
GOLD MEDAL:
ETHNIC SAVAGERY
1

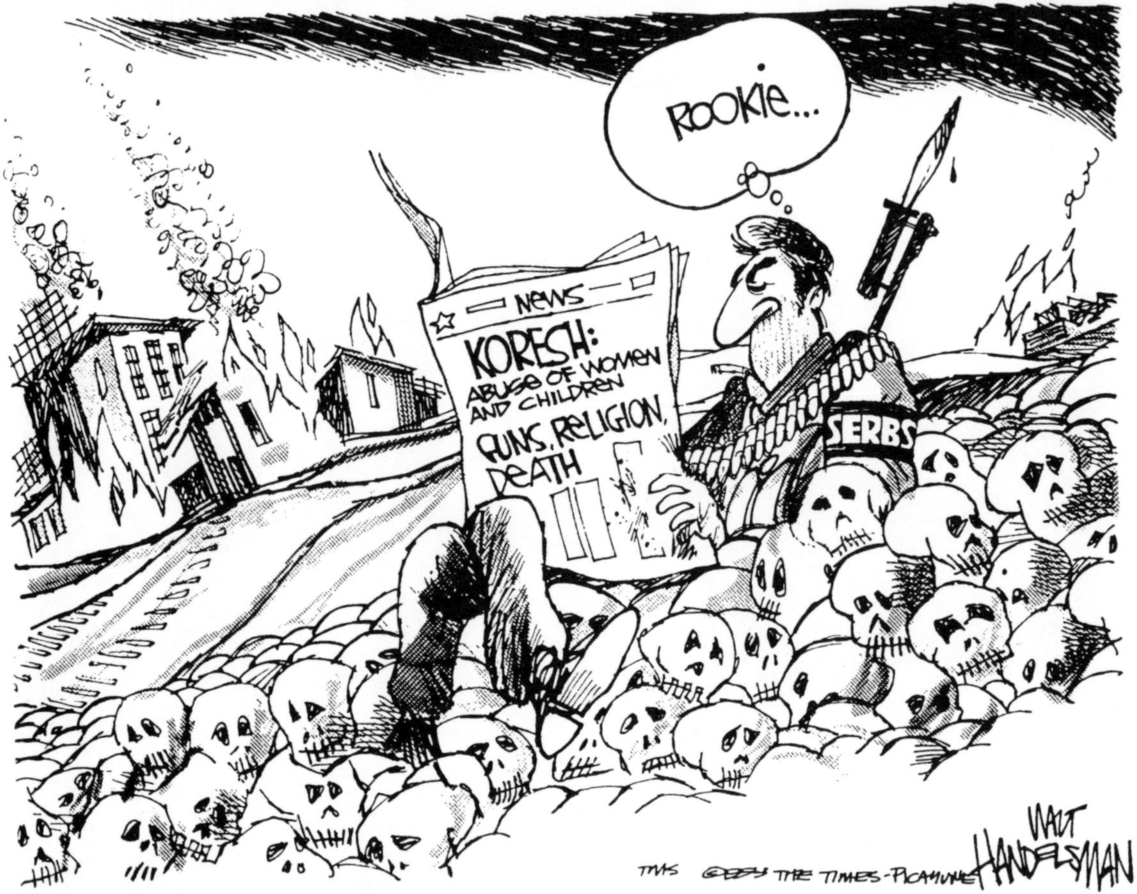
ROOKIE...
NEWS
KORESH:
ABUSE OF WOMEN AND CHILDREN
GUNS, RELIGION, DEATH
SERBS
TMS ©1993 THE TIMES-PICAYUNE
WALT HANDELSMAN

The Gulf War

SCUDs, sorties, smart bombs, and CNN.

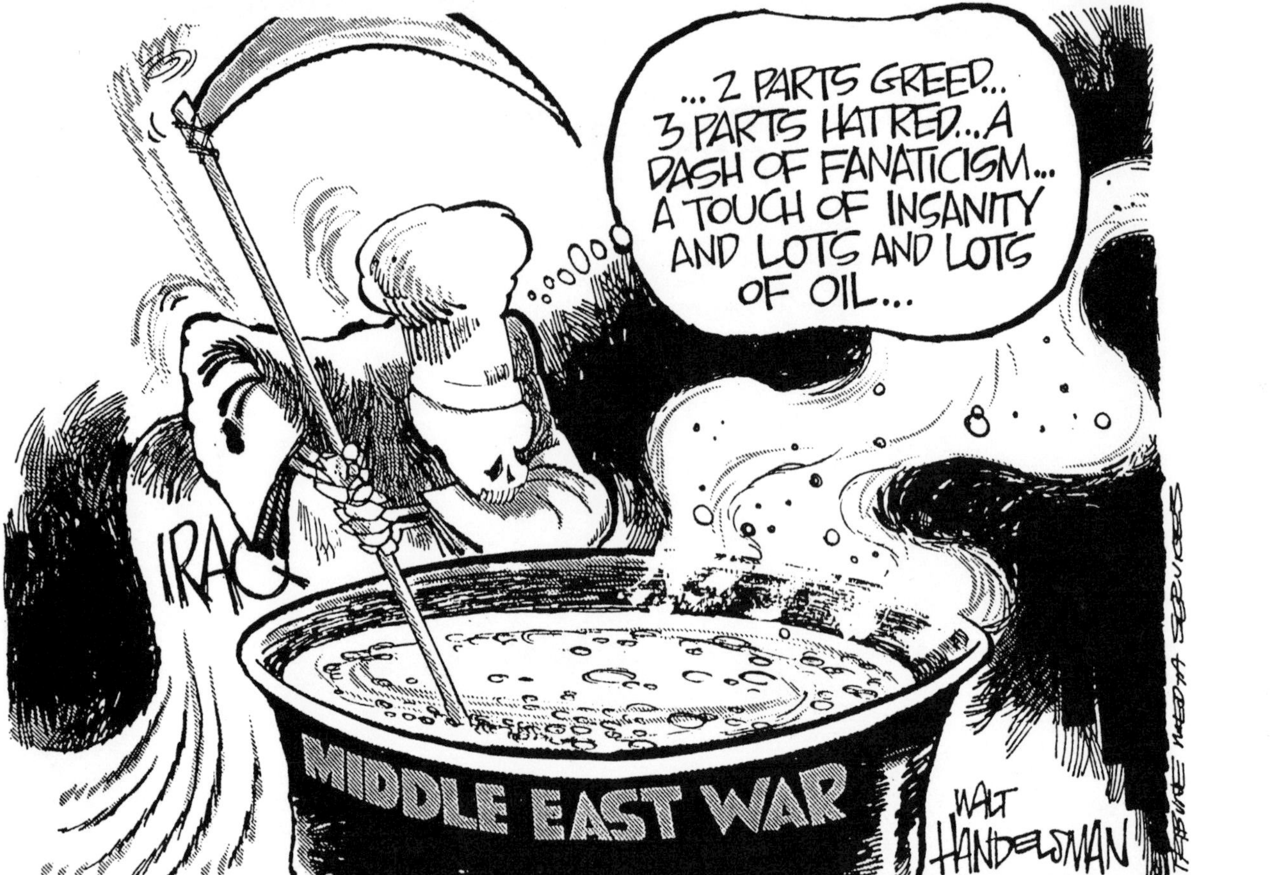
...2 PARTS GREED... 3 PARTS HATRED...A DASH OF FANATICISM... A TOUCH OF INSANITY AND LOTS AND LOTS OF OIL...
IRAQ
MIDDLE EAST WAR
WALT HANDELSMAN
©1990 THE TIMES-PICAYUNE
TRIBUNE MEDIA SERVICES

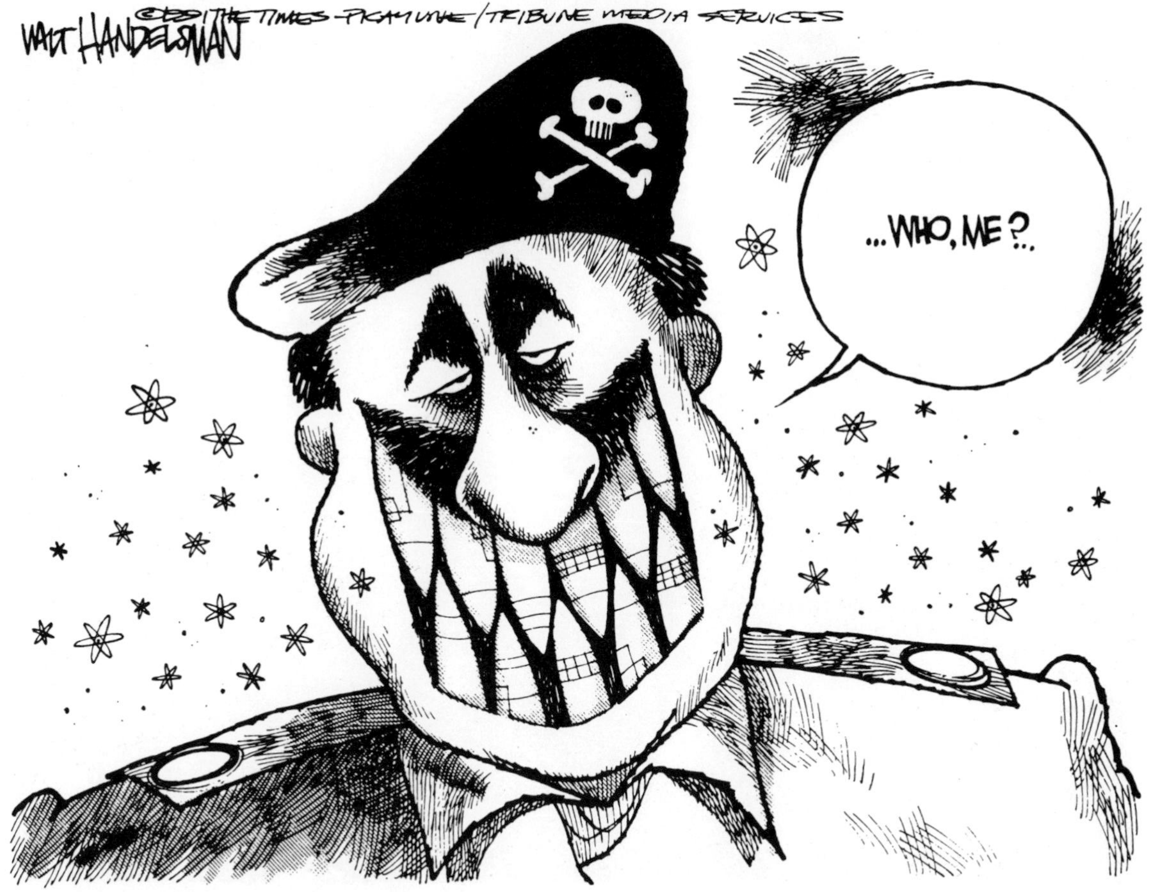
WALT HANDELSMAN
©1991 THE TIMES-PICAYUNE / TRIBUNE MEDIA SERVICES
...WHO, ME ?..

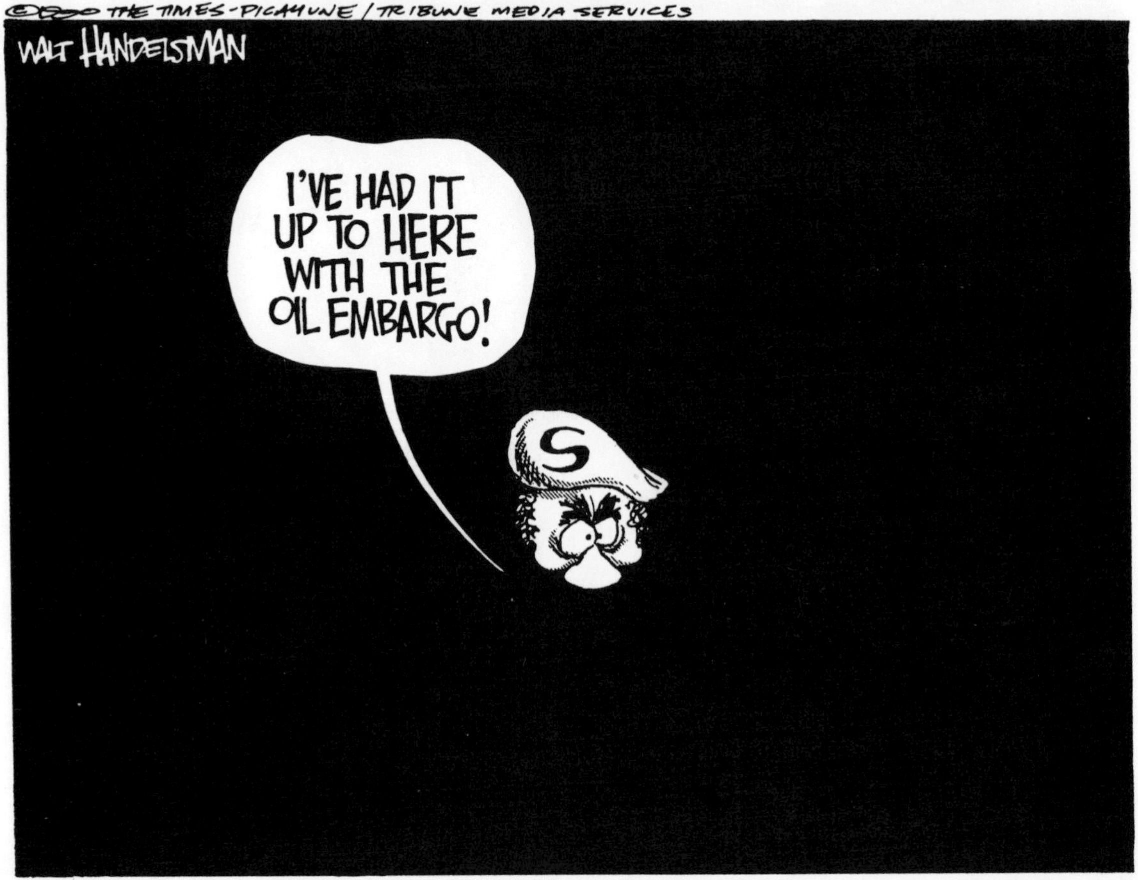
©1990 THE TIMES-PICAYUNE / TRIBUNE MEDIA SERVICES
WALT HANDELSMAN
I'VE HAD IT UP TO HERE WITH THE OIL EMBARGO!
S

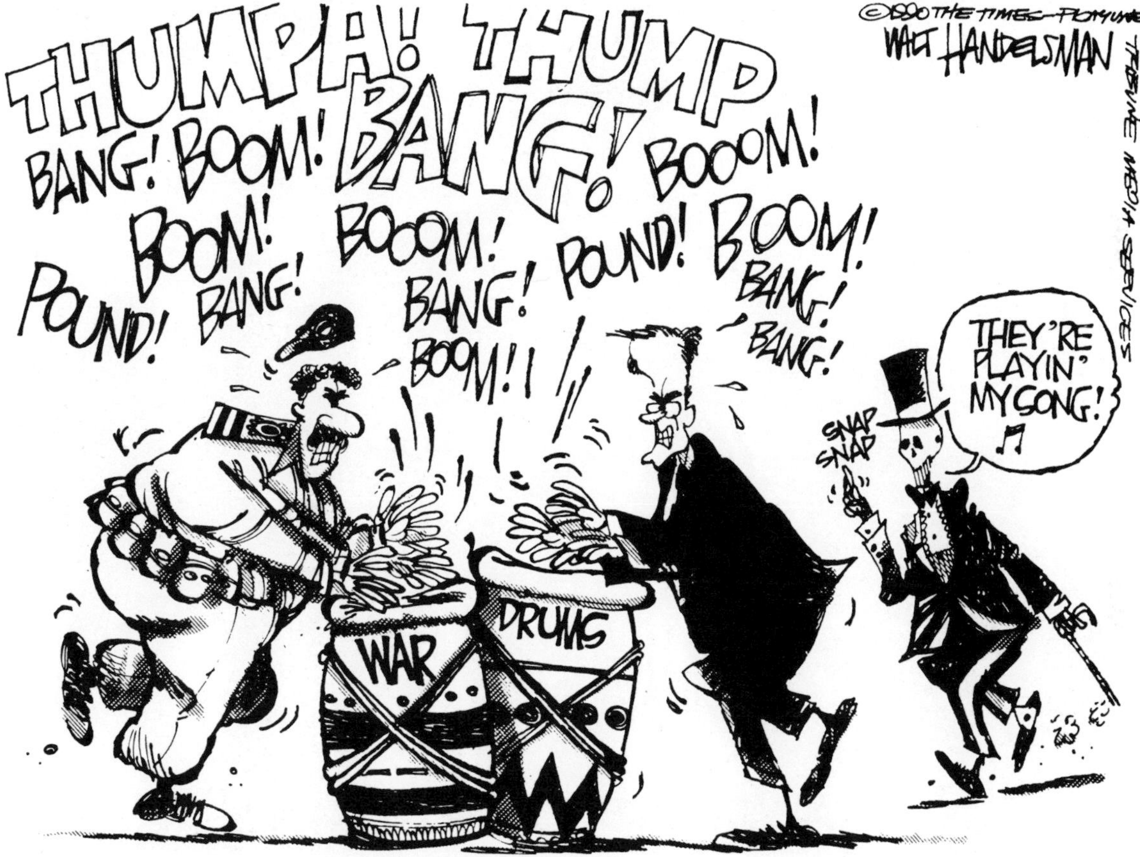
©1990 THE TIMES-PICAYUNE
WALT HANDELSMAN
TRIBUNE MEDIA SERVICES
THUMPA! THUMP
BANG! BOOM! BANG! BOOOM!
BOOM! BOOOM!
POUND! BANG! BANG! POUND! BOOM!
BANG! BANG!
BOOM!
THEY'RE PLAYIN' MY SONG!
SNAP SNAP
WAR
DRUMS

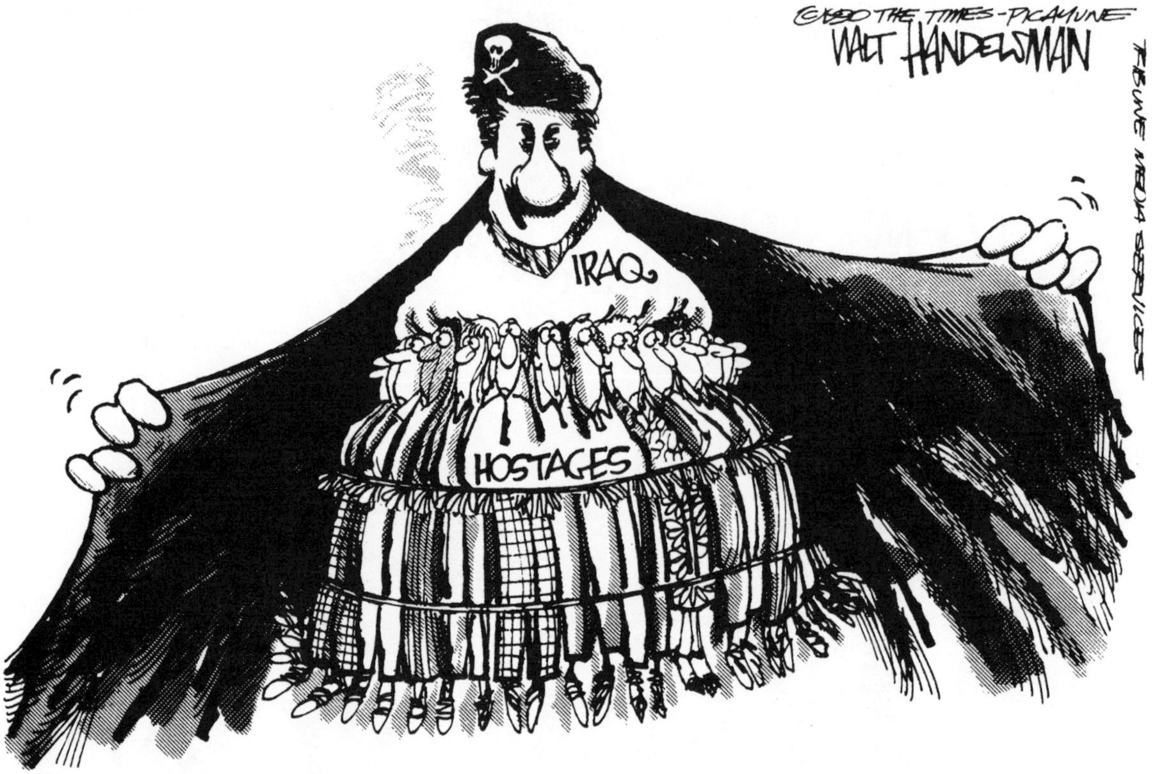
©1990 THE TIMES-PICAYUNE
WALT HANDELSMAN
TRIBUNE MEDIA SERVICES
IRAQ
HOSTAGES

"...GO AHEAD...TAKE YOUR BEST SHOT!"

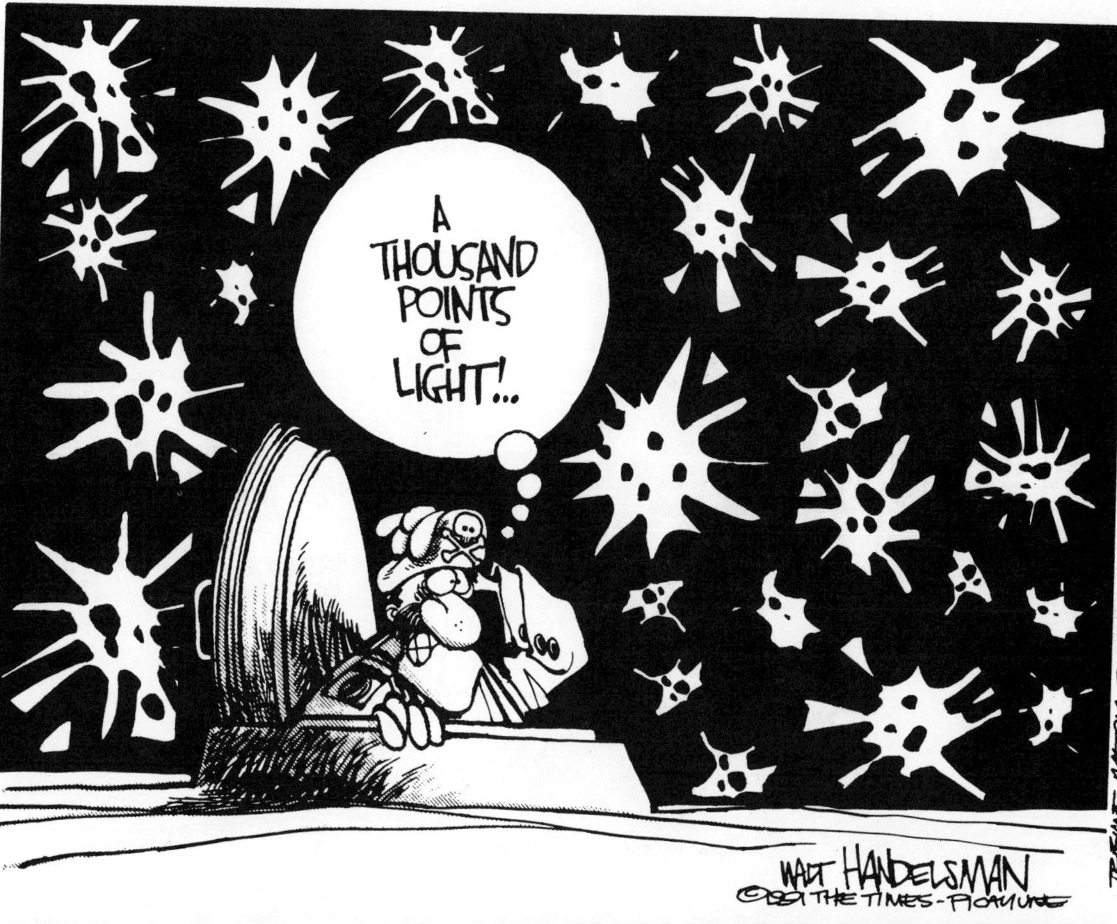
A THOUSAND POINTS OF LIGHT!...
WALT HANDELSMAN
©1991 THE TIMES-PICAYUNE
TRIBUNE MEDIA SERVICES

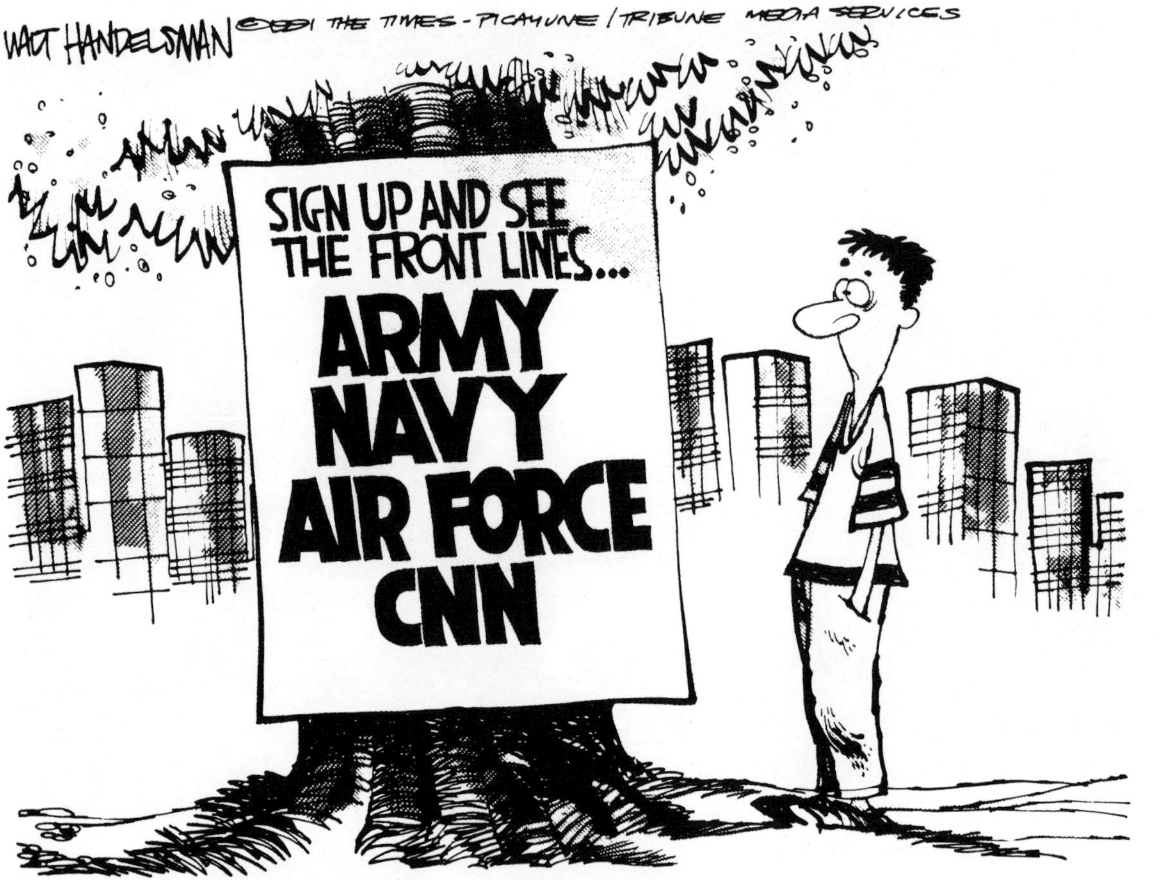
WALT HANDELSMAN ©1991 THE TIMES-PICAYUNE / TRIBUNE MEDIA SERVICES
SIGN UP AND SEE THE FRONT LINES...
ARMY
NAVY
AIR FORCE
CNN

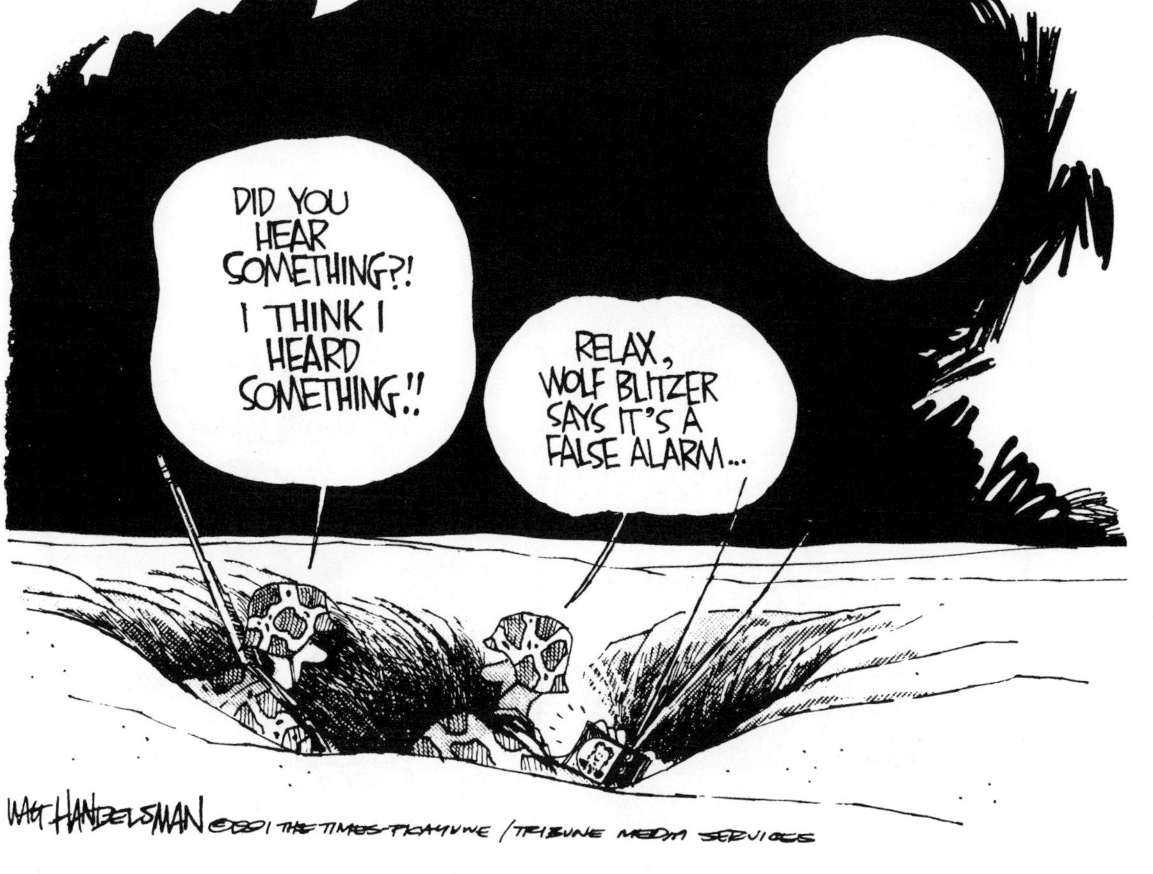
DID YOU HEAR SOMETHING?! I THINK I HEARD SOMETHING!!
RELAX, WOLF BLITZER SAYS IT'S A FALSE ALARM...
WALT HANDELSMAN ©1991 THE TIMES-PICAYUNE / TRIBUNE MEDIA SERVICES

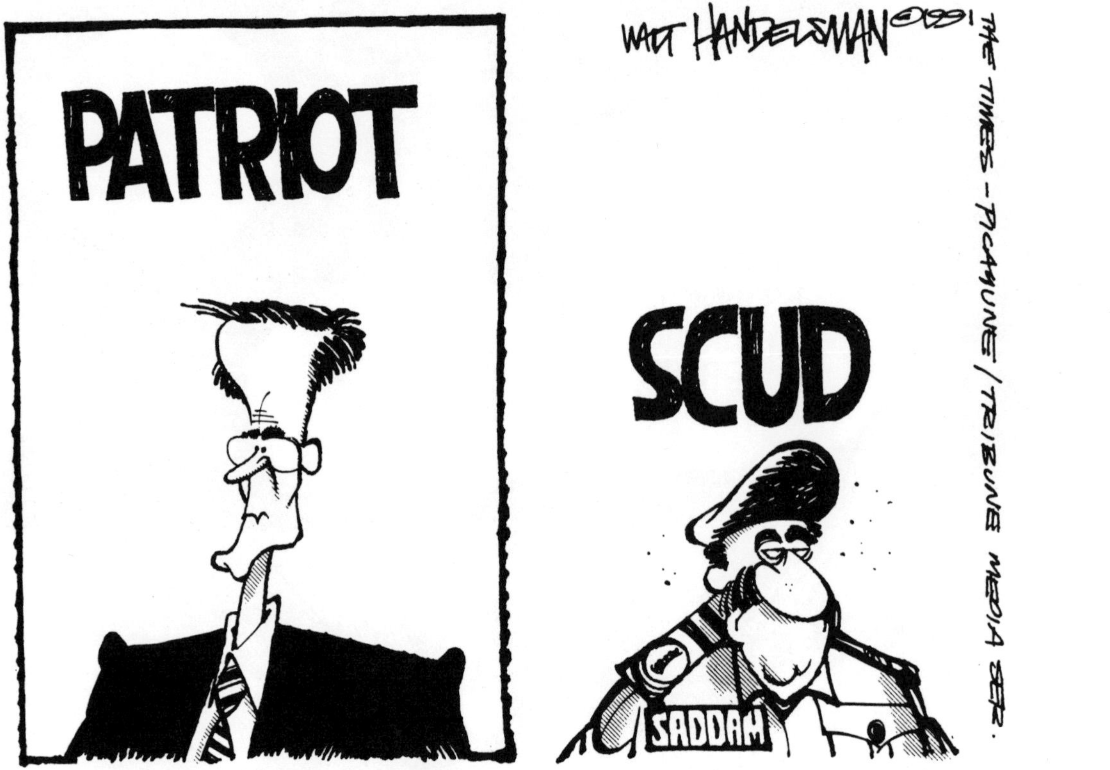
PATRIOT
SCUD
SADDAM
WALT HANDELSMAN ©1991
THE TIMES-PICAYUNE/TRIBUNE MEDIA SER.

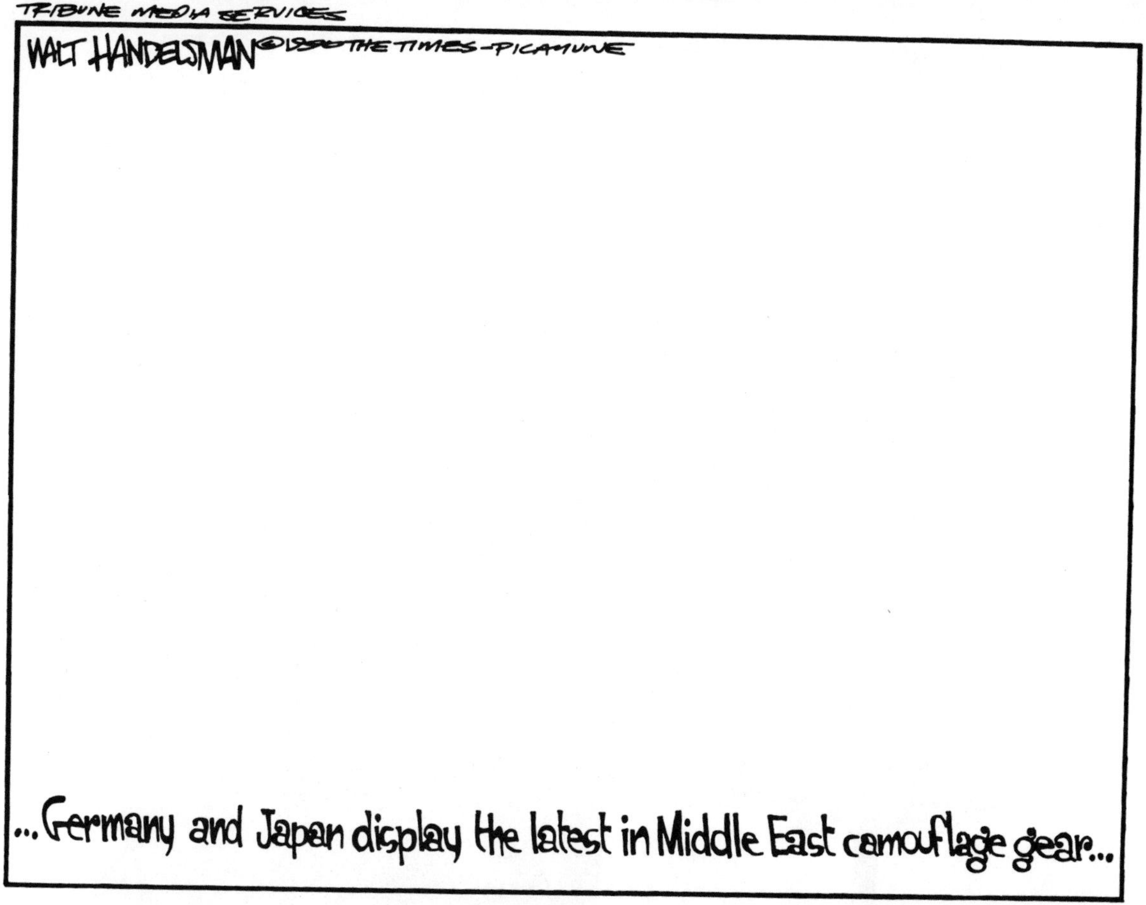
TRIBUNE MEDIA SERVICES
WALT HANDELSMAN ©1990 THE TIMES-PICAYUNE
...Germany and Japan display the latest in Middle East camouflage gear...

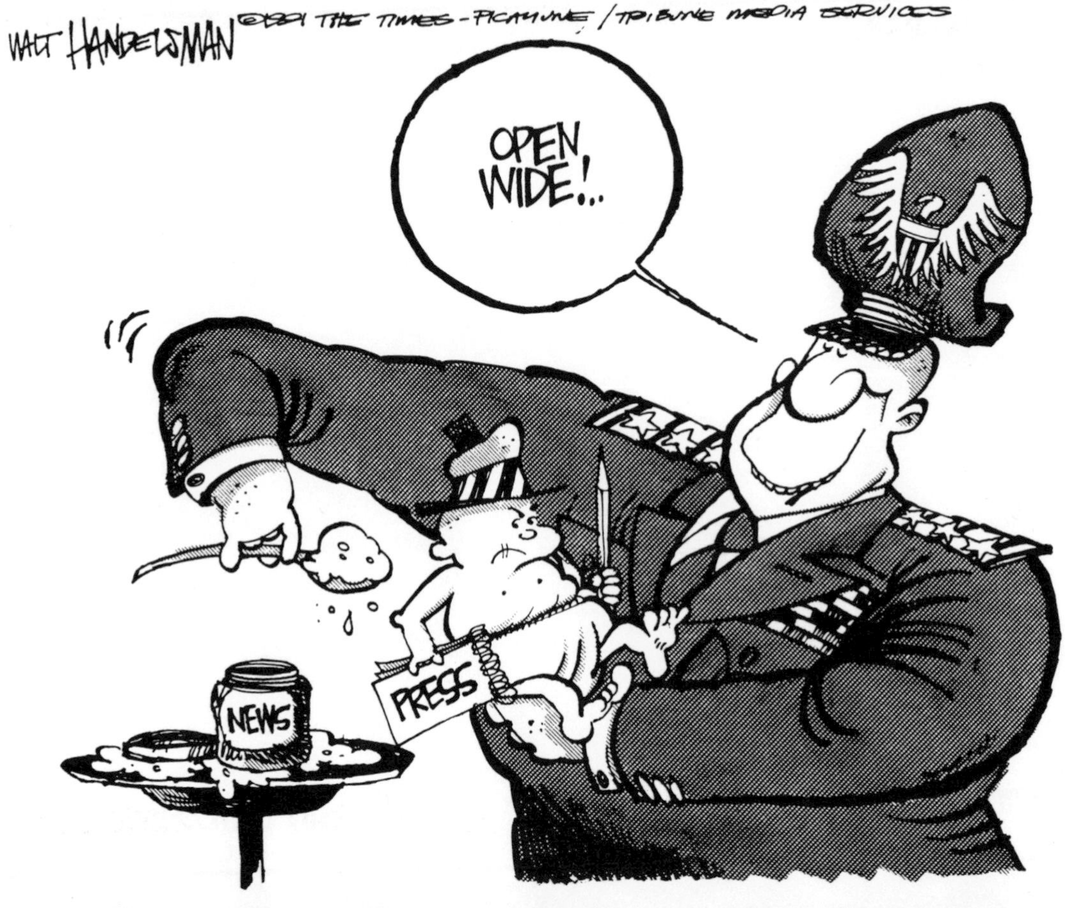
WALT HANDELSMAN ©1991 THE TIMES-PICAYUNE / TRIBUNE MEDIA SERVICES
OPEN WIDE!..
PRESS
NEWS

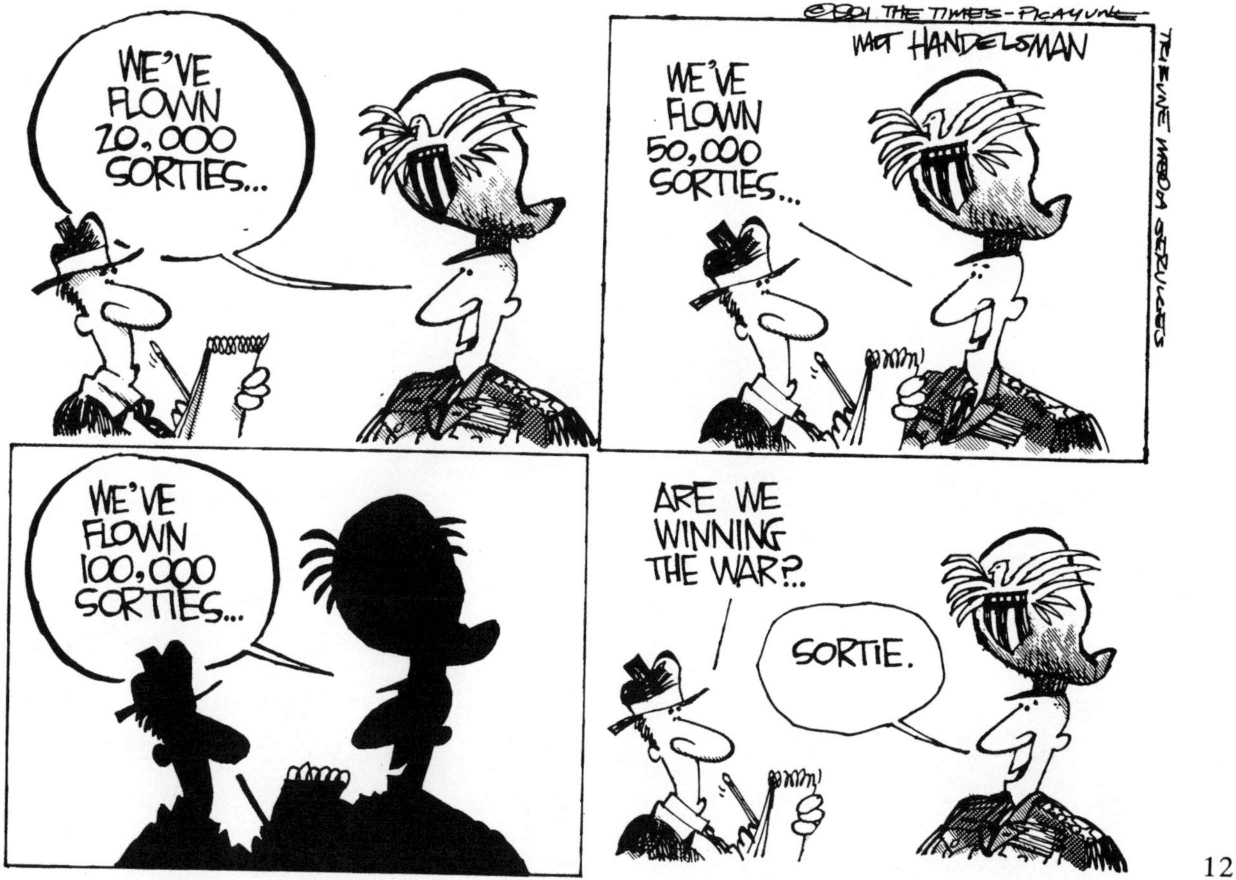
©1991 THE TIMES-PICAYUNE
WALT HANDELSMAN
TRIBUNE MEDIA SERVICES
WE'VE FLOWN 20,000 SORTIES...
WE'VE FLOWN 50,000 SORTIES...
WE'VE FLOWN 100,000 SORTIES...
ARE WE WINNING THE WAR?..
SORTIE.

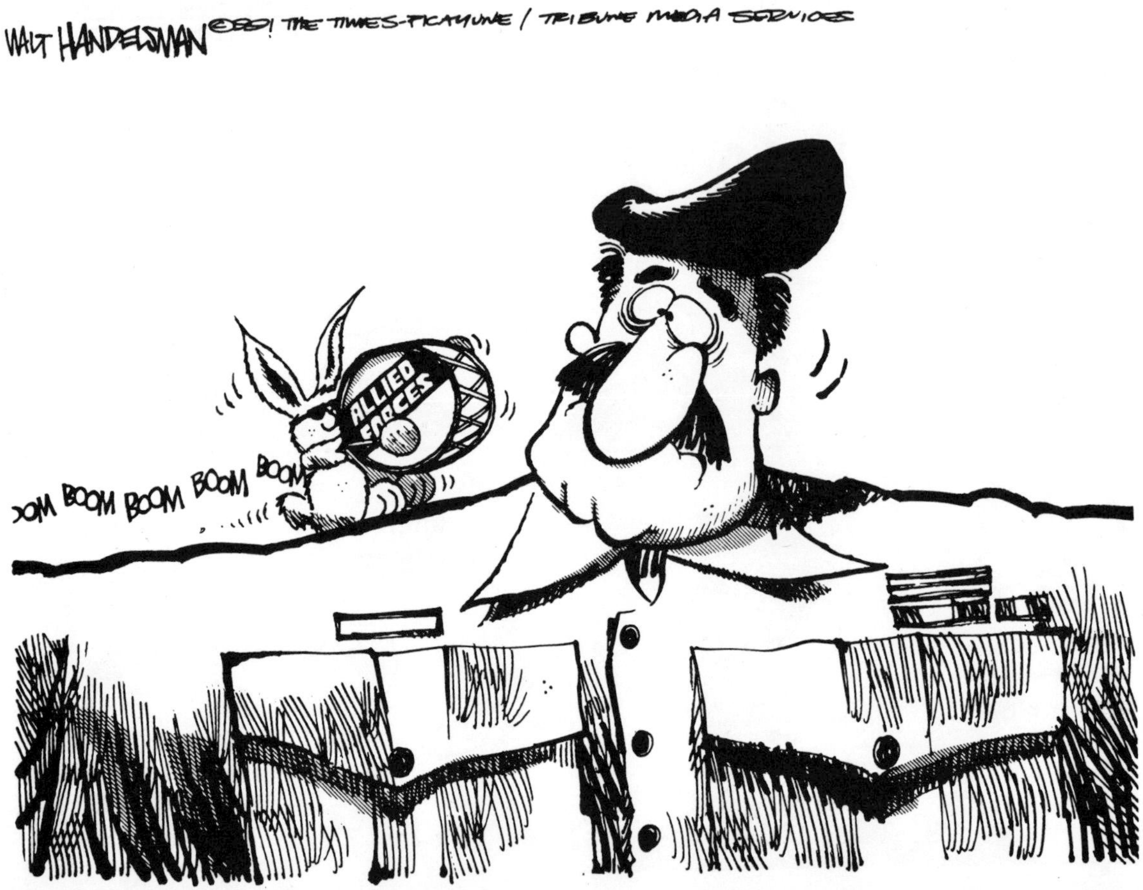

WALT HANDELSMAN ©1991 THE TIMES-PICAYUNE / TRIBUNE MEDIA SERVICES
ALLIED FORCES
OOM BOOM BOOM BOOM BOOM

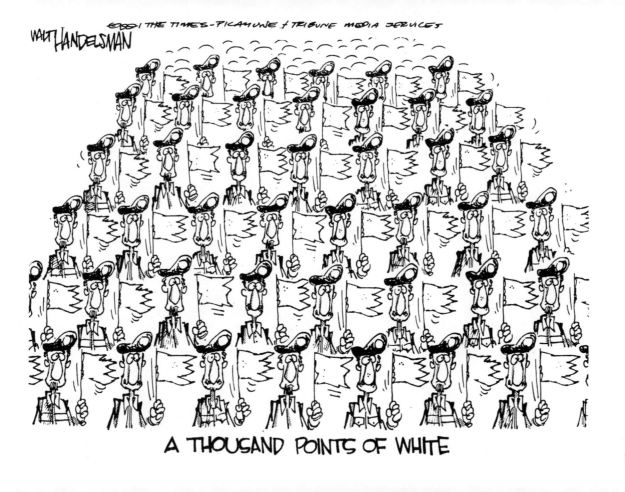

WALT HANDELSMAN

©1991 THE TIMES-PICAYUNE / TRIBUNE MEDIA SERVICES

A THOUSAND POINTS OF WHITE

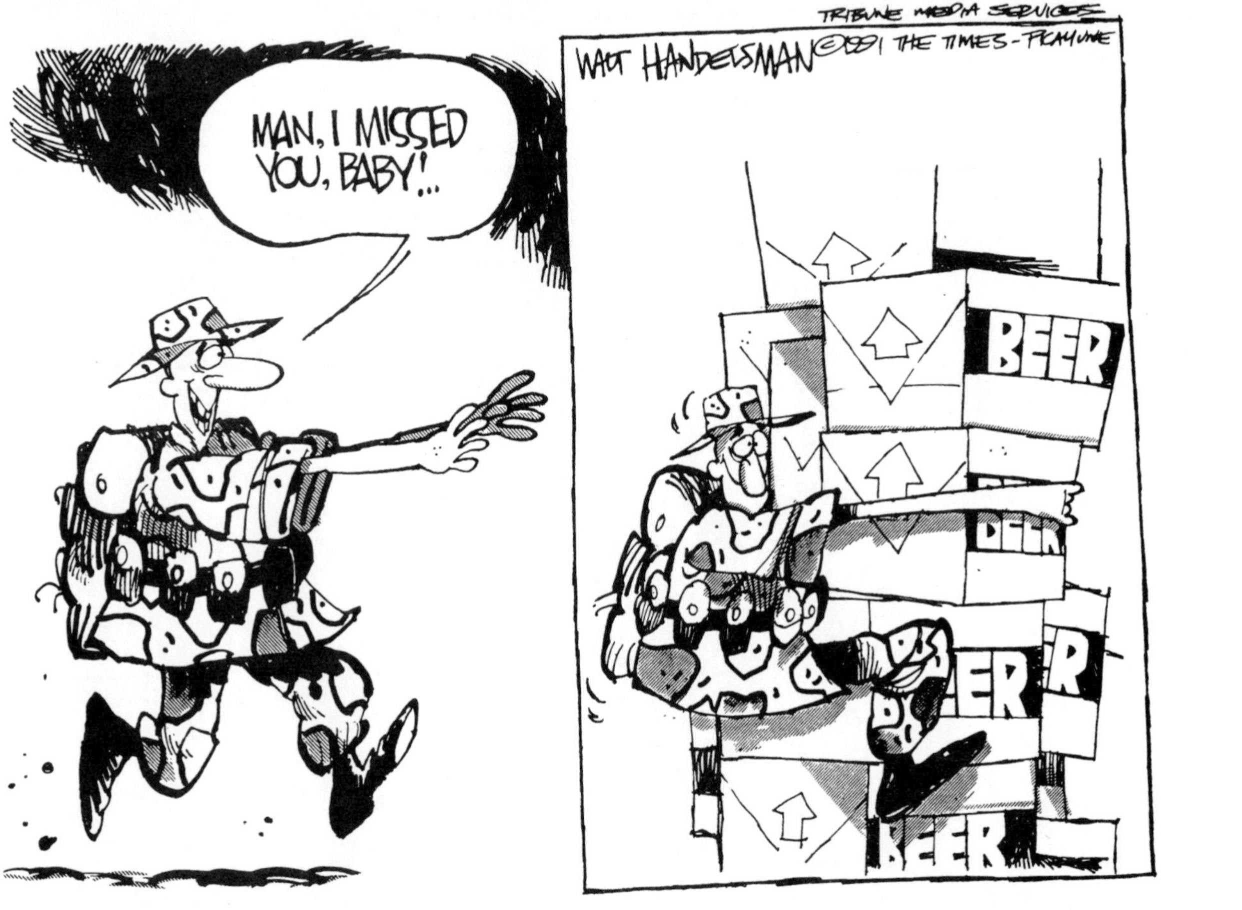
TRIBUNE MEDIA SERVICES
WALT HANDELSMAN ©1991 THE TIMES-PICAYUNE
MAN, I MISSED YOU, BABY!...
BEER

Louisiana:
A Cartoonist's Paradise

A Confederacy of Dunces is a work of fiction. . . . Not!

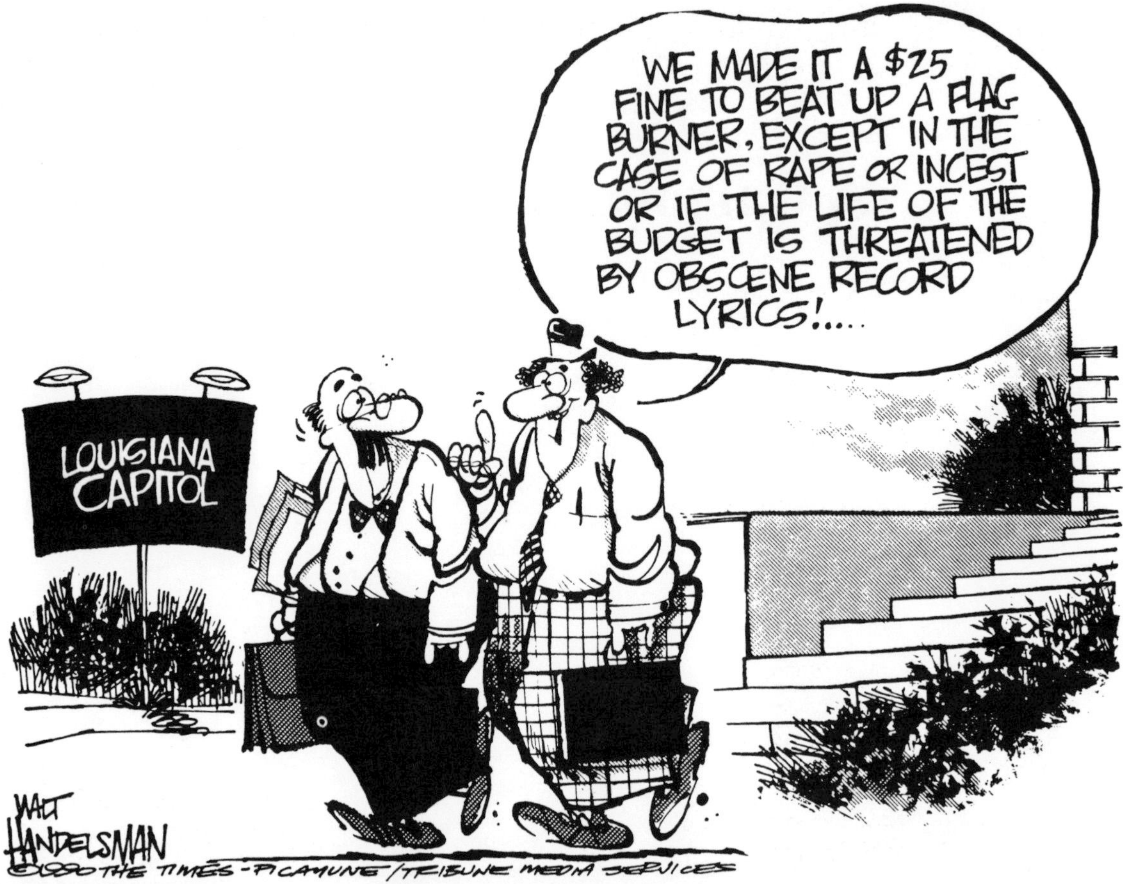
WE MADE IT A $25 FINE TO BEAT UP A FLAG BURNER, EXCEPT IN THE CASE OF RAPE OR INCEST OR IF THE LIFE OF THE BUDGET IS THREATENED BY OBSCENE RECORD LYRICS!....
LOUISIANA CAPITOL
WALT HANDELSMAN
©1990 THE TIMES-PICAYUNE/TRIBUNE MEDIA SERVICES

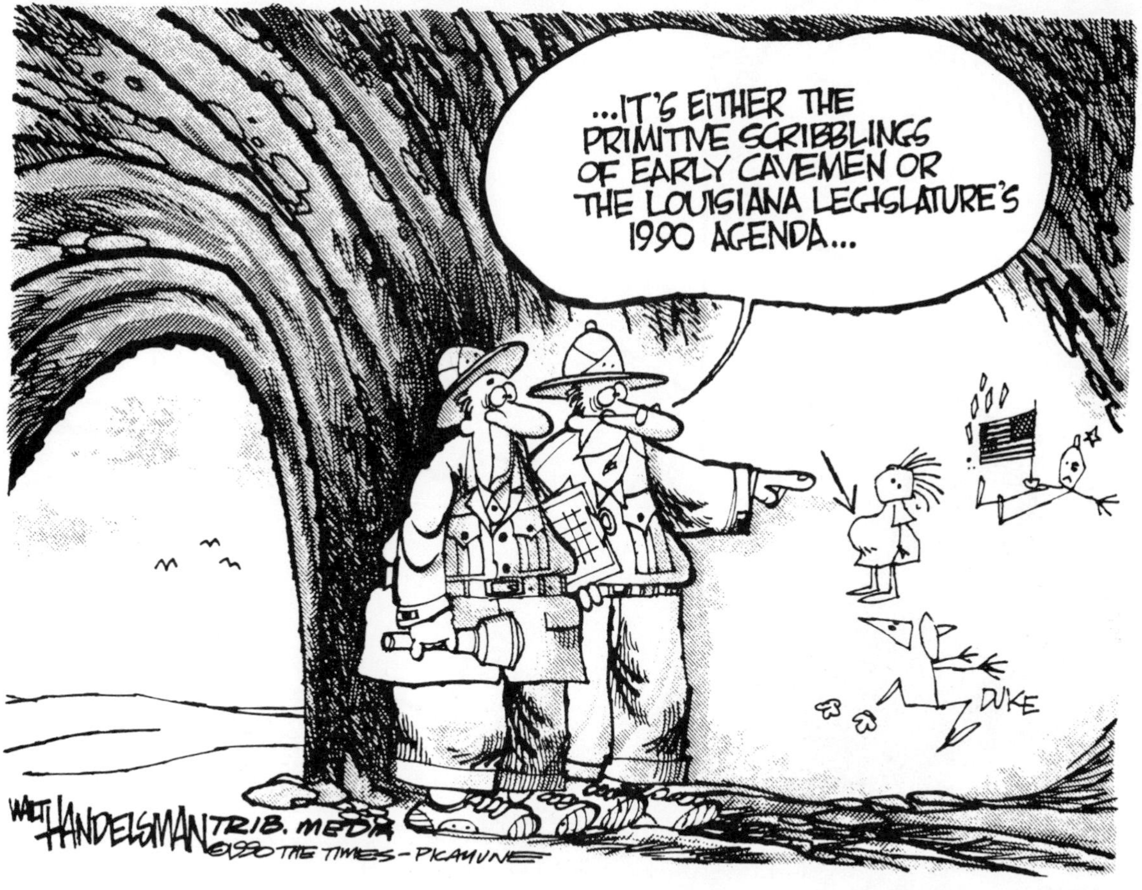
...IT'S EITHER THE PRIMITIVE SCRIBBLINGS OF EARLY CAVEMEN OR THE LOUISIANA LEGISLATURE'S 1990 AGENDA...
DUKE
WALT HANDELSMAN TRIB. MEDIA
©1990 THE TIMES-PICAYUNE

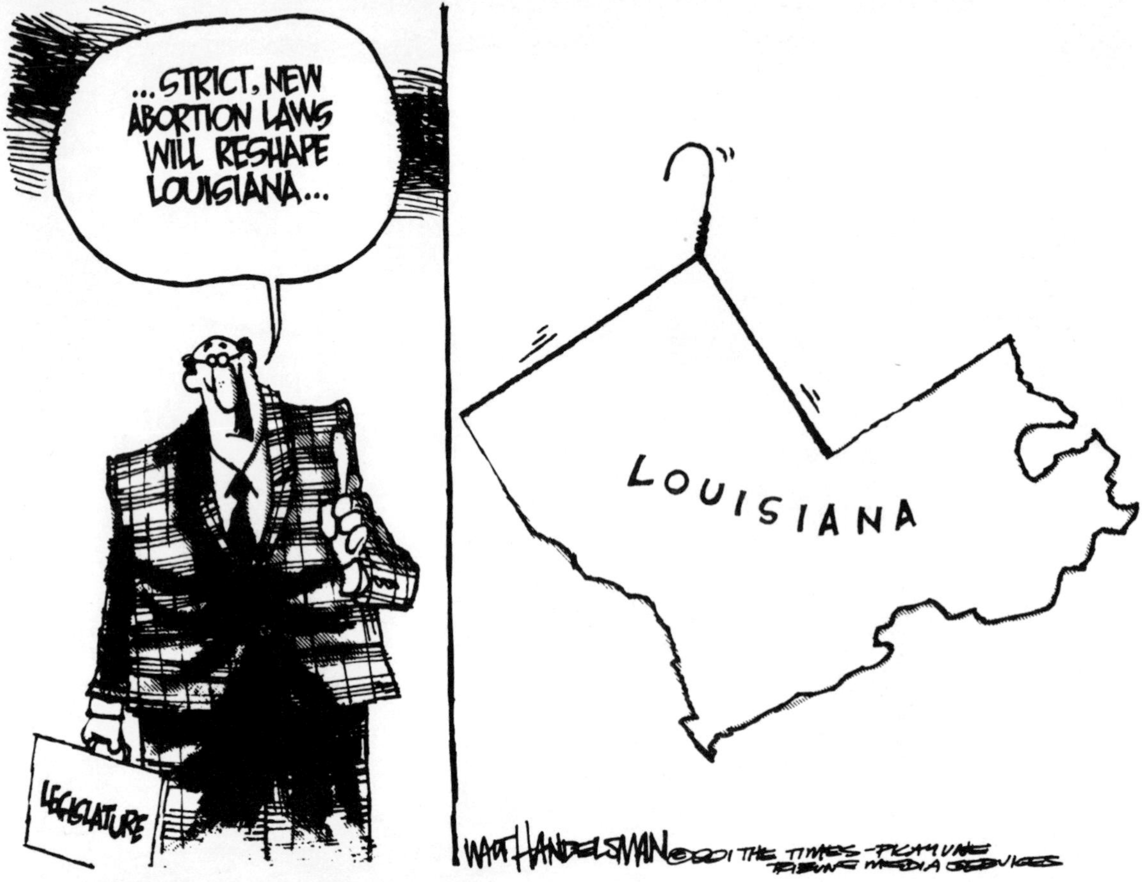
...STRICT, NEW ABORTION LAWS WILL RESHAPE LOUISIANA...
LEGISLATURE
LOUISIANA
WALT HANDELSMAN ©2001 THE TIMES-PICAYUNE TRIBUNE MEDIA SERVICES

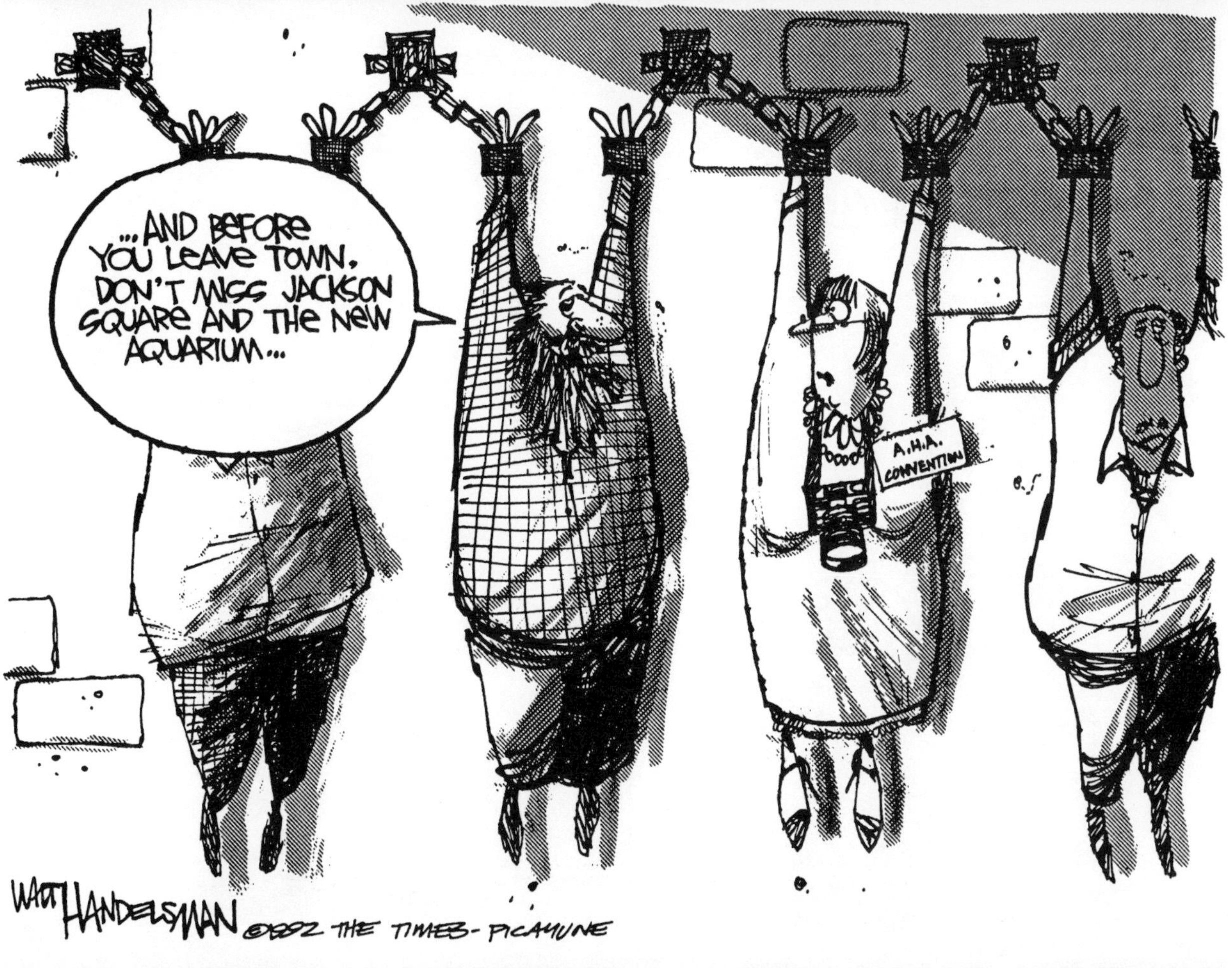
...AND BEFORE YOU LEAVE TOWN, DON'T MISS JACKSON SQUARE AND THE NEW AQUARIUM...
A.H.A. CONVENTION
WALT HANDELSMAN ©1992 THE TIMES-PICAYUNE

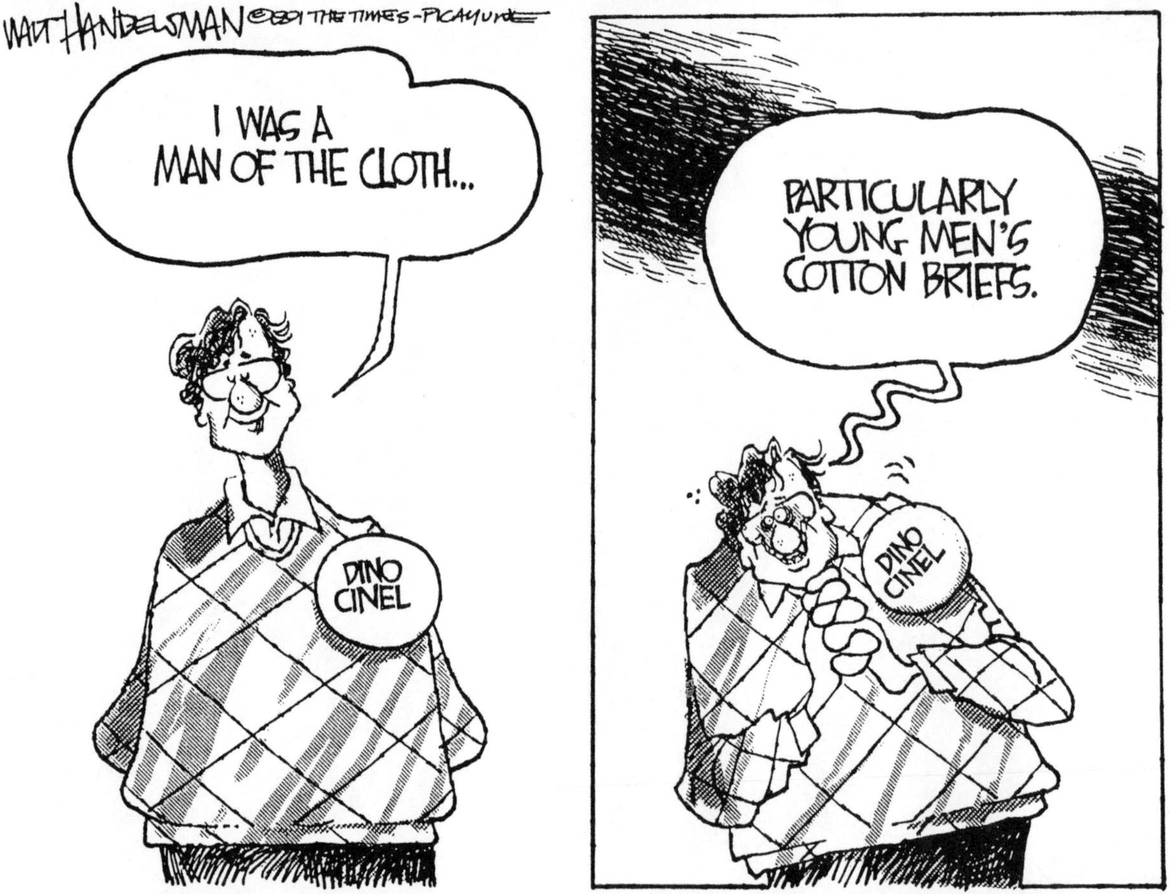
WALT HANDELSMAN ©1991 THE TIMES-PICAYUNE
I WAS A MAN OF THE CLOTH...
DINO CINEL
PARTICULARLY YOUNG MEN'S COTTON BRIEFS.
DINO CINEL

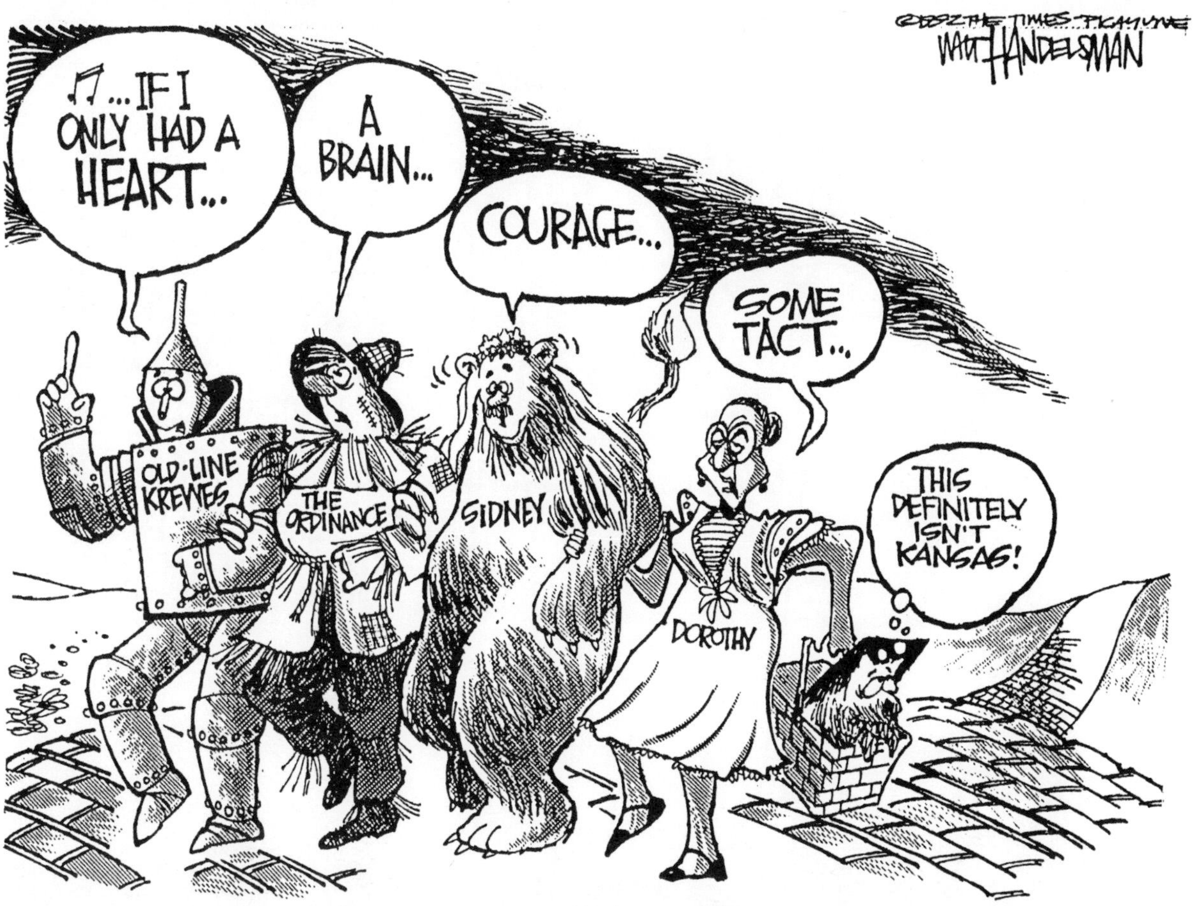
©1992 THE TIMES-PICAYUNE
WALT HANDELSMAN
♫ ... IF I ONLY HAD A HEART...
A BRAIN...
COURAGE...
SOME TACT...
OLD-LINE KREWES
THE ORDINANCE
SIDNEY
DOROTHY
THIS DEFINITELY ISN'T KANSAS!

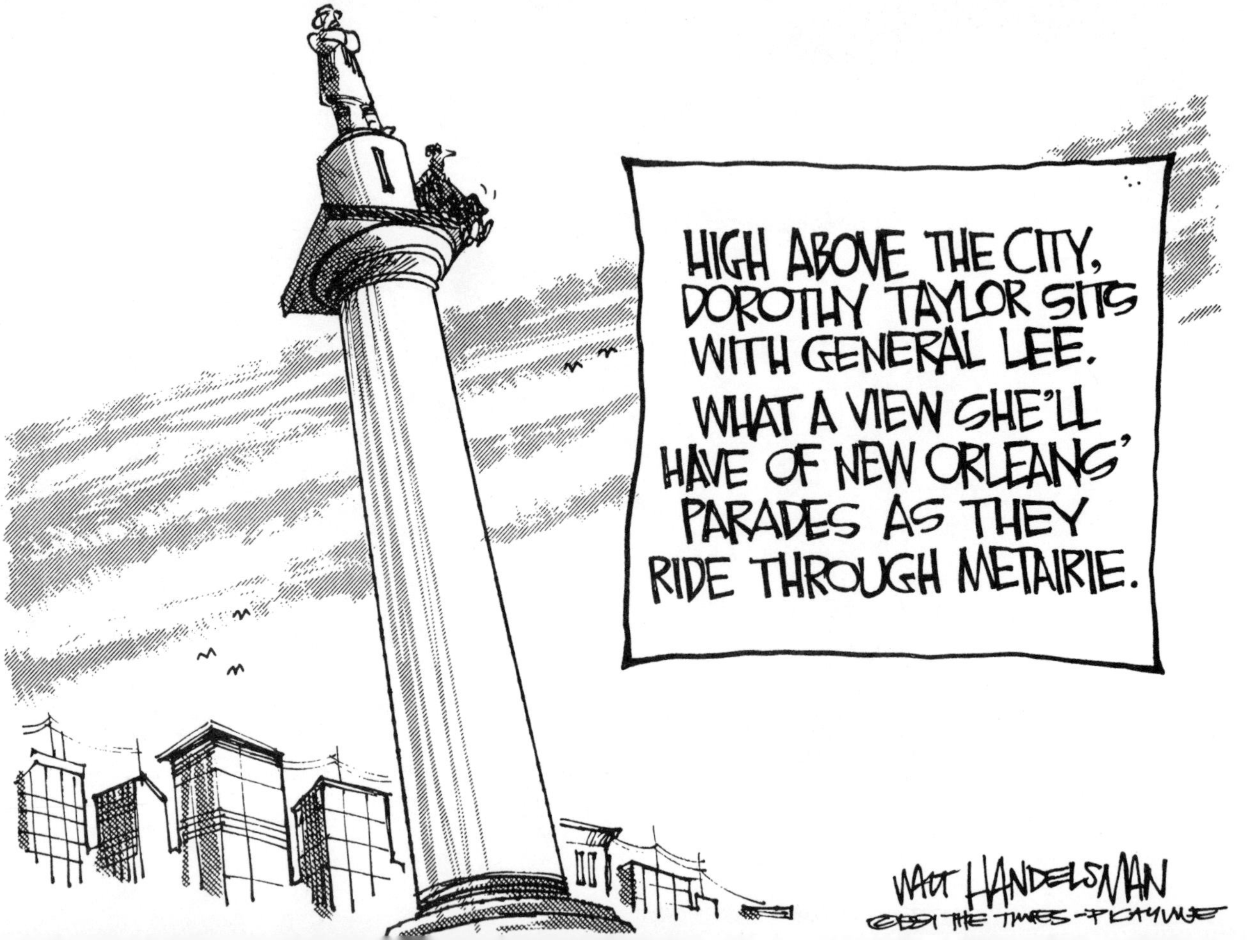
HIGH ABOVE THE CITY, DOROTHY TAYLOR SITS WITH GENERAL LEE.
WHAT A VIEW SHE'LL HAVE OF NEW ORLEANS' PARADES AS THEY RIDE THROUGH METAIRIE.
WALT HANDELSMAN
©1991 THE TIMES-PICAYUNE

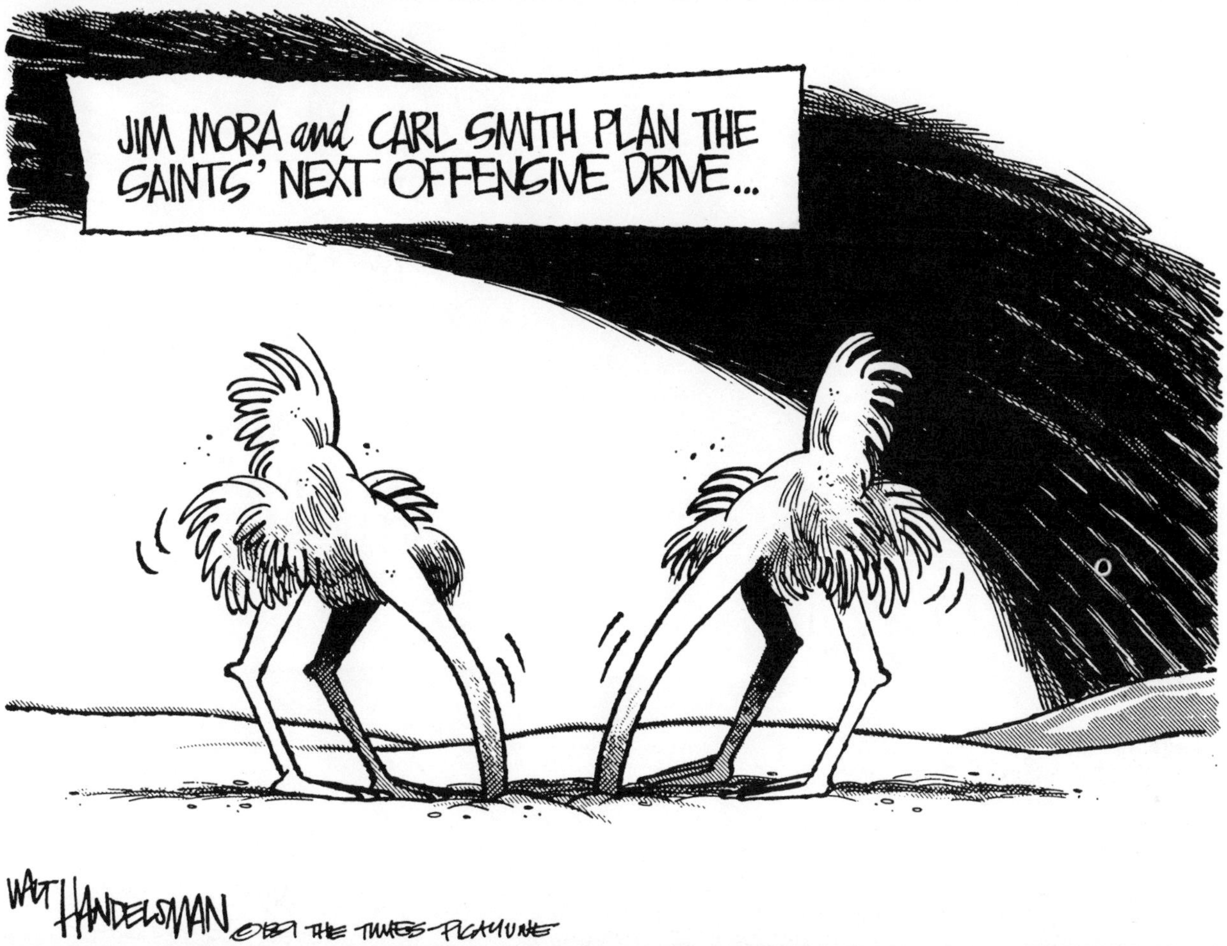
JIM MORA and CARL SMITH PLAN THE SAINTS' NEXT OFFENSIVE DRIVE...
WALT HANDELSMAN

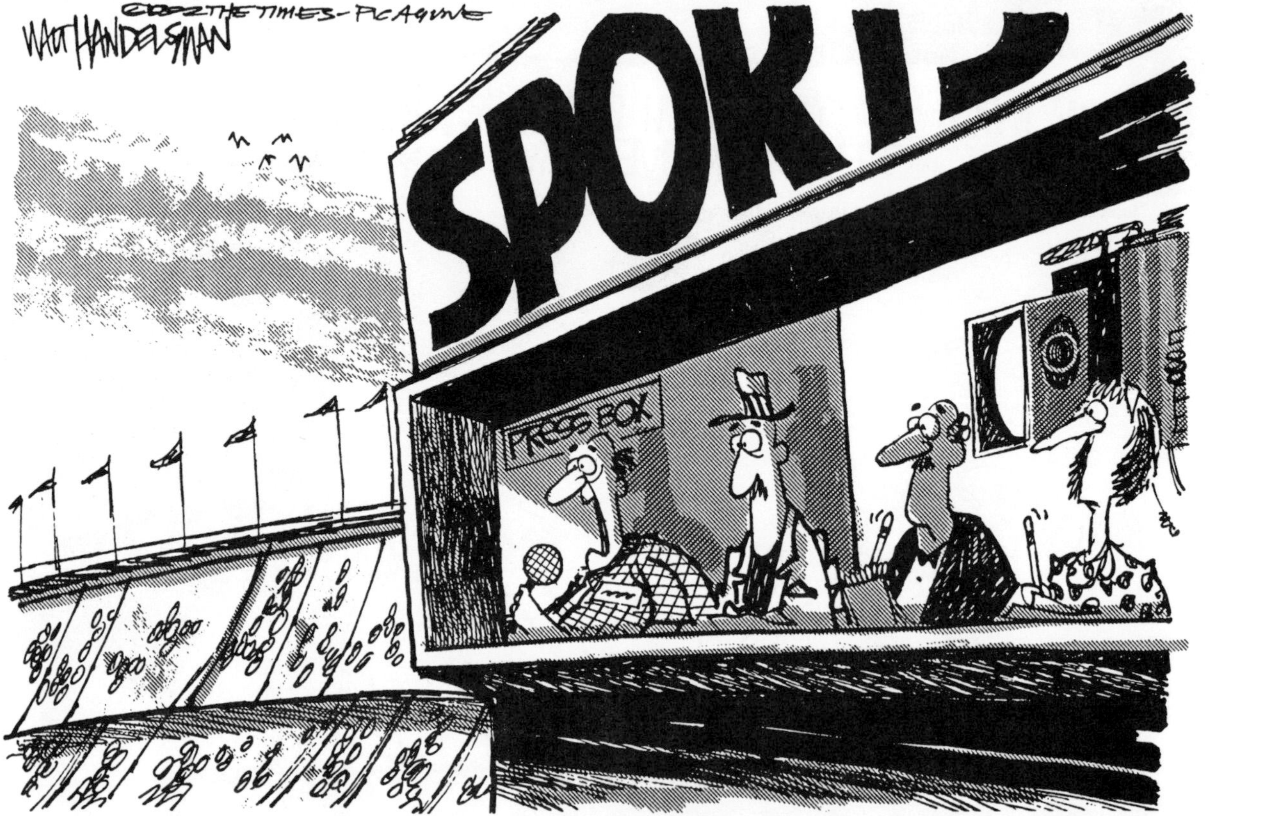
WALT HANDELSMAN
THE TIMES-PICAYUNE
PRESS BOX

"...HANG ON, SPORTS FANS... WITH 3 MINUTES TO GO AND THE SAINTS LEADING 127 to 3 THIS IS STILL ANYBODY'S GAME!..."

Duke vs. Edwards:
The Race from Hell

You know your state's in trouble when a collective sigh of relief goes up because Edwin Edwards has been elected governor.

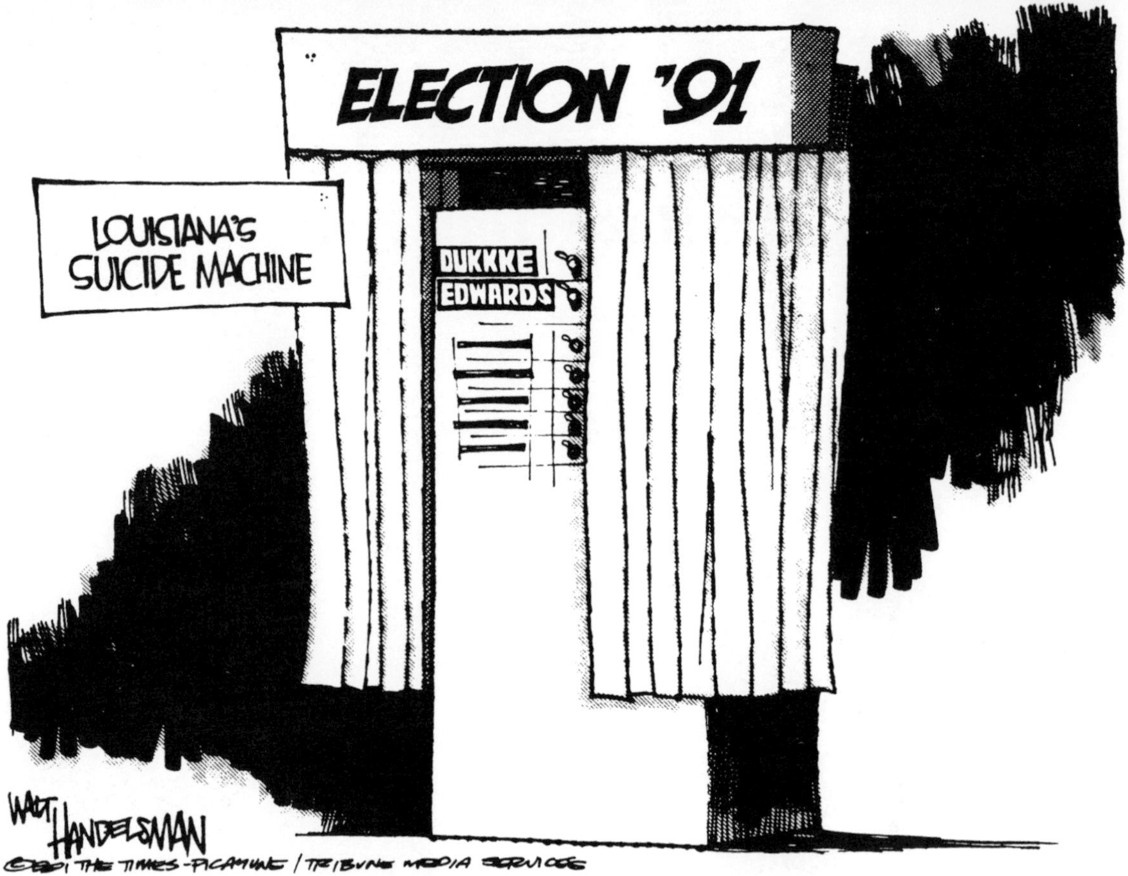
ELECTION '91
LOUISIANA'S SUICIDE MACHINE
DUKKKE
EDWARDS
WALT HANDELSMAN
©1991 THE TIMES-PICAYUNE / TRIBUNE MEDIA SERVICES

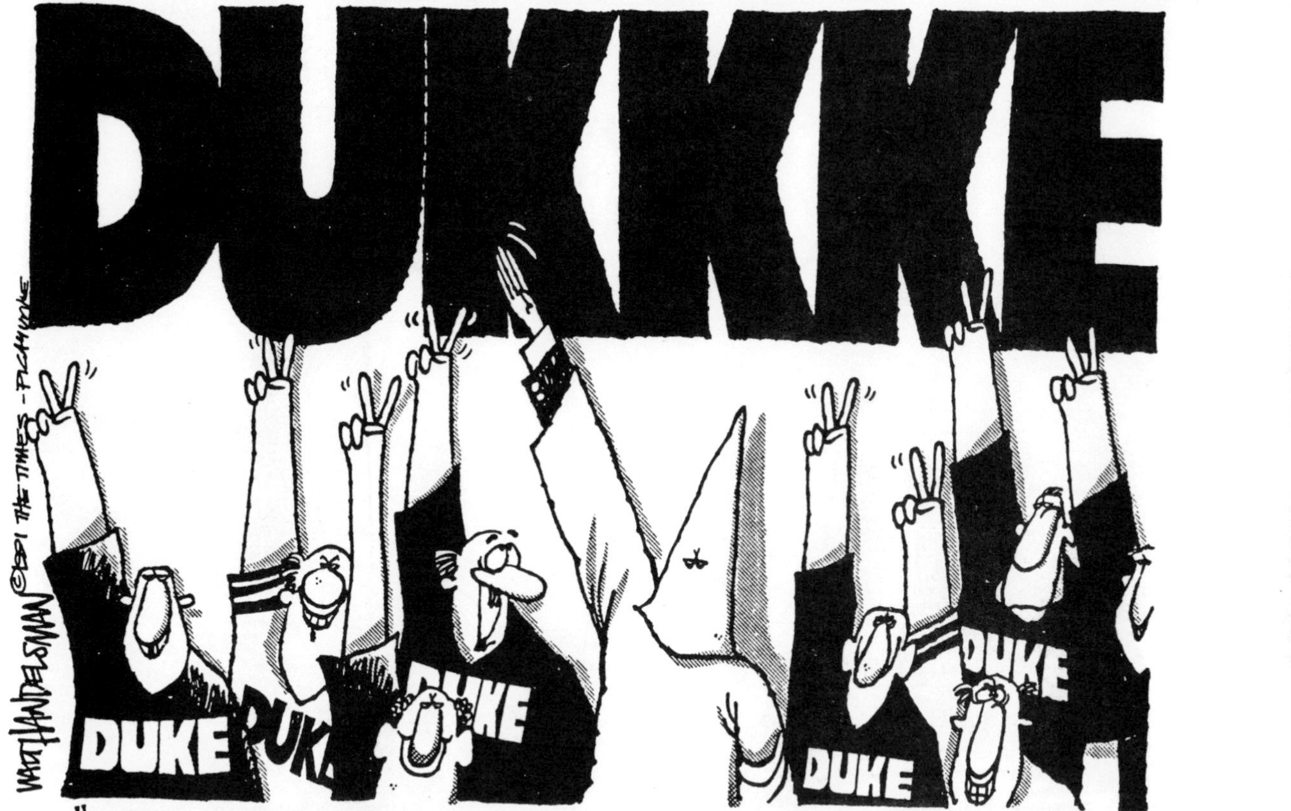
DUKKKE
DUKE
DUKE
DUKE
DUKE
DUKE
WALT HANDELSMAN ©1991 THE TIMES-PICAYUNE
"... TWO FINGERS, DAVID!.. JUST USE TWO FINGERS!... LIKE THIS..."

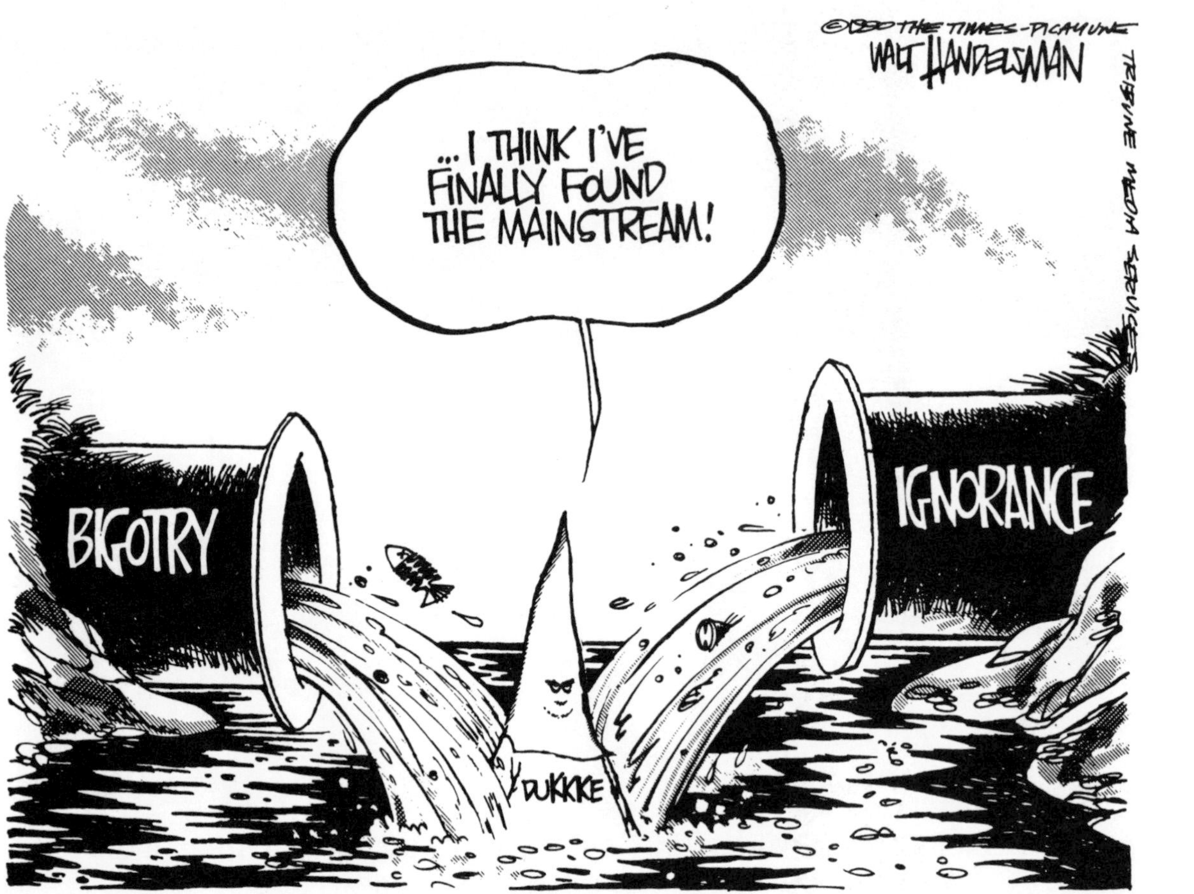
© THE TIMES-PICAYUNE
WALT HANDELSMAN
TRIBUNE MEDIA SERVICES
...I THINK I'VE FINALLY FOUND THE MAINSTREAM!
BIGOTRY
IGNORANCE
DUKKKE

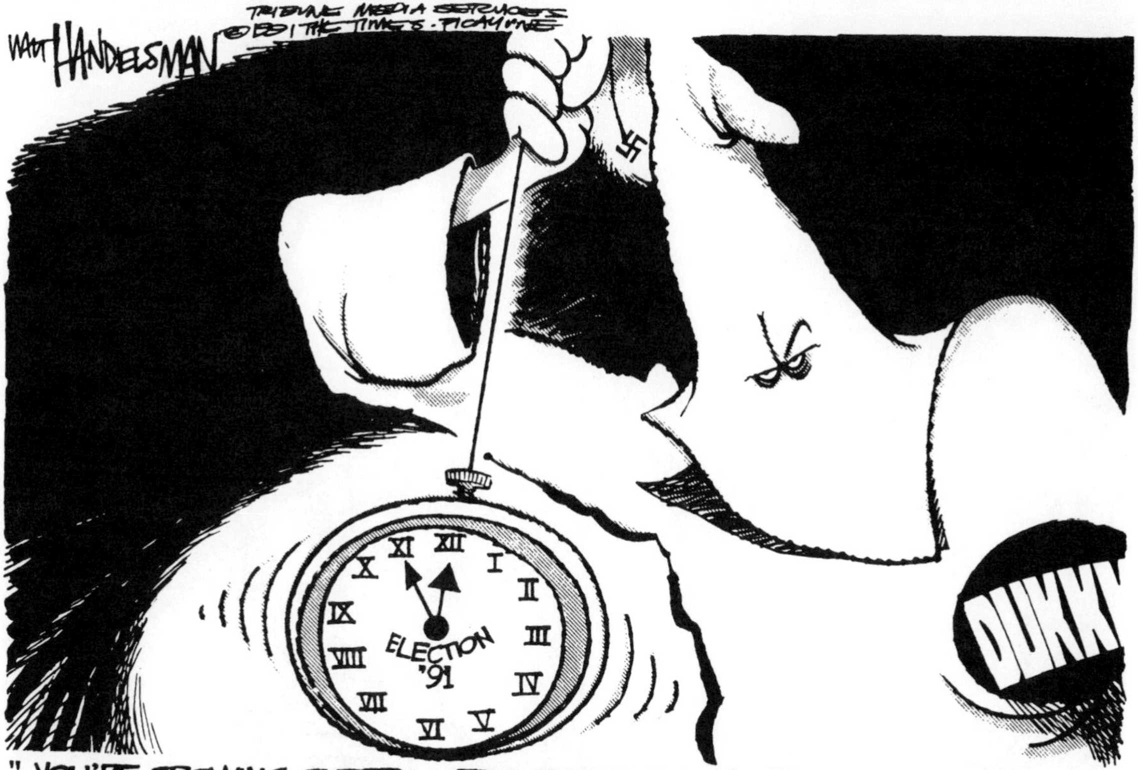
WALT HANDELSMAN
ELECTION '91
DUKK

"...YOU'RE GROWING SLEEPY... VERY SLEEEEEPY... MY PAST IS FADING... FAAAAADING... PAY NOOO ATTENTION.... NOOOO ATTENTION AT ALL... IT'S ALL LIBERAL LIES... SLEEEEPY... AND THE NEWS MEDIA...SLEEPY... EVERYTHING WILL BE FINE ... SLEEEEEEPY... VOTE ... FOR... DUKE.........

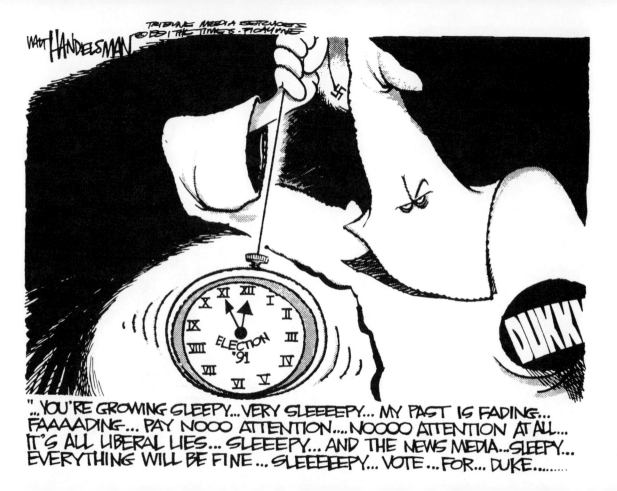

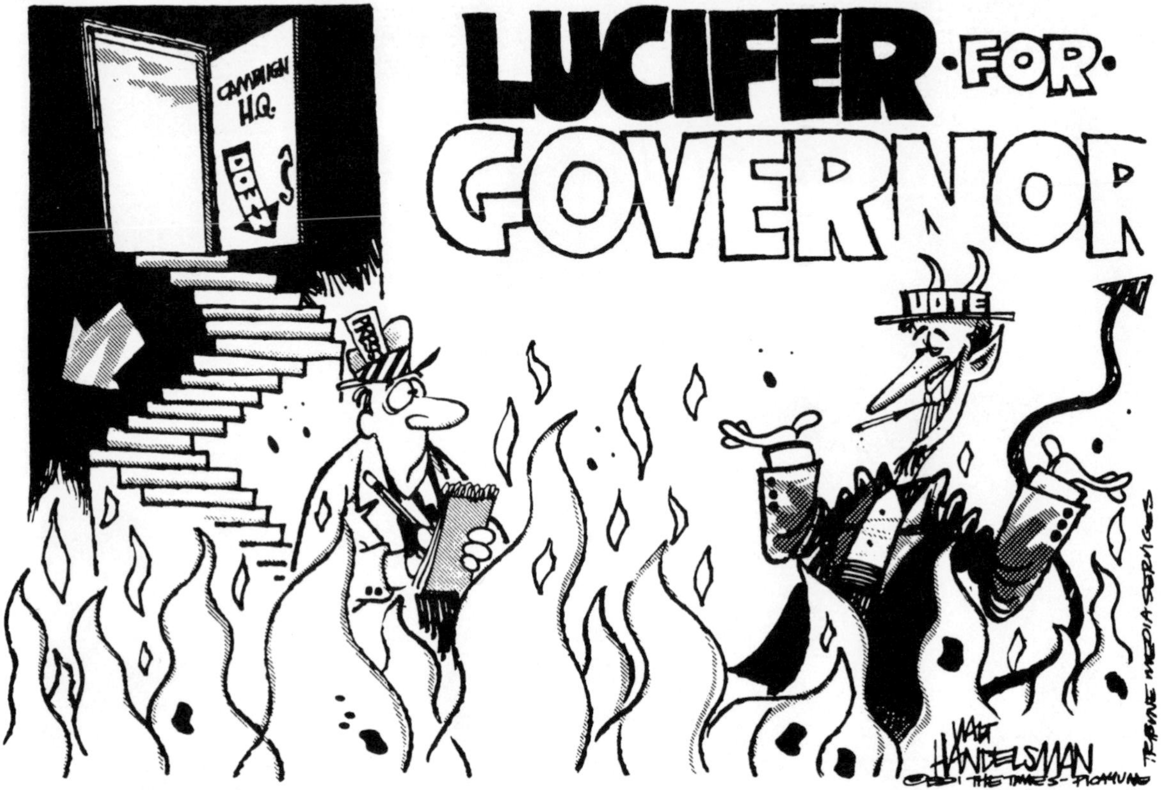
LUCIFER ·FOR· GOVERNOR
CAMPAIGN H.Q.
DOWN
PRESS
VOTE
WALT HANDELSMAN
©1991 THE TIMES-PICAYUNE
TRIBUNE MEDIA SERVICES

"...OKAY, OKAY... I WAS A LITTLE *INTOLERANT* IN MY YOUTH... SO WHO'S PERFECT?..."

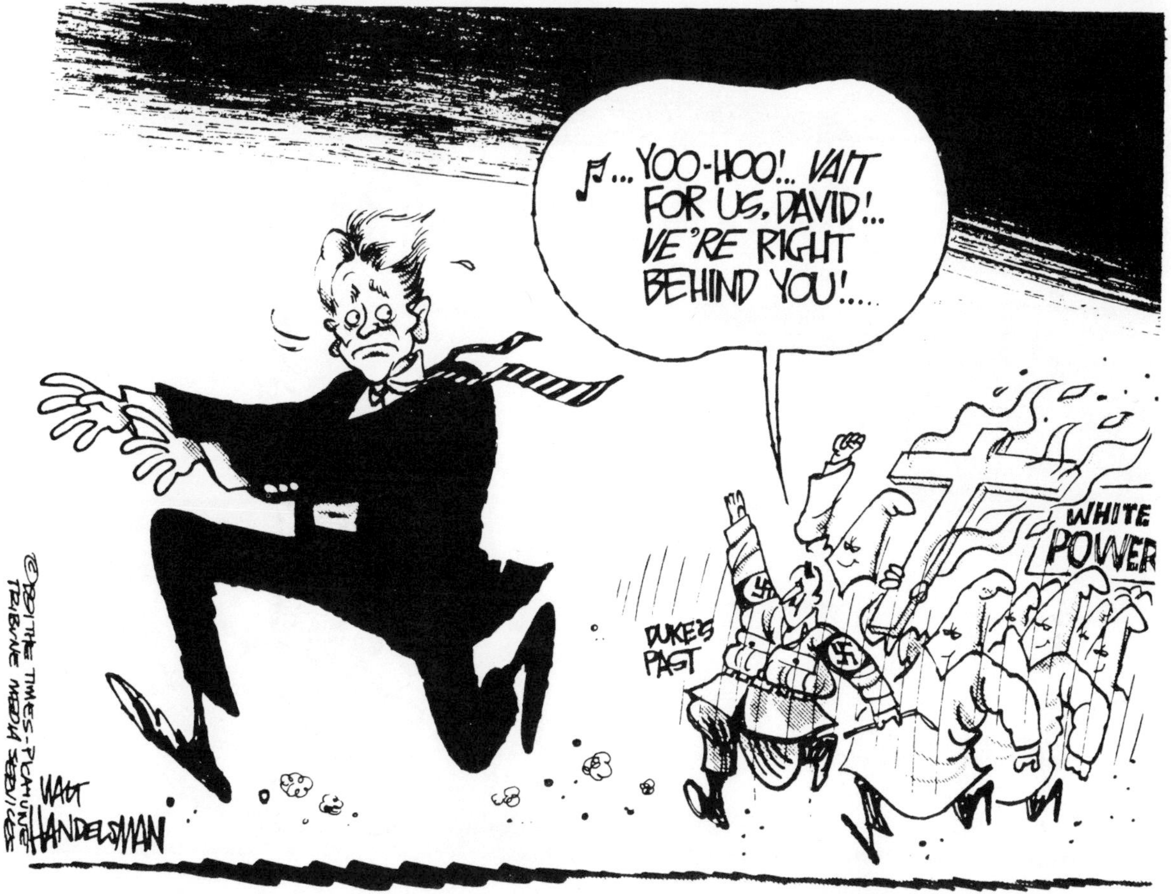

...YOO-HOO!.. VAIT FOR US, DAVID!... VE'RE RIGHT BEHIND YOU!....
WHITE POWER
DUKE'S PAST
WALT HANDELSMAN

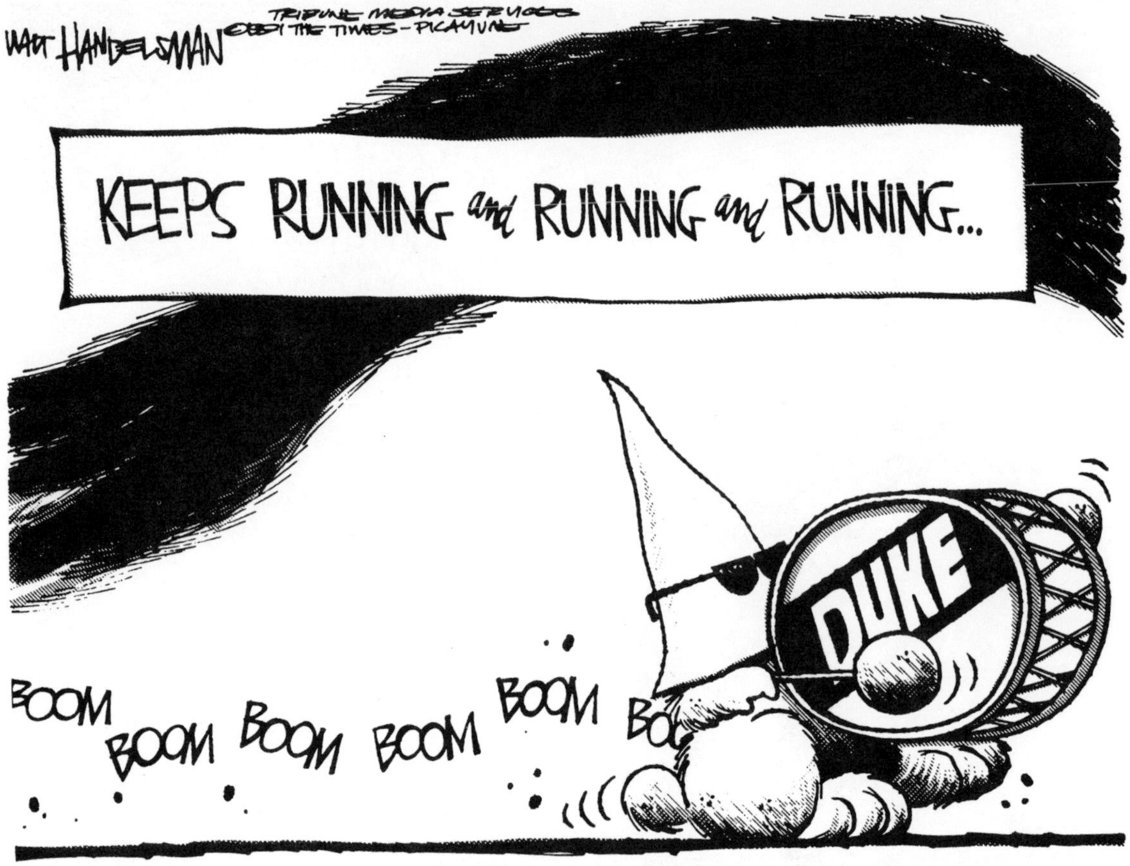
WALT HANDELSMAN
TRIBUNE MEDIA SERVICES
THE TIMES-PICAYUNE
KEEPS RUNNING and RUNNING and RUNNING...
DUKE
BOOM
BOOM
BOOM
BOOM
BOOM

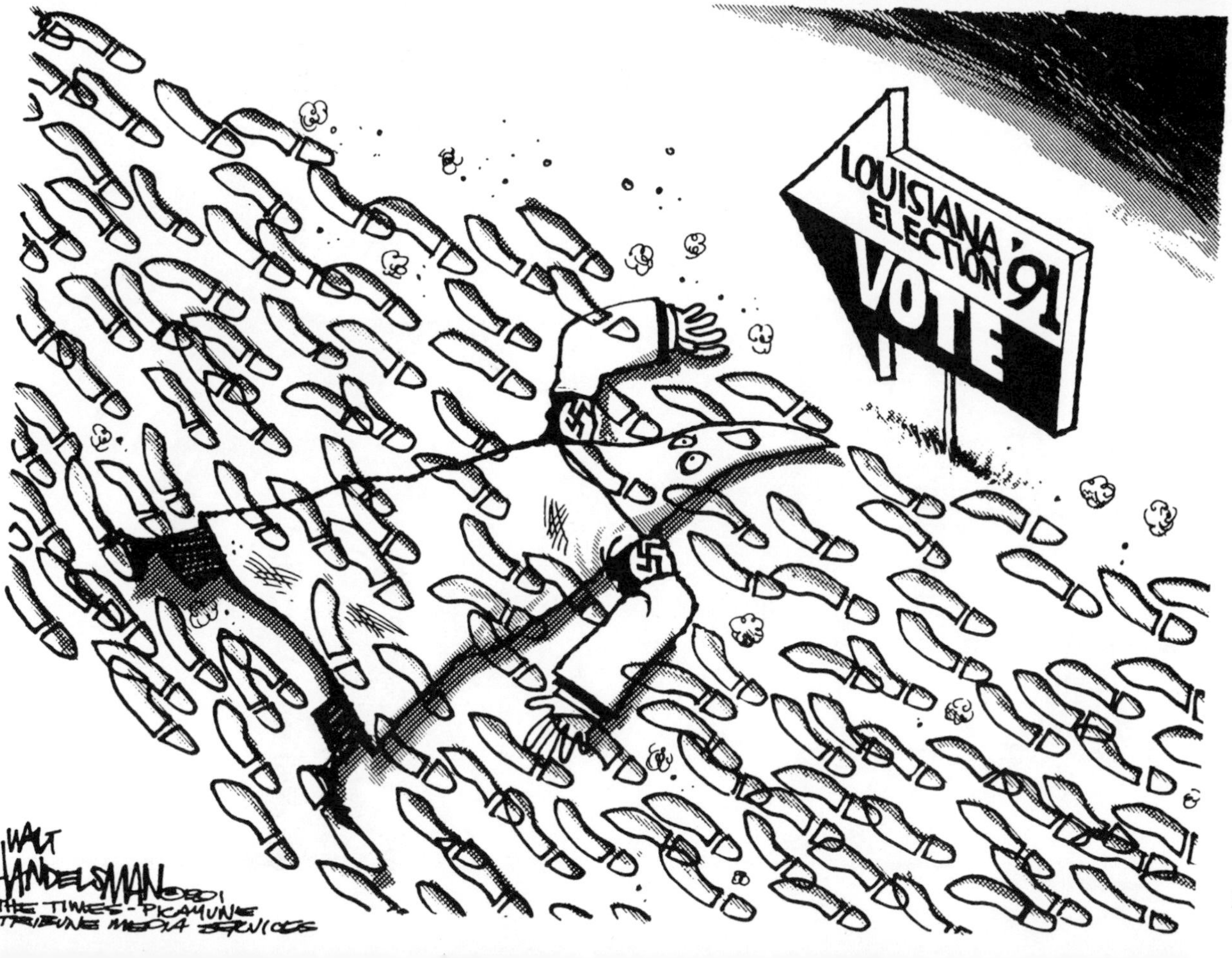
LOUISIANA ELECTION '91
VOTE
WALT HANDELSMAN ©'91
THE TIMES-PICAYUNE
•TRIBUNE MEDIA SERVICES

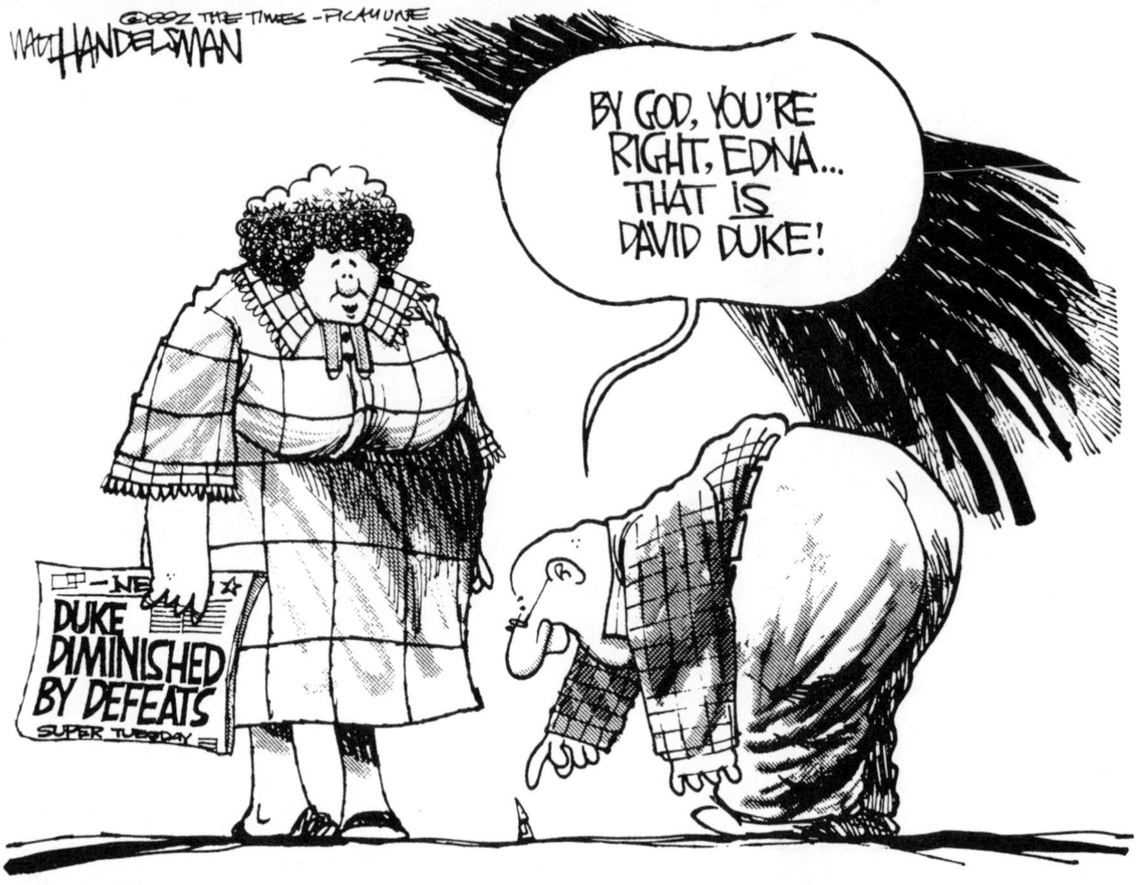
©1992 THE TIMES-PICAYUNE
WALT HANDELSMAN
BY GOD, YOU'RE RIGHT, EDNA... THAT IS DAVID DUKE!
DUKE DIMINISHED BY DEFEATS
SUPER TUESDAY

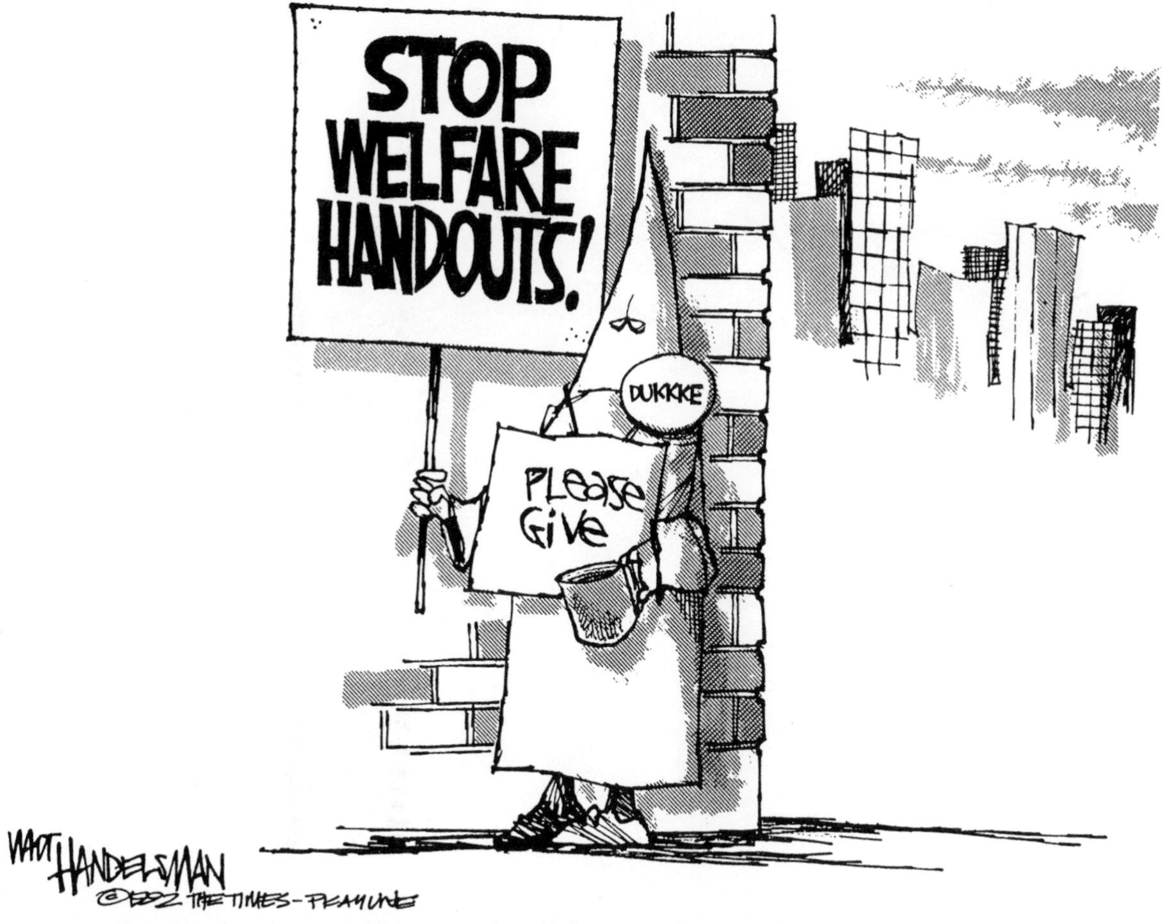
STOP WELFARE HANDOUTS!
DUKKKE
PLEASE GIVE
WALT HANDELSMAN
©1992 THE TIMES-PICAYUNE

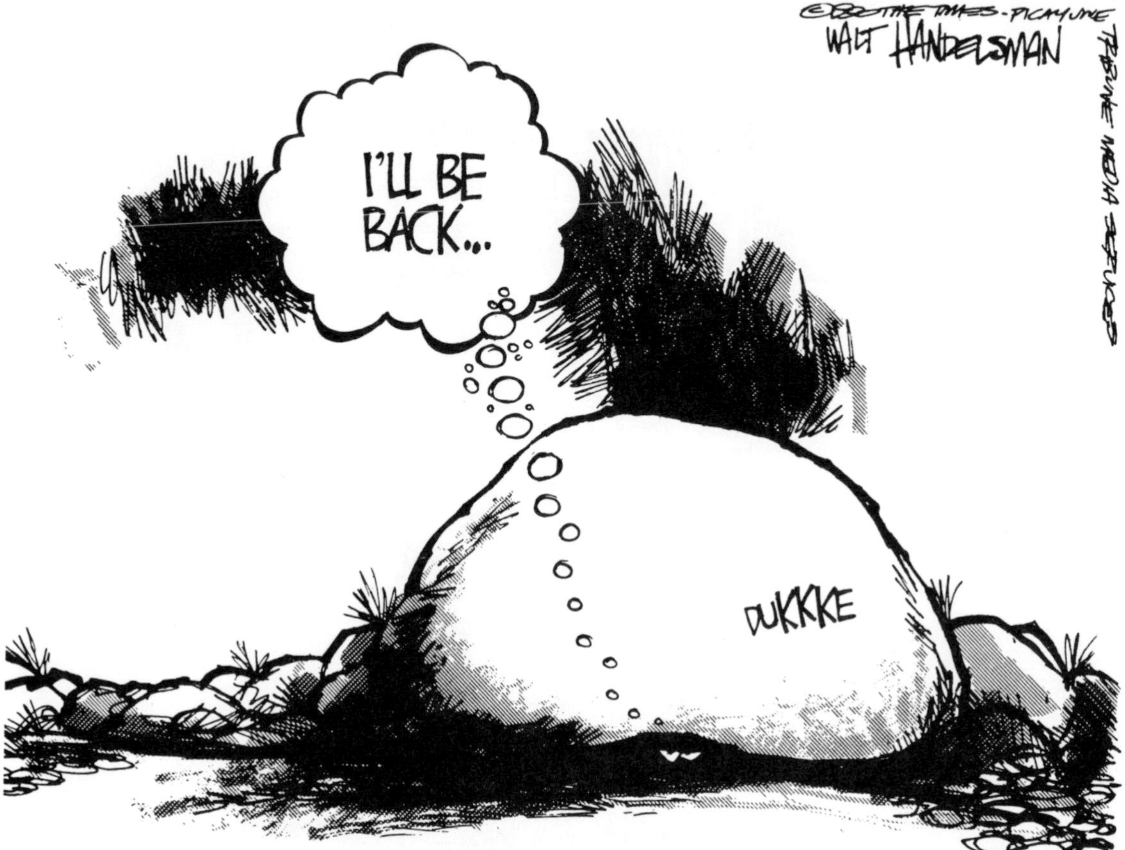

THE TIMES-PICAYUNE
WALT HANDELSMAN
TRIBUNE MEDIA SERVICES
I'LL BE BACK...
DUKKKE

Louisiana's Royal Flush

Edwards and the Legislature gamble with our future.

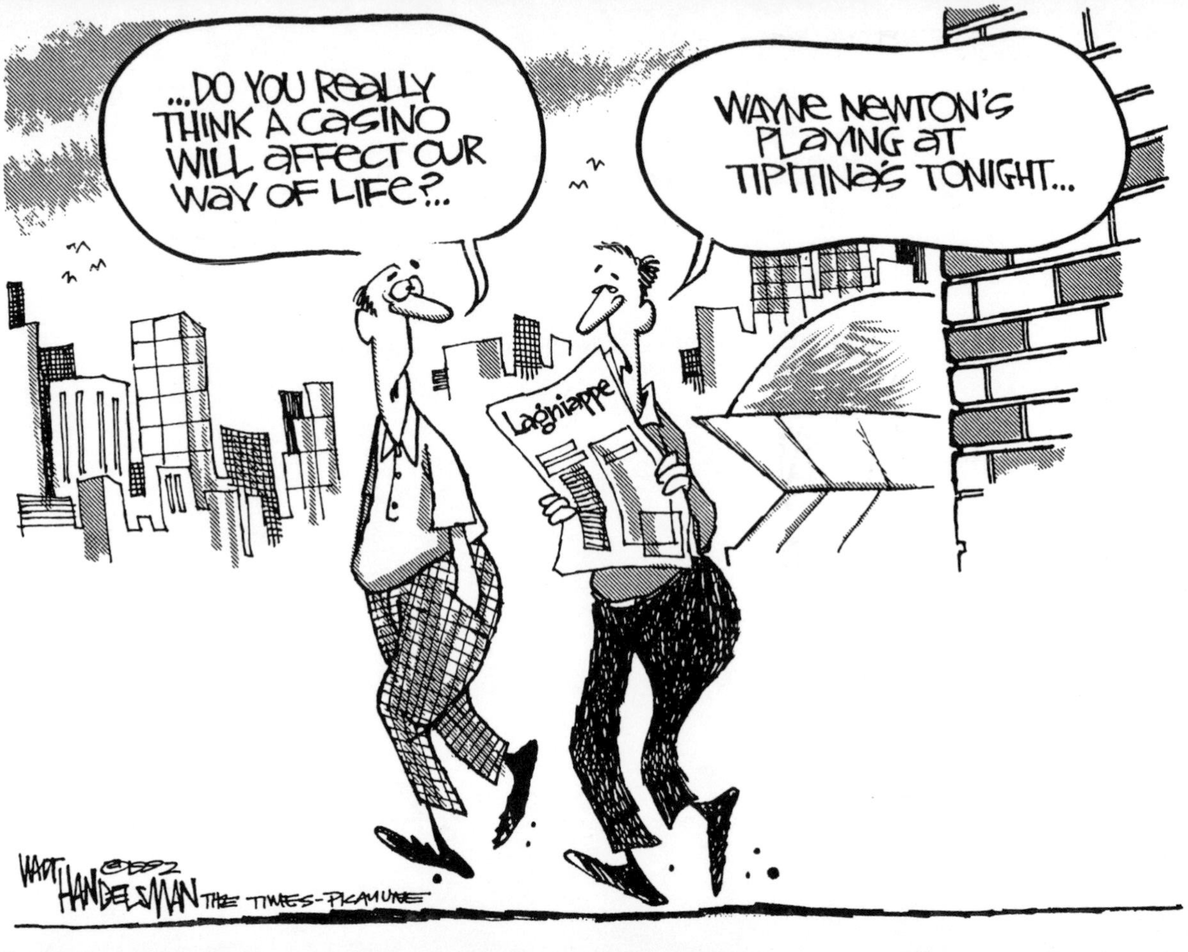
...DO YOU REALLY THINK A CASINO WILL AFFECT OUR WAY OF LIFE?...
WAYNE NEWTON'S PLAYING AT TIPITINA'S TONIGHT...
Lagniappe
WALT HANDELSMAN ©1992 THE TIMES-PICAYUNE

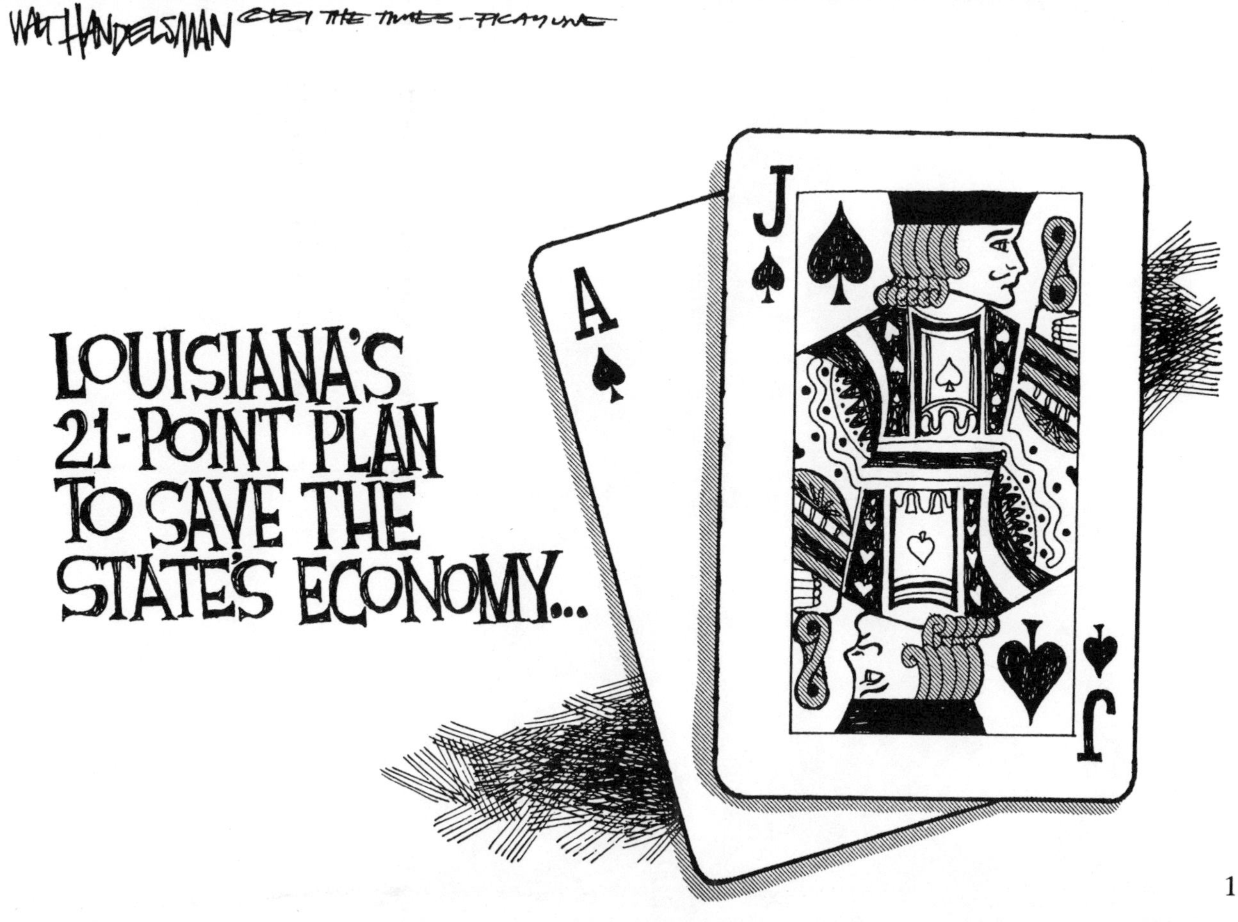
WALT HANDELSMAN
THE TIMES-PICAYUNE
LOUISIANA'S 21-POINT PLAN TO SAVE THE STATE'S ECONOMY...
A
J
J

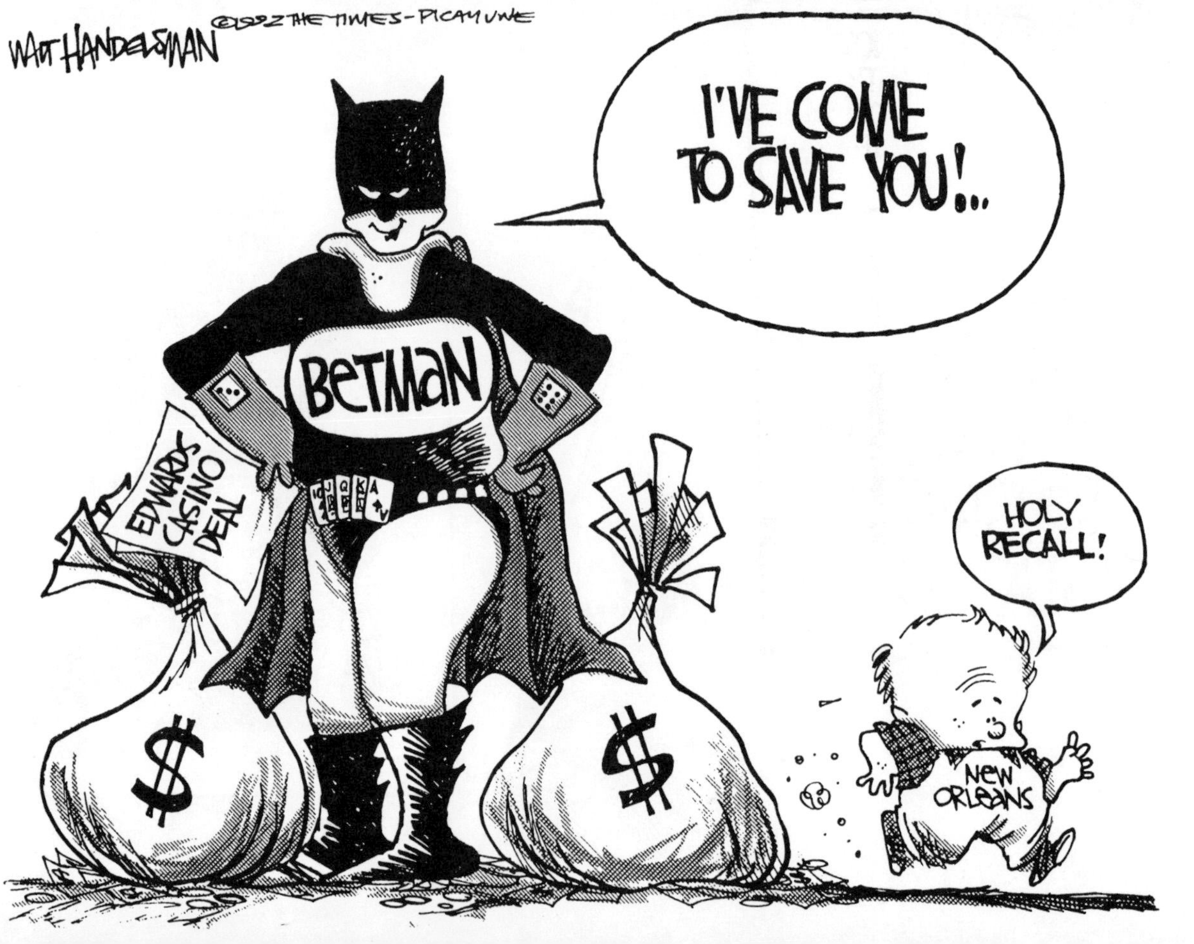
WALT HANDELSMAN
©1992 THE TIMES-PICAYUNE
I'VE COME TO SAVE YOU!...
BETMAN
EDWARDS CASINO DEAL
HOLY RECALL!
NEW ORLEANS

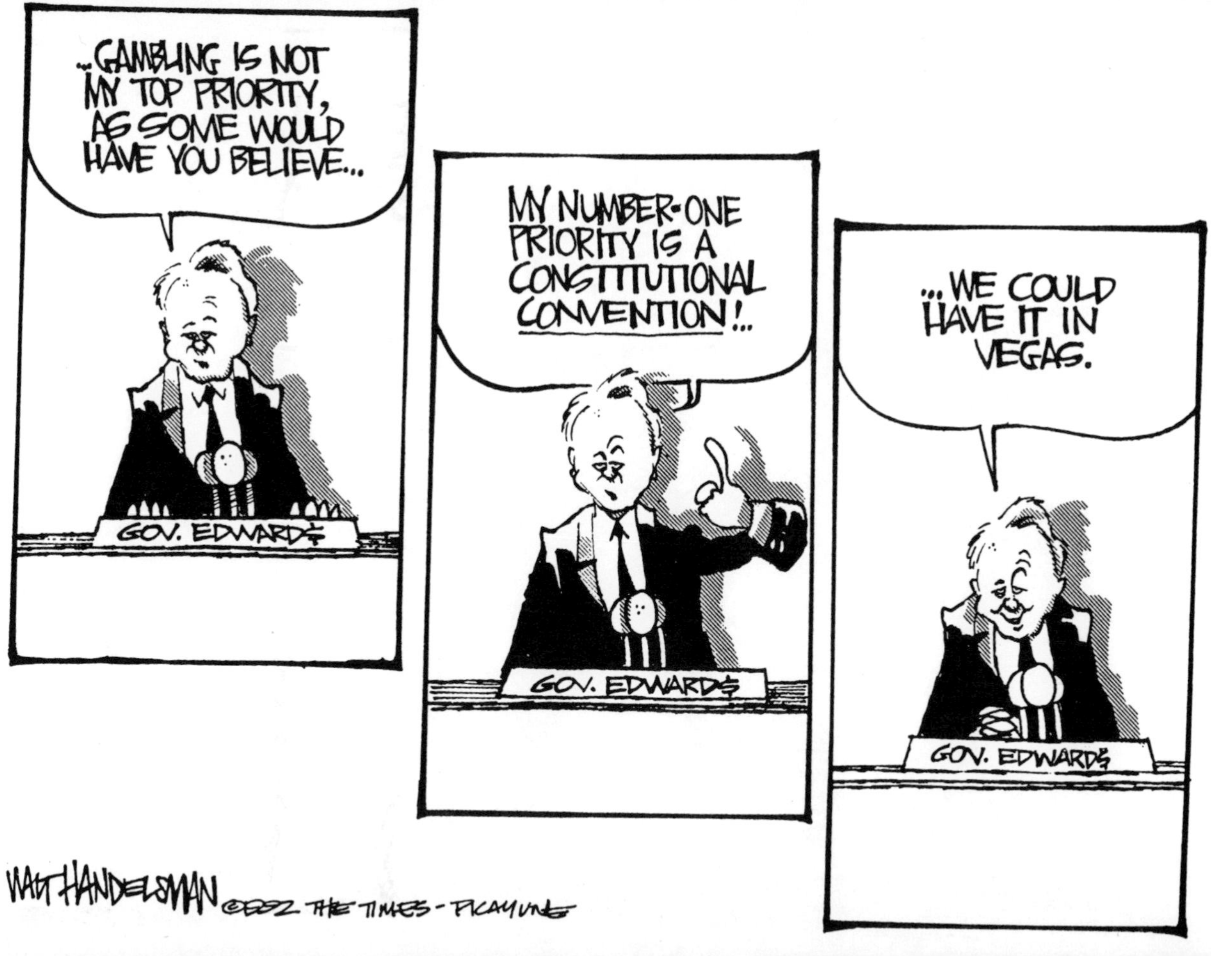
...GAMBLING IS NOT MY TOP PRIORITY, AS SOME WOULD HAVE YOU BELIEVE...
GOV. EDWARDS
MY NUMBER-ONE PRIORITY IS A CONSTITUTIONAL CONVENTION!..
GOV. EDWARDS
...WE COULD HAVE IT IN VEGAS.
GOV. EDWARDS
WALT HANDELSMAN ©1992 THE TIMES-PICAYUNE

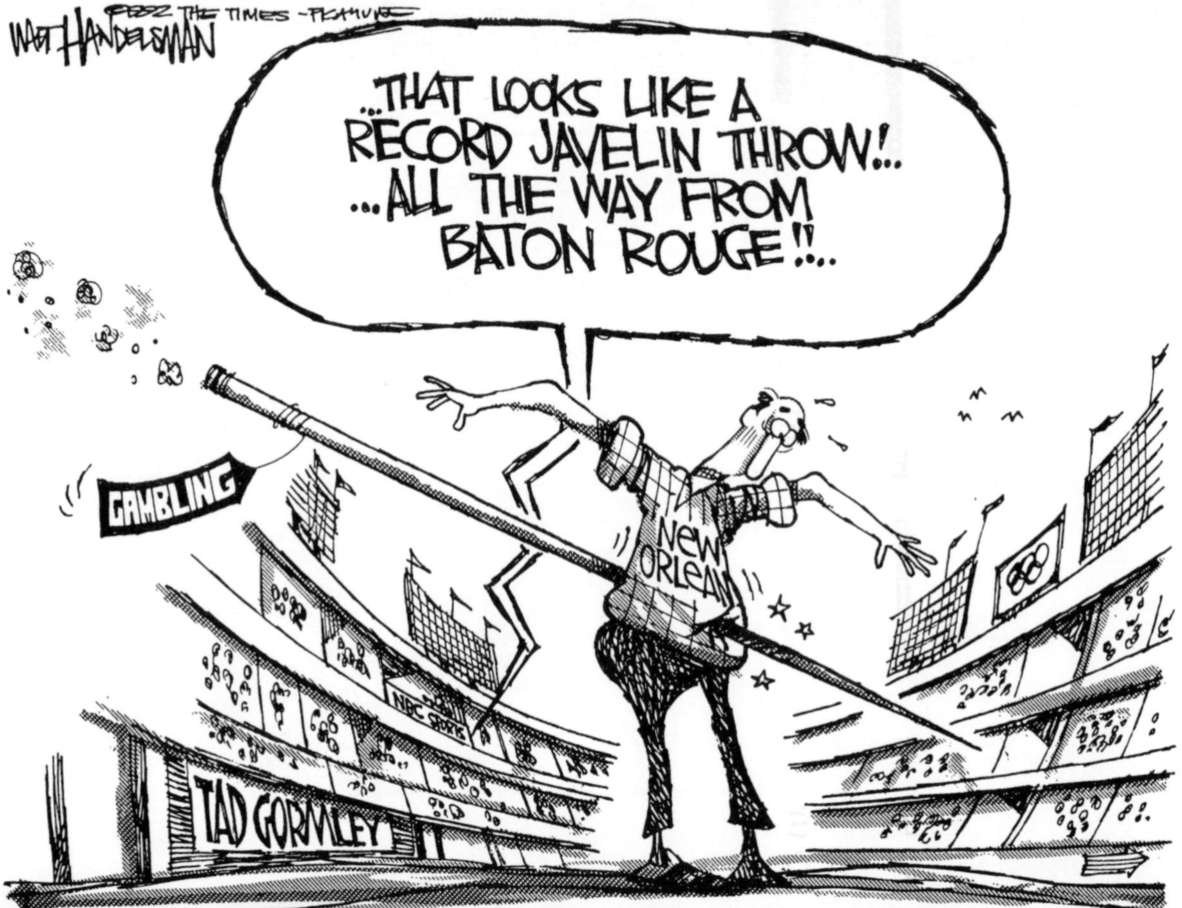
WALT HANDELSMAN
©1992 THE TIMES-PICAYUNE
...THAT LOOKS LIKE A RECORD JAVELIN THROW!... ...ALL THE WAY FROM BATON ROUGE!!...
GAMBLING
NEW ORLEAN
NBC SPORTS
TAD GORMLEY

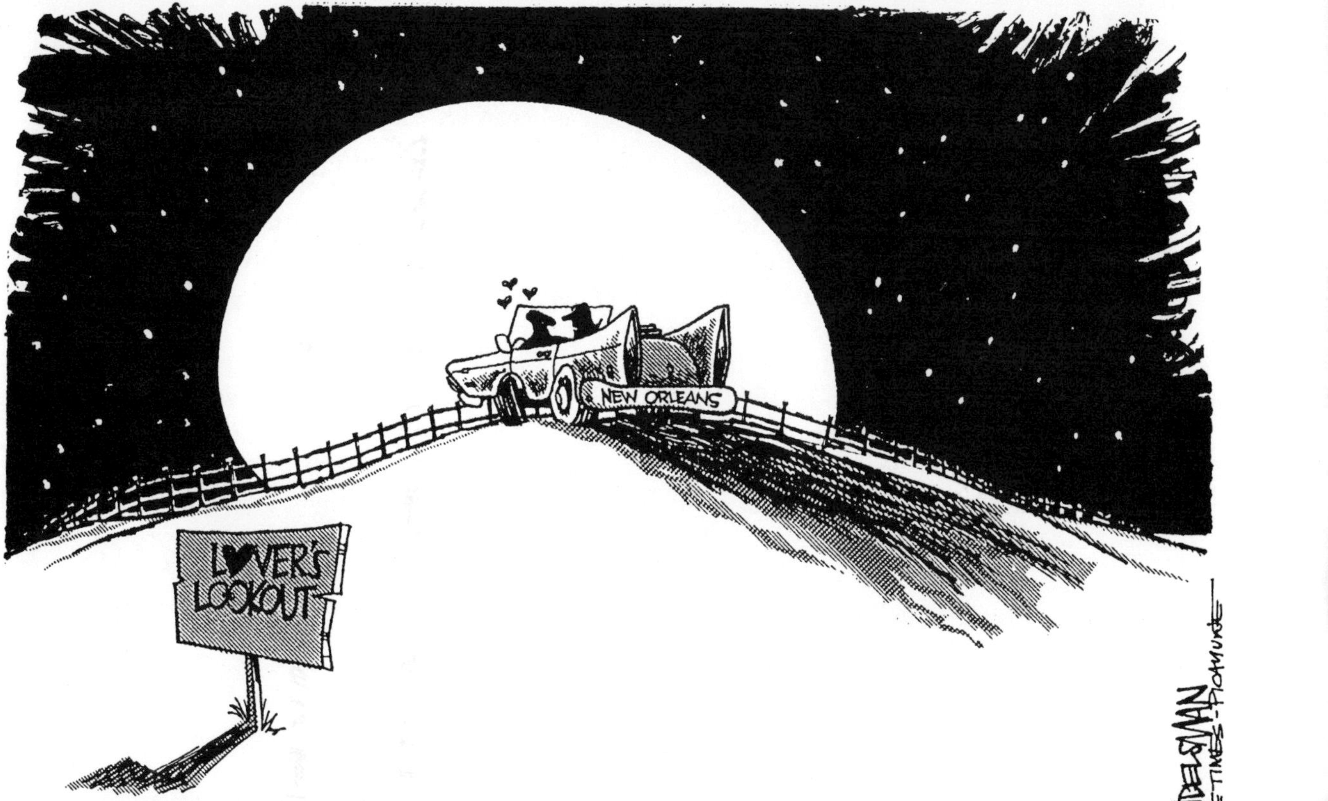
NEW ORLEANS
LOVER'S LOOKOUT

"...GOLLY, MR. HEMMETER, IT ALL SOUNDS SO EXCITING... BUT I'M STILL NOT SURE I'M READY TO GO ALL THE WAY..."

WALT HANDELSMAN ©1992 THE TIMES-PICAYUNE

An atrocious student, Walt Handelsman began his cartooning career in the margins of his math books.

Stumbling into college, he earned an associate's degree in art therapy and then a bachelor's degree in advertising from the University of Cincinnati. He returned to his native Baltimore, where he landed a job at a small advertising agency doing paste-up, layout, and sales for a number of small retail accounts.

He began free-lance editorial cartooning in 1979. It led to his first full-time cartooning job in 1982 with The Patuxent Publishing Corporation in Columbia, Maryland.

In 1985, Walt moved to a daily newspaper, *The Scranton Times* (PA), where, in 1988, he received the National Headliner Award and became nationally syndicated with Tribune Media Services, Inc.

He joined *The Times-Picayune* in 1989. Since then, he has won another National Headliner Award and the Sigma Delta Chi's award for editorial cartooning. Walt, 37, lives in New Orleans with his wife, Jodie and their son, James David.